DOS Customized

Revised and Expanded

DOS Customized

Revised and Expanded

David D. Busch

The first edition of the book was
published as *PC-DOS Customized*

BRADY
New York

B R A D Y

Simon & Schuster, Inc.
Gulf + Western Building
One Gulf + Western Plaza
New York, New York 10023

Distributed by Prentice Hall Trade

Manufactured in the United States of America

10 9 8 7 6 5 4 3 2

Library of Congress Cataloging-in-Publication Data

Busch, David D.
    DOS customized / by David D. Busch.—Rev. and expanded.
    p.   cm.
    Rev. ed. of: PC-DOS customized. 1985.
    "A Brady book."
    Includes index.
    1. PC DOS (Computer operating system) 2. MS-DOS (Computer operating system)
I. Busch, David D. PC-DOS customized.   II. Title.
QA76.76.063B874   1988
005.4'46—dc19   87-28548

ISBN 0-13-655150-5

Contents

Dedication

For Jonathan, Cathy, David Jr., and Michael

Trademarks

IBM, IBM PC,XT,AT,PS/2, Topview, PC-DOS, and Display Write are registered trademarks of International Business Machines Corporation.

MS-DOS, Windows, and Microsoft are registered trademarks of Microsoft Corporation.

Sidekick is a trademark of Borland International.

Lotus and 1-2-3 are trademarks of Lotus Development Corporation.

Intel is a registered trademark of Intel Corporation.

WordStar is a registered trademark of MicroPro International Corporation.

Apple is a registered trademark, and AppleDOS is a trademark of Apple Computer, Inc.

CompuServe is a trademark of CompuServe Information Services, an H & R Block Company.

CP/M is a registered trademark of Digital Research, Inc.

WordPerfect is a trademark of WordPerfect Corporation.

Norton Utilities is a trademark of Norton Computing, Inc.

dBase II and dBase III are registered trademarks of Ashton-Tate.

MCI is a trademark of MCI Telecommunications Corp.

TRS-80 is a trademark of the Radio Shack Division of Tandy Corporation.

The Source is a service mark of Source Telecomputing Corp.

People/Link is a trademark of American Home Network, Inc.

Extended Batch Language is a trademark of Seaware Corp.

Personal REXX is a trademark of Mansfield Software Group.

Pro Command is a trademark of Innovative Technology.

Command Plus is a trademark of ESP Software Systems, Inc.

Wordfinder is a trademark of Microlytics, Inc.

Limits of Liability and Disclaimer of Warranty

The authors and publisher of this book have used their best efforts in preparing this book and the programs contained in it. These efforts include development, research, and testing of the theories and programs to determine their effectiveness. The authors and publisher make no warranty of any kind, expressed or implied, with regard to these programs or the documentation contained in this book. The authors and publisher shall not be liable in any event for incidental or consequential damages in connection with, or arising out of, the furnishing, performance, or use of these programs.

Preface

Dos users of the world unite! Now is the time
for you to take control of your machine and begin doing things *your* way. This
book was written to help you develop personalized commands for MS-DOS or
PC-DOS without having to learn machine language or master the complexities
of assembler. You don't even have to know BASIC! Built right into DOS 2.x and
DOS 3.x are some powerful tools that let you devise your own easy-to-use,
simple-to-remember DOS commands that will bring new power to your IBM
Personal Computer, IBM Personal System/2, or compatible.

This book is a revised and enriched "cookbook" of DOS-enhancing "recipes" that you can use to assemble your own array of commands and features.
But there is much more. You'll learn *how* these commands are created so that
you can combine them, mix and match, or build your own from scratch. Once
you begin your customized DOS, you are limited only by your imagination!
And, with the computer doing more of the work, you'll have more time to let
your thoughts run free.

In *DOS Customized*, you'll learn how to:

- Master the DOS environment to pass information from one program or "command" to another.

- Enable one DOS command (in batch-file form) to call a *second* DOS command—without resorting to DOS 3.3's CALL statement.

- Build your own menu system as a DOS shell to bypass entirely the dreaded DOS prompt.

- Create *interactive* commands that can accept user input.

- Redefine keys so that you can summon disk directories by pressing Alt-A or Alt-B instead of typing DIR A: or DIR B:.

- Customize your system's power-on configuration with the screen colors you want, function key definitions you select, and many other options—including a system prompt that greets you "Ready, Master!" if you choose.

- Change existing commands, like FORMAT, so that they are easier—and safer—to use.

- Control your IBM computer from a remote device.

- Consult a built-in database, using nothing more than DOS commands you have created.

If you're a serious business PC user who is frustrated by DOS' complexity, this book will help you construct a customized DOS that even the newest operator can learn quickly. Experienced DOS users too will find some new tricks here and some useful routines that they can apply directly without having to reinvent the wheel.

This book has one more purpose: Its approach is probably the most unusual but effective way of becoming comfortable with DOS commands. Nearly all the most common and powerful DOS features are introduced and explained, one by one, as they are applied to developing new DOS commands. You'll learn tricks about MODE, CTTY, CHKDSK, RESTORE, and BACKUP that you never dreamed were possible. Every special batch-file language command will be explored and put through the wringer to squeeze out every function and capability.

By the end of the book, you'll not only be comfortable with bypassing DOS with commands of your own, but also will know a great deal about how to use SORT, MORE, and FIND, I/O redirection, and dozens of other DOS 2.x and 3.x features. You'll find, as thousands of others have, that this "learn by doing" approach is a painless way to master the use of your IBM PC, PS/2, or compatible!

Introduction

LET'S BE HONEST. DOS WASN'T WRITTEN FOR YOU: IT
was created by programmers for programmers. How else can you explain the
existence of a TREE command in an operating system that at the same time
forces you to describe your most complex files in eight characters (plus a three-
character extension) or less? DOS bristles with rarely used features, while tasks
that you are likely to do a dozen or more times a day, such as apply a name to
files, are cumbersome or inconvenient. This proves that the operating system
wasn't created with the end-user in mind.

In fact, each new release of DOS, from 1.1 to 3.3 and any later versions we
are likely to see, have had to address the difficulty that most intelligent business
users face when viewing the cryptic A> or C> prompt. Fixes have been patched
on fixes so that DOS has evolved from allowing you to reformat (or erase) your
hard disk by simply pressing any key when asked, to requiring you to explicitly
type Y, to asking you to confirm by entering the hard disk's volume label before
proceeding with the destructive task. An operating system that catered to the
end-user would simply separate the FORMAT command into two separate commands; one to format floppy disks and a different command for performing low-
level or high-level formatting of a fixed disk.

MS-DOS and PC-DOS abound with such examples. Windowing environments and the Presentation Manager of OS/2, and even entire computer systems like the Macintosh have been developed to bypass the mysteries of the DOS command line.

SOME BACKGROUND

In 1984, I began work on my own contribution to deciphering DOS arcana with a book called *PC-DOS Customized*. It provided neophyte and advanced user alike with simple techniques for taming DOS batch files and BASIC programs. The book, the first on the market totally dedicated to "souping up" DOS, was published in 1985 by the same Brady Communications publishing division that is now part of Simon & Schuster. Despite its modest length (only 166 pages), the book generated a gratifying response from DOS users, who still often write me with questions and suggestions for additions to the book, many of which have been included here. Eventually, *PC-DOS Customized* became the springboard for the monthly "DR. DOS" column voted the most popular in the now-defunct *PC Companion Magazine*.

MS-DOS and PC-DOS have come a long way since the first edition of the book. Undocumented features of earlier releases have become undocumented nonfeatures of later versions. Interesting, but not especially useful aspects of DOS, such as the DOS environment, have become treasures of possibilities. Entire subcultures of PC users have grown up developing and using extended batch file language enhancements that add even *more* capabilities to DOS.

At the same time, new commands in latest releases of DOS, from 3.0 to 3.3, such as LABEL and CALL boost the operating system's power and flexibility.

PHILOSOPHY BEHIND *DOS CUSTOMIZED*

As a result, it seemed prudent not to merely update *PC-DOS Customized* to include new information. Rather, an extensive overhaul that would enlarge upon and enhance the original concept was called for. We've kept the ideas and basic tutorial information that made the original book popular, but we've also more than doubled the size of the text by packing it full of the exciting new techniques that have been developed for DOS in the past three years.

If you purchased and liked *PC-DOS Customized*, you'll find this book to be like an old friend who has grown with new experiences. The 48 batch file utilities introduced in *PC-DOS Customized* have been augmented by 60 percent with new routines—including several machine language programs that give DOS additional capabilities. New chapters have been written on using the DOS environment, creating a security system, three or four different ways of writing menus and DOS "shells," and communicating with DOS through interactive batch files. An entire chapter is devoted to customizing your AUTOEXEC.BAT file with examples of features you never dreamed possible in a start-up file. There is even a chapter on making further enhancements to DOS through public domain utilities and shareware programs. We'll show you how to find them and when to use them. Make no mistake: old friends will find *DOS Customized* well worth their investment in the upgrade.

New purchasers should find this book a rewarding, educational experience. Given the new amount of legroom granted by Brady, we have been able to stretch out and *explain* concepts you may have found glossed over in other books. Extra examples, in the form of working batch files, guide you to in-depth understanding while sparking ideas for your own, personalized customization routines.

If you want to become proficient with DOS and streamline your working methods, you'll find the effort entertaining and rewarding. After all, there is a lot of life left in DOS and is highly unlikely to vanish from the PC scene anytime soon. The new OS/2 for the line of IBM PS/2 computers is large (well over a megabyte of memory), complex, and costly. None of the ten million or more current users of 8088 or 8086-based PCs will be able to use OS/2 without an expensive hardware add-on. Nor will those purchasing the "new" generation PS/2 Model 30 or Model 25 have access to the new operating system.

Only users with 80286- or 80386-based computers like the PC/AT and the middle and high end PS/2 line can use OS/2, and such users will make up only the tiniest fraction of computers in the workplace through 1989, at least. The transition should be a slow one, if only because of the sheer numbers of 8088 and 8086 computers still working satisfactorily.

The typical lag in availability of suitable software will prolong this transition. Most early users of OS/2 will find themselves confined by Microsoft's DOS 3 "compatibility box" that allows them to run existing DOS applications. Several years after the PC/AT's introduction very few software packages can take advantage of the 80286's capabilities, even though the installed base is many times larger than the PS/2 line will be able to boast for some time. Given a huge market of existing PCs, if you were a programmer, would you write software that would run on the computers owned by those customers—*plus* run on the PS/2 computers within the compatibility box—or would you write software that would operate *only* on the PS/2 computers?

So, this book was written for the 90 to 95 percent of you who will be happily using—and modifying—various versions of MS-DOS and PC-DOS for the foreseeable future.

This is not to say that DOS is perfect. In fact, overcoming DOS' shortcomings is a key purpose of this book. PC-DOS, in all its incarnations from DOS 1.0 through DOS 3.x and beyond, often is criticized for its faults: It is somewhat slow, critics assert, particularly in its handling of screen displays, tempting programmers to bypass DOS entirely and access the computer's ROM routines directly. That, of course, leads to the potential incompatibility problems that a standard DOS is designed to avoid.

Because DOS descends from the venerable CP/M operating system, it retains some of the drawbacks of Digital Research's pride and joy. Yes, it *does* seem silly to use an operating system too dumb to search the other available drives and directories when it can't find a file. But the critics sometimes forget that DOS bristles with tools allowing even novice user to customize the operating system to meet their needs. In fact, one of the first things shown in the book is how to set up DOS so that it *will* search other drives and directories for certain types of programs.

Unlike some operating systems, if you don't like the way your DOS behaves, often you can change it to suit you. And this book will be your key to customizing DOS 2.x and 3.x. Users of the IBM computers and compatibles don't have to learn complex DOS commands. Instead, they can create a customized set of commands that are easier to remember, quicker to type in, and which bypass complex syntax.

All the hard work has already been done. *DOS Customized* is a cookbook of scores of new capabilities that supply a useful array of new DOS commands. Readers who just want to run applications and aren't especially interested in understanding the complexities of DOS can use these methods as a shortcut to streamlined, friendlier DOS operation. The author, however, also supplies detailed explanations of how to harness the power of batch files, a simple installable device driver, and other tools. The more advanced user can learn from these descriptions and go on to design custom DOS commands.

Either way, no knowledge of machine or assembly language is required. In several cases, machine language routines are given to enhance DOS capabilities. If you insist, though, you'll never have to use DEBUG. Simple BASIC programs create the machine language programs for you, automatically.

KEY FEATURES OF *DOS CUSTOMIZED*

For the most part, this book relies on routines that show how to manipulate the commands already built into DOS to make the operating system much easier to use. For example:

- Tired of typing "DIR B:", or of remembering to hit Shift to get the colon instead of a semicolon? A simple routine allows you to just type A or B, or C, in upper- or lowercase, to see that disk's directory. If you like, you can choose to have the directory shown to you a page at a time or across the full width of the screen, automatically—still by typing only a single letter.

- Boot up into a configuration of *your* choice. Have special function key definitions installed and waiting for you. The screen color combination can be preset, and the screen centered each time you turn on your computer. If you like, the screen prompt can be a message of *your* choosing, and the current time and date can be displayed automatically in the upper right corner of the screen. Dozens of other start-up options can be yours.

- Manipulate data and files from DOS in complex ways, without complex commands. Use DOS to give you an always-accessible phone directory or a catalog of programs on your disks. Sort files by fields of your choice. Copy files and add them to other files quickly.

- Set up automatic, simple-to-use menu "shells" that can be used by operators who know little or nothing about DOS. Three different menu methods are given that will insulate your operators from the DOS prompt and get them quickly into the application program of their choice.

- Introduce the idea of "subroutines" to batch files by using the DOS environment in creative ways. Pass information from one batch file to another, and customize DOS for particular users by defining an environment variable with "their" information.

DOS Customized shows you how to simplify your operations *without* adding new rules and problems. For example, many of the tasks are carried out through the use of sophisticated batch files. We'll show you how to "hide" all these files in a subdirectory, BATCHES, and then show DOS how to find them, as needed, through a simple PATH command. This PATH command itself is embedded in the boot-up AUTOEXEC.BAT file. Once the files have been placed on the user's disk or hard disk, the new commands are readily available even though "invisible" to routine DIR commands.

All the new commands were designed for ease of use. Instead of remembering the syntax for the MORE filter, the user can type:

```
        LOOK filename b
or
        LOOK b:filename
```

Using the batch file LOOK.BAT, DOS will TYPE the file specified by filename on B:, and use the MORE filter to display a page at a time. Typing KEYS 1 or KEYS 2 can turn customized DOS function key definitions on, while KEYS OFF can return them to their normal DOS definitions, or set up a specialized function key definition file. This book not only offers many different, flexible new

DOS commands, but also shows readers how they can further customize their operating system. Best of all, the methods used can be easily understood by any IBM PC user. Customizing your DOS doesn't have to be a painful experience. In fact, this book may be the fastest shortcut to DOS fluency available.

HOW TO USE THIS BOOK

If you already understand batch files thoroughly, you may want to pore over the table of contents or index and choose a routine you need. Just remember that it is *not* necessary to type in the line numbers given with each batch file for clarity. Several BASIC programs in this book have nonoptional line numbers. You'll find lots of batch file tricks you might not know and even veteran users may wish to read the accompanying explanations. Less experienced readers should start at the beginning of the book, where useful concepts are introduced and explained with examples. By the time you've finished, you'll understand how to use your new DOS commands, and, more important, how to create your own.

If you're not dedicated to complete mastery of your IBM computer, you may still type in and use any of the modules in this book. Simply read Appendix A to glean the absolute minimum needed. Once you've used a few of these routines to streamline your work, though, you'll probably be back for more.

IMPORTANT NOTES

Experience has shown that this type of book appeals to computer owners with varying levels of expertise. For clarity and consistency in presentation, all the routines follow a similar format. Where necessary, HELP lines give a brief explanation of a command's function and syntax. Some of these lines will not be needed by an experienced user and may seem to make the routine needlessly long.

If you are a beginning user, I urge you to type in all the routines exactly as they appear. The remarks, HELP, extra labels, and other information help you keep the various routines separate and their functions understandable.

Experienced users should not snort with disgust if they find a six-line routine that does nothing more than display a disk directory. Remember that you too were a beginner once and that even the simplest concepts so readily apparent today once may have confused you. If you understand a line's function and think that it is superfluous, then leave it out. It is much better to have too much information in programs or routines than too little. Readers found that some of the simplest routines in the original version of this book helped them understand DOS complexities more easily.

You should also, note, however, that extraneous lines in a batch file *will* slow down the file somewhat. Feel free to delete the extra lines once you understand how a file operates to gain maximum performance.

By the end of this book every reader should be an expert who can modify all the routines presented here to do their job better and more efficiently.

One final note: examine the instructions that accompany each batch file carefully. When compared with BASIC, the error trapping for batch files is somewhat clumsy. To check for all possible improper entries would make some batch files so long as to be impractical. Many readers will want to type in files from this book for their own use. Therefore, we've tried to keep the routines as short as possible without sacrificing features.

Where the choice of options is limited, the modules in this book do check for validity. In other cases, it is quite easy to enter nonsense that will mean nothing to the new DOS command you are creating. These routines are neither foolproof nor idiot-proof (it's been said that anyone can make a mistake; only an idiot insists on it). That's quite similar, however, to the situation with real DOS commands, which are terribly unforgiving of syntax errors. Your new DOS commands actually can be *more* sophisticated in that regard than traditional DOS commands. Read the accompanying instructions, and you'll be on your way to using your new commands freely.

DOS DIFFERENCES

All the routines presented were developed and tested using DOS 3.1 or DOS 3.3. They will also work, as written, with DOS 2.0, 2.1, or 3.2. Because of some notable bugs, DOS 3.0 is not recommended. Note that there have been some small changes between DOS 2.1 and 3.0 and higher in the handling of batch files. There are some changes that you can make (such as using a period to set off remarks) that may work fine with DOS 2.x but will *not* be compatible with DOS 3.0 or higher. Make such changes only at your own risk.

In addition, some notable bugs in DOS 3.0 were solved in later versions. A few routines in this book, particularly those using the environment, may not function with DOS 3.0. We've pointed these out where appropriate. In the meantime, the reader is urged to upgrade from DOS 3.0 to 3.1 or later versions if at all possible. Differences between DOS 3.1, 3.2, and 3.3, although minor, can be significant: These are covered in the relevant sections.

DOS 3.3 has two ways of accessing another batch file from within a given batch file, while earlier versions (2.0 to 3.2) have only one: the COMMAND command. Since most readers of this book won't have access to DOS 3.3 and its CALL command, we've stuck for the most part with the syntax that is compatible with *all* DOS versions in releases 2.x and 3.x. Some few routines do take advantage of specific features of later versions of DOS, such as XCOPY, or expansion of the size of the environment. These will be noted as they are explained.

SUMMARY

This introduction gave a brief overview of why *DOS Customized* was written and a glimpse at some of the topics that will be covered. We also offer some tips on how to use the book as well as a discussion of which DOS versions are most suitable for the techniques described in the chapters to follow.

Before we can get into some meaty new DOS customizing routines, it will be useful to learn something about DOS itself and the concept of batch files. Both are covered in detail in the following two chapters. Even if you know something about DOS and its background, we think you'll want to read through this discussion for an even more detailed background on the program you use most—DOS.

1

What is DOS?

INTRODUCTION

Can you guess which software program is the most widely used on IBM PCs and compatibles in the world? No, WordStar doesn't qualify. That venerable word-processing program has sold millions of copies and is used by countless others with their PCs, but it isn't the most used software for personal computers. Nor is Lotus 1-2-3, or some other obvious choice the champion. In fact, your operating system, MS-DOS or PC-DOS, is the one software package used without fail by almost every owner of an IBM PC or compatible. Aside from a few installations where Xenix or a version of Digital Research Corporation's CP/M-86 or Concurrent DOS are in use (and they are themselves operating systems), you use a version of DOS as published by Microsoft (as MS-DOS) and enhanced by IBM (as PC-DOS) every time you turn on your computer.

Some users may not *see* DOS, as their computers have been set up for them with a shell or special environment like Microsoft Windows to insulate them from the vagaries of the operating system. But rest assured that underneath the shell, DOS is operating to give the software the services it needs to open and close disk files, and, most likely, to communicate with devices like the screen, keyboard, printers, and modems.

It's surprising then that so many PC users know so little about the software they use most. You may not need to know the inner workings of your automobile to drive to the store, but it is handy to know some rudimentary details, such as how to change a tire, give a jump-start, or manually close the power moon-roof if it starts to rain and your battery is dead. Beyond that, you may want to know how to improve performance by adding larger tires or spoiler to reduce wind resistance.

This chapter will launch you on the way to learning for yourself how to jump-start DOS, and augment it with routines that streamline your working procedures. We'll start off with a few details on what a disk operating system is, the history of DOS, and why it is important to you.

DOS: A STERN TASKMASTER

Let's face it: DOS can be intimidating. New PC users can usually unpack their computer, plug in the monitor and power cord, and turn the system on with little difficulty. Computers are so much a part of the workplace today that even a neophyte confronted with a PC may know enough to insert a floppy disk labeled "DOS" in Drive A: when powering up. It is even increasingly likely that the new user will be seated in front of a system equipped with a hard disk, and may have had DOS installed at the computer store or by a knowledgeable friend or associate in the organization.

After a few minutes, while the power-on self-test runs (POST-time, the wags call it), the new user's trepidation is answered by real, actual messages appearing on the screen. The computer may or may not ask for the correct date or time. Other things will happen on the screen. Then the new user is faced with the DOS prompt, the necessity that was probably the mother of the term "user unfriendly."

What is that "A>" or "C>" *for*, anyway?

We promised you that it is not necessary to learn machine language or assembler to customize your DOS 2.x and 3.x. You may find it useful, though, to learn something about DOS itself. Certainly, the inner workings of the disk operating system (DOS) can safely remain clouded in the nether regions of computer esoterica. You *will* want to have some understanding of what DOS is so that you can use its tools better. After all, you mastered the remote control of your color television to change channels and adjust the tint from your easy chair. DOS is only slightly more complex to program than the typical 14-day, 7-event, 81-channel VCR. When we are finished customizing DOS to our needs, it will be considerably less complicated to use.

Any user will need to learn the basics of DOS, which controls your disk drives, the storage and loading of your programs and data, and other functions of the IBM PC. Barring an unexpected takeover by Microsoft Windows, or TopView or OS/2's new Presentation Manager, most users will find themselves interfacing regularly with DOS.

Even if all you want to do is run applications (programs such as WordPerfect or Lotus 1-2-3), you'll find it useful to learn how to format a disk, copy and erase files, view a list of files on your disk, and do other operations. This book will explain new and sophisticated uses even for simple DOS commands, like DIR. However, to avoid starting at absolute square one, we assume that you can already do rudimentary tasks; that is, you can turn on the computer, run simple programs, and handle the basics of formatting disks and using the PC. That's all you really need to know, however.

Someday, more users will be insulated from DOS by application managers and windowing "environments" like Windows. For the most part, that will come with more advanced machines, like the PS/2 line, that have memory to spare and microprocessors fast and powerful enough to manage multiple tasks. Until that time, digest this useful information, which makes your PC easier to use.

MICROCOMPUTER BASICS

Any computer consists of a microprocessor, such as the 8088 chip used in the IBM PC, PC-XT, Convertible, and their defunct brethren, the Portable PC and PCjr. Many compatibles use the 8088, or a faster version of it, like the 8088-2. There is also the 8086 microprocessor, such as that used in the IBM PS/2 Model 30, and the 80286 or 80386 chips used in the original PC-AT, PC-XT 286, and the PS/2 models above the basic Model 30.

The microprocessor is the "heart" of the computer. It contains individual memory locations called *registers* and a set of instructions that can be accessed by the programming. Depending on the numbers or *bytes* loaded into the registers, the microprocessor performs calculations or sends instructions to DOS or to other hardware components of the system.

All the "computing" of a personal computer is performed in the central microprocessing unit (called variously the MPU or CPU—depending on the erudition of the speaker), and in specialized coprocessors that may be attached to the system. For example, an 8088-based PC may be equipped with an 8087 microprocessor that takes or "offloads" the math calculation chores to free the main processor for its other tasks. Microprocessors can also be found in peripheral equipment to control intelligent disk drives, graphics boards, and other components.

The speed of computers using these microprocessors is generally measured in megahertz (abbreviated Mhz) and can range from the slow 4.77 Mhz of the original IBM PC to the breathtaking 20-Mhz speed demons with 80286 or 80386 microprocessors.

Don't be misled, though. The processor's "clock" speed is only one measure of how fast the computer operates—that is, how many instructions can be handled per second. Other factors also must be considered. For example, how many of those clock cycles are actually used to do work? Slow memory, for example, may mandate one or more "wait" states in which the computer pauses between instructions, slowing speed. The computer computes faster than the memory chips installed in the system can store or retrieve data, forcing the microprocessor to mark time before carrying out the next instruction.

Also important in computer speed is the power of the microprocessor's instruction set itself and the presence of a coprocessor chip. More advanced microprocessor chips have more powerful instructions—like commands or statements in BASIC—which theoretically can accomplish more within a given clock cycle. The latest chips also have extra "modes" such as the protected mode of the 80286 microprocessor and the "virtual 8086" mode of the 80386 chip. These allow accessing more memory or setting up multiple "computers," each of which can be assigned a separate task. These innovations can multiply the effective power of a computer by two or three—or more.

Specialized coprocessors, such as the 8087 or 80287 math coprocessors can offload a task like number crunching, performing it more quickly than the main microprocessor alone, and theoretically allowing for faster operation.

Unlike faster clock speeds, more powerful instruction sets and coprocessor add-ons only produce speedier operation with software geared to take advantage of these capabilities. As a result, an 80286-based computer with a math coprocessor operating at 6 Mhz may only match the speed of—not outrun—an 8088-2 computer operating at 7 Mhz, if the software can't take advantage of the coprocessor's potential.

Another key component of computer systems that affect performance is memory of the random access and/or read-only type (RAM and ROM). The speed of the RAM (memory can be rated as 150-, 200-, or 250-nanosecond speeds, for example), and the efficiency of the programs in ROM can affect overall speed of the system.

RAM and ROM simply store programs that tell the microprocessor what computing functions to carry out or supply data that is used to arrive at results. Temporary programs are loaded into RAM, which also can store the data used by the software. More permanent instructions or programs can be stored in ROM form for ready access to the computer at all times.

Also important are various peripherals, such as the keyboard, CRT, and storage devices. Peripherals furnish a way to move this information from a mass storage medium to memory or to preserve this data for later use. These devices also allow us to direct output to a screen or printer, where we can view it.

In many types of applications, the peripherals control how fast the computer operates. Even an original IBM PC can handle data faster than the speediest hard disk drive can supply it. Some applications use data that resides entirely in memory, as in the case of Lotus spreadsheets. These applications, which involve much number crunching, are heavily processor-bound. The speed of a disk drive, for example, will slow down Lotus 1-2-3 only when loading or saving a spreadsheet.

Other disk-bound applications require frequent access to disk files. These include large and complex programs that are written to operate even on PCs with limited memory. Since the software can't all be loaded into memory at once, the computer loads various modules, or overlays, into the available memory, and then substitutes other overlays from disk as required. The original WordStar, created for computers with 64 Kbytes (64K) of memory, was such a program.

Applications frequently access large data files that are stored on disk, requiring frequent accesses that again slow down operations. Printers, too, can slow down a PC (hence the creation of printer "spoolers" and "buffers" to parcel out print files in the background, or to receive large quantities of text faster than the printer can accept it.) Even tasks such as writing to the screen can be limiting in very rapidly operating programs. As a result, much incompatibility among PCs and clones results from programmers taking nonstandard shortcuts to speed up this operation.

INTRODUCING DOS

The disk operating system, or DOS, is the final link in determining computer power and speed. To work properly, the functions mentioned so far must be supervised and controlled by some sort of "operating system" or "input/output system." IBM Personal Computers have a certain amount of this control permanently built-in, in a read-only memory (ROM) chip that contains the ROM-BIOS (Read Only Memory—Basic Input Output System). ROM is a type of memory that cannot be written to by the user; its contents can only be read. Note also that special *erasable* programmable ROM chips, or EPROMs, can be reprogrammed or "burned" after exposure to ultraviolet light. More recently, *electrically* erasable programmable ROM (EEPROMs) have become available.

The ROM-BIOS has, among other functions, bootstrap instructions that tell the computer what to do when it is first powered on. These are not particularly complex functions, when compared to the instructions needed to handle the computer's complete operation.

These instructions differ among the various IBM computers. The now-departed PCjr was particularly different, because it could use its built-in BASIC or Cartridge BASIC. The 8088-based PCs also have a built-in BASIC but it is rarely used.

In general, the powerup sequence goes like this: When the IBM PC is turned on, the ROM-BIOS will perform certain system checks and examine memory (the POST). That's why it takes longer for a PC with 640K of memory to "boot up" than one with 128K. On newer PCs, or those with a special ROM chip, if the door to Drive A: is left open or it is closed but contains no disk, the machine will next try to load a more complete "operating system" from the hard disk, Drive C:. Otherwise, it will look for that OS on Drive A:. (In mid-1987, Tandy introduced a novel PC-clone that contains DOS on a ROM chip.)

If the system is found in neither place, an 8088-based PC will turn over control to its one large built-in program, ROM BASIC. Once you are lodged in this simplest of PC BASICs, you are limited to the commands given. Programs can be written, run, and even SAVEd—but only to cassette. Disks cannot be used because access to them, as well as many other advanced features, requires a special operating system called a "disk operating system," or DOS for short.

DOS used by the IBM computers is called PC-DOS. This is a version of MS-DOS produced by Microsoft for IBM. The so-called IBM "compatibles" and "clones" also use PC-DOS or MS-DOS. Generally, DOS is simply referred to by its release number—DOS 2.1, DOS 3.3, and so on.

There are other operating systems, of course. Apple II-series computers use AppleDOS (there was even a DOS 3.3), which now has been mostly supplanted by ProDOS. OS/2, UNIX, XENIX, Concurrent PC-DOS from Digital Research, and other DOSs, particularly those intended for the 80386 processor (These are frequently called "control programs."), also exist for the IBM PC. In this book, when we refer to DOS, we refer to MS-DOS or PC-DOS versions 2.x or 3.x.

Today's DOS actually descends from CP/M, which, if not the first operating system for microcomputers, was the most widely used for earlier systems. CP/M was developed by Digital Research in the mid-1970s as an operating system for a family of microprocessors, including the 8080, 8085, and Z80 chips—all 8-bit microprocessors.

CP/M was also updated for the 16-bit "big brothers" of that family, notably the 8086, 8088, and 80x86 microprocessors used in IBM PCs and compatibles, as CP/M-86 and a multitasking system called Concurrent PC-DOS. There is also a multiuser version of this operating system.

The present MS-DOS and PC-DOS were adapted from an operating system developed for the 8088 microprocessor by programmer Tim Paterson, co-owner of Seattle Computer Products. The OS was purchased by Microsoft and licensed to IBM before the introduction of the first IBM PC in April 1981.

DOS works with routines built into the ROM-BIOS to supervise the control of your computer's hardware. Some functions, such as the handling of video display memory in computers other than the PCjr, are taken care of by special controller boards. That is why certain programs, such as Microsoft's Flight Simulator, can "bypass" DOS to address your screen. That is also why computers that do not have this ROM-level compatibility with the IBM PC (the PCjr was one) cannot run programs that use such tricks. Most functions, though, flow through the operating system, which forms an integral part of your computer. For the most part, today's clone computers have been engineered with functionally equivalent ROM-BIOS so that they appear identical to the operating system and programs, even if the coding within them is different (as required to avoid copyright violations).

A large or complex DOS isn't all in memory at once. The essential and most frequently used commands are loaded into memory and kept there for use at any time, even if your start-up disk is removed (if you are using a floppy-disk-based system.) That's why you may use DIR, COPY, and other commands, which are called "internal" DOS commands, anytime after start up.

These commands are controlled by a command "processor" called COM-MAND.COM, which is loaded into memory when you start DOS. If an application program requires enough memory, it may take over the RAM used by COMMAND.COM, overwriting it. That is, floppy-disk users will sometimes leave an application to be greeted by a message "Insert disk with Com-mand.Com In Drive A:" The command processor must be reloaded before you can use any of DOS' internal commands again. Hard disk users, of course, almost never see this message, because COMMAND.COM is always available to DOS on the hard disk.

Other DOS commands are "external" commands. Rather than being part of DOS itself and loaded into memory, these commands are actually separate programs, with names like FORMAT.COM. Though they are programs in their own right (just as DOS is a program, too), the external commands form an essential part of DOS, necessary for you to carry out the full range of DOS functions. You can tell DOS to copy several programs, format a disk, list a program, or perform a series of tasks, all with simple chains of commands.

Each new release of DOS brings new commands and capabilities. For example, DOS 3.0 introduced LABEL.COM, which allows the user to rename a disk with an 11-character label. Previously, it had been necessary to remember to label a disk volume when formatting (using the /V option), or resort to a clumsy utility program. Now, disk renaming is "built-in," thanks to the new LABEL external command.

Many DOS commands are actually tools to build and use other commands. These are the key to customizing your DOS. For example, by typing:

```
PROMPT "your message"
```

you can replace the familiar A> or B> prompt with a message of your choice. Typing just PROMPT, with no set of characters (or "string") following it will return the system to normal.

If you had to sit down and type PROMPT "Ready Master!" every time you turned on your computer, you'd soon tire of the exercise, and would rightly feel that your DOS had *not* truly been customized. So, in later chapters, we'll show you how to use these features, incorporate your changes into DOS "permanently," and produce a disk operating system that does things your way with a minimum of fuss.

CHANGES IN DOS

As you probably know, DOS comes in different versions. The first IBM PC-DOS, Version 1.0, was not used by many who lived to tell about it. That DOS was quickly supplanted by DOS 1.1, which became the most widely used version before 1983. When the PC-XT was introduced early that year, DOS 2.0 was unveiled. DOS 2.0 had some features similar to those in XENIX, Microsoft's version of Bell Laboratories' UNIX operating system.

In general, a new release of MS-DOS and PC-DOS comes in response to the IBM's introduction of a new product. The first eight DOS versions are listed in Table 1-1.

Table 1-1. Versions of DOS

Release	Date	Product
1.0	8/81	IBM PC, single sided drives
1.1	5/82	Double-sided disk drives
2.0	3/83	IBM PC-XT, hard disk drives
2.1	10/83	PCjr, half-height drives
3.0	08/84	PC-AT, 1.2-megabyte floppy
3.1	03/85	IBM PC Network
3.2	12/85	PC Convertible, 720K 3.5-inch disks
3.3	04/87	IBM PS/2, 1.44M 3.5-inch disk drives

DOS 2.0 had many improvements over DOS 1.1. All users gained from 2.0's ability to format disks with more capacity (each track was divided into nine 512-byte sectors instead of eight), making roughly 360K available on a double-sided disk, versus 320K with DOS 1.1. DOS 2.0 and beyond will automatically recognize and use the older disk format, so that no one (other than those who chose to remain with DOS 1.1) was left behind.

Hard-disk users reaped most of the benefits from the new capability of dividing a disk into many different subdirectories. However, this book will show how even users of floppy-based systems can use subdirectories.

DOS 2.1, introduced with the IBM PCjr, contained some changes to make the DOS compatible with the low-end machine. Then, when the IBM PC-AT heralded the next generation of IBM computers with a true-16-bit 80286 microprocessor chip, PC-DOS 3.0 was unleashed. This version of DOS, along with its successor, DOS 3.1 (which was announced, but not available, at the same time because it had some networking features that had yet to be completely implemented) is generally compatible with the earlier versions. A much larger DOS, its system files take up 36K of memory, compared with DOS 2.1's 24K.

Each new version of DOS generally adds capabilities for new hardware, usually new types of disk drives. In addition, most later releases of DOS brought useful new features not dependent on hardware innovations. For example, DOS 2.0 improved on DOS 1.1 by providing the ability to install customized device drivers for more flexible interfacing of peripherals of all types. Extended keyboard and screen control allowed redefining keys and handling the screen more flexibly. DOS 3.0 brought the capability to mark files as read-only with the new ATTRIB command and expanded the ways in which keyboard layout and date and time formats can be configured.

Some of the techniques described in this book require DOS 3.x or later, although most work equally well with DOS 2.x. Where a special feature is unique to DOS 3.0, 3.1, 3.2, and so on, that will be explained. We'll also assume that you already know basic DOS commands that are used with a floppy-disk-based system, such as FORMAT, COPY, DIR, and so on. We won't bore you with discussions on how to name files, use wildcards, or copy a file from one disk drive to another.

DOS 2.1 has remained as a standard even after the introduction of DOS 3.x because floppy-disk users had little incentive to upgrade to an operating system that took up more memory and disk space, and offered few new features, other than the ability to specify a label for a disk even after formatting had been completed. Hard disk users find more advantages in DOS 3.x, particularly with DOS 3.2 and later versions, which have interesting new features, such as DRIVER.SYS (which allows the user to create an alternative identifier for a drive.)

A user with a 64K PC system couldn't use DOS 3.x under any circumstances. A minimum of 96K, or 128K with a hard disk, are required. This is almost a moot point since most computers sold these days have a minimum of 256K to 640K of memory. Many in fact are sold with a megabyte or more, and 256K memory chip sets currently sell in the $30 range. It's almost inconceivable that anyone who can afford an IBM PC would not have at least the 256K that can be installed right on the motherboard of the PC's sold in the last few years.

Because DOS 3.0 and above does use extra memory and the features it offers are not overwhelmingly advantageous, it has been entirely practical for a user to stay with DOS 2.1, which many users have done. However, those who want to keep up with the latest software technology or can use the convenience of some of the new features, an upgrade makes both logical and economic sense.

A key new feature of DOS 3.0 to 3.3 and later is the ability to handle hard disks, single-sided and double-sided conventional disk drives, the high-density 1.2-megabyte drives, 5.25-inch drives, as well as the 720K- and 1.44-megabyte 3.5-inch diskettes found in the PC Convertible and PS/2 computers.

Although many of the features of this book work with DOS 1.1, to get the most from your custom DOS, you really need specialized commands, such as PATH, and subdirectories, which will be explained in detail. The upgrade to DOS 2.1, or 3.x costs only a few dollars, and this option should be taken by any serious PC user. If nothing else, you'll gain faster disk operation (16 percent faster), and a 12 percent increase in floppy disk storage. The only drawback to the later DOS' is that they use more memory. DOS 2.0 and beyond really require 128K to take advantage of all the features. And using some of the best features, such as "RAM" disks (using memory to simulate disk drives) as well as the top application programs all call for more memory than that. With memory prices so low, the extra RAM required of the newest DOS should not be a controlling factor.

Therefore, this book has been written solely for DOS 2.0 and later, and the routines and programs are guaranteed to work only with those operating systems. DOS 3.1 or later is strongly recommended to get the most from this book and the features of DOS.

A QUICK DOS COMPARISON

For those of you who are contemplating upgrading from DOS 1.1 to 2.1 (if there are any of you left) or, as is more likely, from 2.1 to 3.1 or later, here is a brief discussion of some of the major differences between DOS versions. The DOS manual supplied with each more completely explains each feature.

Version 1.1 to Version 2.0

Here's a breakdown of some of the enhancements to DOS that Version 2.0 added to the features available in Version 1.1. Those of special interest to readers of this book are:

- You can create a special file of commands that DOS will read each time it starts up. This file, called CONFIG.SYS, differs from your AUTOEXEC.BAT file. It allows defining special *drivers* for peripherals such as RAM disks, the keyboard, or screen. The use of AUTOEXEC.BAT and CONFIG.SYS will be explained completely later in this book.

- Starting with DOS 2.0, the operating system will support one or more fixed disk drives, which can be used to start up or "boot" the system. The fixed drives can be divided into more than one operating system, so you may partition one for PC-DOS and another for CP/M-86 or XENIX if you wish.

- DOS 2.0 increased potential disk capacity, thanks to the ability to use nine-sector 5.25-inch disks, rather than the eight-sector formatting used previously.

- Tree-structured directories were introduced, allowing subdirectories within any given directory or subdirectory. This feature allows dividing up your disk into logical areas and grouping programs or data in convenient order.

- Disk volume labels—the ability to name disks, but only during FORMAT, or through the use of a special utility program not included with DOS.

- Extended keyboard and screen control. Starting with DOS 2.0, the user can redefine keys from DOS, control the color of the screen, and move the cursor with special character sequences. These capabilities are explained and used extensively in this book.

- Redirection of input and output. DOS may cause a program to receive its input from a source other than the keyboard, such as a file, or to send its output to a destination other than the screen, for example, another file. In between, you may use "filters" that can sort or otherwise manipulate the data.

- DOS 2.0 and later versions have many new commands, such as CLS (clear screen), ASSIGN (reassign disk drive letters, that is, change Drive A: into Drive B:), PATH (used with tree-structured directories), and PROMPT (change the system prompt).

- Previous DOS 1.1 commands were enhanced with DOS 2.0. CHKDSK, DIR, ERASE, and FORMAT are among the commands with new features.

- As mentioned, DOS 2.0 also introduced the ability to install a customized device driver for character or block-oriented devices. This feature will be explained in the following chapters.

Enhancements From DOS 2.0 To DOS 3.0 and Later

A significant group of enhancements of DOS 3.x are of special interest to users of this book:

- Files can be marked as read-only with ATTRIB.

- LABEL can add, change, or delete a volume label.

- SELECT enables users to choose the keyboard layout and date and time format they want to use.

- COUNTRY can be included in the CONFIG.SYS file to "permanently" install a date and time format.

- Virtual disks, or "RAM" disks, can be automatically installed when DOS is booted. Previous versions of DOS also allowed RAM disks, but the user had to supply the software from another source, such as the vendor of a multifunction or memory board. With DOS 3.0, the VDISK.SYS device driver was supplied, with the capability of installing such disks automatically with statements in CONFIG.SYS.

- The maximum number of drives that can be accessed can be customized, using the LASTDRIVE statement in the CONFIG.SYS file.

- Besides 5.25-inch disks, DOS 3.0 introduced provisions for 1.2-megabyte 5.25 inch high-capacity disks, while DOS 3.2 and 3.3 added 720K and 1.44-megabyte 3.5-inch disks on computers equipped with the proper controller.

- Enhanced commands support the higher capacity disk drives: FORMAT, BACKUP, RESTORE, DISKCOMP, and DISKCOPY all allow for the 1.2-megabyte drives. DATE supports additional date formats.

- DOS 3.2 added the XCOPY command for new copying features and support for 3.5-inch diskettes as well as the aforementioned DRIVER.SYS device driver.

- DOS 3.2 also introduced the APPEND command, which allows users to specify path searches for all types of files, not just system files ending in .EXE, .COM, and .BAT extensions.

- DOS 3.3 adds features like CALL, which allows batch files to call other batch files. This DOS was initially available only as PC-DOS, with Microsoft's "generic" version following some months later. Unfortunately, it also had problems with hard disks, which were cleared up in short order. These two factors caused a delay in getting the latest version of DOS out to a broad number of users.

These are by no means all the enhancements of either DOS, and the explanations are skimpy. Those that you need to understand to customize your DOS will be explained as we go along. In fact, nearly every command available in

DOS will be addressed separately, and you'll be shown how you can use these features in new ways to customize DOS.

SUMMARY

This chapter has served as your introduction to microprocessors and DOS. We looked at some of the theory behind the microprocessor and some of the factors that can affect computer speed and power. These included the power of the microprocessor chip and its instructions, the speed of the peripherals and memory and whether the software, including the operating system, takes advantage of these capabilities.

The concept of the operating system itself was discussed, along with some history of MS-DOS and PC-DOS. The various differences of the DOS versions from 1.0 to 3.3 were explored. The versions of DOS supported by this book and the rationale behind the use of DOS 2.0 to 3.3 were also explained.

Next, we'll need to explore one of the key tools of DOS for managing information: the file—including data files, program files, and a special type of file called the *batch* file. These topics are taken up in the next chapter.

2

What is a Batch File?

INTRODUCTION

Batch files contain lists of commands that DOS examines and carries out as if you had entered them from the keyboard. You can chain together these commands and incorporate powerful options that allow the batch file to act in different ways, depending on the way the file is invoked. Batch files form the most important single concept in this book. In fact, most of the modules presented here are themselves nothing more than batch files, with a few enhancements added occasionally through machine language utilities.

If you know nothing more about batch files other than that your bootup disk has a file called AUTOEXEC.BAT—or even if you know less—this chapter will offer the introduction you need. We'll start at the beginning with a discussion of the different types of files found on a diskette, and move on to what makes a batch file different and, for our purposes, potentially very useful.

WHAT IS A FILE?

A file has much in common with the files found in your office filing cabinet—groups of information placed in a folder because the data is related in some way. Paper files usually have some features in common, such as a label to

14

identify the folder and a place where the folder belongs so that you can find it rapidly. The amount of information that can be placed in a given file may be limited by the size of the file drawer.

Computer files are also collections of information, stored in electronic or *machine-readable* form, rather than in hard-copy or *human-readable* format. A typical floppy disk or hard disk contains many different groups of such programs and data, and each of these are considered as separate files. Like paper files, computer files have a label, called a file name, that identifies that file uniquely. No other file on a single disk can have the same file name, although that name also includes a full description of the file's location relative to the other files. That is, the *path* used to find a file is actually part of its file name. We'll discuss paths extensively in Chapter 7 and other sections of this book.

Once created or copied to a disk, a file remains in the same place on that disk until it is moved by copying to a different place—similar to how a file folder remains in a given drawer or cabinet until it is moved. An index, called the disk directory, tells us where we can find the file.

The files themselves are stored as bytes on the disk, with DOS keeping track of which disk sectors are assigned or allocated to which particular file. Files don't have to be stored in consecutive sectors on the disk. DOS automatically makes use of available scattered sections of the disk by filling them with portions of a file stored, if necessary in nonconsecutive, or *noncontiguous* form. Computers make a distinction between *logical* features and *physical* features so that a *logical* disk file consists of consecutive sectors of data even though the *physical* file sectors may be scattered all over the disk surface.

Another logical distinction is in the file's format. All files are nothing more than bytes stored on the disk. However, DOS makes many distinctions between different types of files. For example, a file can be an application program that can be executed by DOS (usually with a .COM or .EXE extension). Such programs are nothing more than a set of instructions that tells the computer how to perform a task. Lotus 1-2-3 and WordPerfect are examples of application programs, which perform a useful function unrelated to the computer itself. That is, the program handles a task like word processing, telecommunications, graphics, database management, and so on.

Utilities are another type of program file, used for a computer housekeeping task. The Norton Utilities, which can help "unerase" files, sort disk directories, and perform other chores are among the most well-known IBM-oriented utility programs. However, DOS external commands like FORMAT.COM can also be considered utility programs as can most of the operating system itself. That would included the program that accepts and processes all the commands you type in from DOS, COMMAND.COM. Usually, COMMAND.COM is loaded into memory and used from there, but when DOS must reclaim that memory temporarily it then must reload the disk file COMMAND.COM to continue. All these are different types of files.

The interpreter BASICA or GW-BASIC is yet another file. Interpreters are unique in that they actually simulate *other* programs by using instructions from the data files that make up your BASIC programs.

Of course, files do not have to be programs. Some files cannot be directly executed by DOS. Your word processing program or database manager stores its information on the disk in the form of a file. Such files have a *file structure* determined by the applications program that creates the file. Generally, other software cannot use those data files unless they have been programmed to access that particular file structure.

ASCII CODE AND FILES

A file can be as simple as a few lines of text consisting only of the letters A to Z, numbers, punctuation, and so forth. These characters are often called alphanumerics, since they consist of the alphabet as well as numbers. Such characters are stored using a set of consistent code numbers (the computer handles only numbers, remember) called ASCII (pronounced *askey*), after the American Standard Code for Information Interchange. The ASCII code uses numbers from 0 to 127 to define a total of 128 different characters, including 52 alpha characters (26 upper and 26 lowercase), the numerals 0 through 9, and common punctuation marks and symbols.

Table 2-1 shows some of the printable ASCII characters.

Table 2-1. Some Printable ASCII Characters

<Space>	32	@	64		96		
!	33	A	65	a	97		
"	34	B	66	b	98		
#	35	C	67	c	99		
$	36	D	68	d	100		
%	37	E	69	e	101		
&	38	F	70	f	102		
`	39	G	71	g	103		
(	40	H	72	h	104		
)	41	I	73	i	105		
*	42	J	74	j	106		
+	43	K	75	k	107		
,	44	L	76	l	108		
-	44	M	77	m	109		
.	45	N	78	n	110		
-	46	O	79	o	111		
0	48	P	80	p	112		
1	49	Q	81	q	113		
2	50	R	82	r	114		
3	51	S	83	s	115		

Table 2-1. Some Printable ASCII Characters (Continued)

4	52	T	84	t	116
5	53	U	85	u	117
6	54	V	86	v	118
7	55	W	87	w	119
8	56	X	88	x	120
9	57	Y	89	y	121
:	58	Z	90	z	122
;	59	[	91	{	123
<	60	\	92	|	124
=	61	]	93	}	125
>	62	^	94	~	125
?	63	—	95	^	127

The characters from 0 to 31 usually are control characters, represented by special symbols not available on all printers, or by graphics symbols. Starting with ASCII symbol 127, the characters are special alpha characters needed for languages (such as the n with a tilde above it used in Spanish), or graphics characters defined by IBM.

A single computer memory location can store one eight-bit byte. Each of the binary digits (bits) in a byte can be either a 1 or a 0, so numbers from 00000000 to 11111111 (binary) can be expressed in each byte. That corresponds to the decimal values 0 to 255 so that there are 256 different possible code numbers that can be indicated by one byte. The ASCII code requires only 128 of those combinations. So, actually, only seven of the eight bits in the byte can designate any of the 128 different codes (01111111 binary being 127 in decimal), or any of the characters shown in the table above. That's why you often hear some files referred to as "7-bit ASCII." The application program using those files can *ignore* the eighth bit entirely, if the programmer so desires, because it gives no additional useful information.

However, if all 256 characters are used by a computer, as in the IBM PC, as mentioned, an additional 128 non-ASCII characters can be defined. These are *not* standardized between computer systems. IBM uses them for Greek letters and special math symbols and to generate characters that draw lines and boxes on the screen.

So, when we are talking about ASCII files, we mean files that use *only* the first 128 characters of the standard ASCII character set, and usually only the characters shown in the table. You may view the contents of such a file by entering TYPE "filename" at the keyboard. DOS prints the contents of the file to the screen. If the file is *not* pure ASCII, you will know it by the odd characters, beeps, and other garbage that results.

You can create ASCII files using EDLIN or simply by COPYing from the keyboard console to a disk file. The latter is accomplished by typing:

```
COPY CON:"filename" <ENTER>
This is a line of text.
```

You may hit ENTER as many times as you like to start a new line of text, or finish the file by pressing F6. That function key sends a Control-Z character to the file. Control-Z is widely used by DOS and application programs as an end-of-file marker for ASCII text.

So, you may create ASCII files using COPY CON, just as outlined above. You can't edit those files, though, without another facility. If you want to make a change, the entire file must be retyped. For very short, say one or two-line ASCII files, this is no bother at all. Simply enter TYPE "filename" to view what was previously in the file, should you need to, and COPY CON to enter the new line or lines.

BATCH FILES: A SPECIAL KIND OF ASCII FILE

More ways of entering ASCII files will be covered in Chapter 3. The discussion to this point was a basis for the introduction of the concept of batch files. These are a special kind of ASCII text file, which always contain the extension .BAT, which makes batch files what is called a "system file." Others lumped in that category are those ending with .EXE or .COM extensions. System files have one attribute in common: They may be summoned simply by typing their "root" name—the part of the name before the extension, as long as you are logged onto the drive and directory that contains that file, or have instructed DOS how to find it through a PATH command (the concept of PATH and subdirectories are covered in Chapter 7 of this book.)

For example, you run BASIC.COM or FORMAT.COM just by typing BASIC or FORMAT. When the PC sees a file name consisting of a legal word with no extension, it first looks to see if a .COM or .EXE file with that root exists—in that order. If so, it runs that program. Next, it looks to see if a .BAT file has that root. In that case, DOS looks at each line of text and tries to carry it out as if it were entered at the keyboard. Certain special rules for batch files apply in this case. If no .COM or .EXE or .BAT file with the root exists, and there is no other file by that name (if there is an extension, such as .BAS, it will not match) then the BAD COMMAND OR FILE NAME error message is displayed.

So, you can see that a batch file, called D.BAT, consisting of a single line:

```
DIR A:
```

causes DOS to display a directory of Drive A: every time you typed just D<ENTER> at the keyboard. That is, this would be true as long as you did not have a file called D.EXE or D.COM on that disk directory and the file D.BAT were either available in the current directory or residing in a directory pointed to by PATH. DOS looks for the .COM or .EXE extensions first, again, in that order. For this reason, you could not have a batch file called FORMAT.BAT or BASIC.BAT, if either FORMAT.COM or BASIC.COM were in that disk directory. Batch files cannot have the same root name as DOS internal commands, either, so DIR.BAT is invalid.

Most other names are fine, however. Do you see that we could create commands or lists of commands of our choice, and then call them up by typing the root word of the batch file? Suppose D.BAT consisted of:

DIR A: /W

Here each time you typed D < ENTER >, you would see a directory of Drive A: displayed in the wide format. Try it now at your computer.

1. From the DOS prompt, type COPY CON:D.BAT.

2. Press Enter (or Return, depending on your computer system's keyboard nomenclature).

3. Type: DIR A: /W.

4. Press F6 followed by Enter.

5. DOS will respond:
   (1) Files Copied.

Now, test out this batch file by typing D from the DOS prompt. If you followed the directions carefully, DOS responds to your new command by displaying a directory of Drive A: in wide format.

One special batch file you should know about is called AUTOEXEC.BAT. When your PC is powered up, it looks for that file in the startup disk's root directory. If AUTOEXEC.BAT is found, its commands are executed automatically, without your needing to do anything.

AUTOEXEC.BAT is a good way to customize your system. You can choose the program that you want the computer to run when it is turned on. For example, if you want the PC to operate as an unattended host computer during certain hours of the night, you may connect it to a timer and autoanswer modem and insert the name of your host communication program in the AUTOEXEC.BAT file. Then, when the timer turns the computer on, the host program runs automatically.

AUTOEXEC.BAT can also run utilities that set the system clock to a clock board you've installed, activate a RAM drive (if different from DOS 3.0's

VDISK), or do other tasks on powerup. A RAM drive, a "false" disk drive created by setting aside part of memory, is thus much faster than either a floppy or fixed disk. A thorough discussion of AUTOEXEC.BAT and how to customize it appears in Chapter 13.

Batch files are one of the most popular DOS "customizing" tools available, because even the neophyte can create long lists of commands that can be called by typing the batch file's root name. Try this:

1. From the DOS prompt type COPY CON:ALL.BAT

2. Type these lines:

   DIR A: /W <Enter>

   DIR B: /P <Enter>

   DIR C: <F6> <Enter>

3. DOS will respond:

   (1) Files Copied.

Now, type ALL from the DOS prompt. If you have a system with two floppy disks and a hard disk, DOS shows you directories of all three drives. Those with a hard disk and a single floppy disk will be shown a directory of the disk in Drive A:, then prompted to load a disk for Drive B:, and then shown a directory of Drive C:. If you have only two floppy disk drives and no Drive C:, DOS reports that an invalid drive was specified, but no harm is done.

As you will learn, batch files are particularly flexible because DOS offers a simple batch file "language" that allows choosing one course of action or another based on various conditions, including instructions the user types in along with the batch file command. Later in this book, we'll show you a modification that will allow even more flexibility by permitting user input *during* the batch file's operation.

SUMMARY

This chapter gave an introduction to file concept, with the analogy of the common business file cabinet. We discovered how programs, data, and even DOS itself are stored on disks as files. Special types of files, especially ASCII files, were discussed, with examples of how they can be created using COPY CON.

Batch files, a special kind of ASCII file, are system files like .COM and .EXE files that can be called directly from DOS by typing their root name. Several uses for batch files, AUTOEXEC.BAT in particular, were discussed. The idea of batch file "language" and programming was introduced.

We'll continue with batch files shortly. In the next chapter, you'll want to take the time to learn about some of the tools used to work with DOS. These will include several alternate ways of writing and editing batch files.

3

Some DOS Tools:
EDLIN and DEBUG

INTRODUCTION

Before we can begin customizing DOS, let's learn about some of the tools that we use to shape the operating system to our will. Now is a good time to learn one of the various ways of entering ASCII text at your PC so that you can create and edit the batch files you'll be shown throughout this book. We'll cover various different ways to enter batch files. You'll learn the quickest and easiest way: using COPY CON to type in the file directly from the keyboard. We'll also present an introduction to EDLIN, DOS' "free" text editor, with some examples. A simple batch file will be created using EDLIN, then modified to show you how the various commands work.

ENTERING BATCH FILES USING COPY CON:

As mentioned in the last chapter, you can enter short batch files (or any ASCII text for that matter) by copying from the console (the keyboard) to a file. To activate this mode, type COPY CON:*filename*, where *filename* is the name of the file you wish to create. If a file already exists by that name on the currently logged disk drive and directory, it will be replaced (in other words, erased) without warning. So, be careful when using COPY CON:.

To review: after you have typed the file name and pressed Enter, the DOS cursor drops down a line and waits for you to type your ASCII text. When you have finished an individual line, press Enter. You may backspace within a line to retype the text, but once you have pressed Enter and dropped down to the next line, there is no way to edit that line without typing the whole file again.

When finished typing the text, you may end the file by pressing F6 (assuming the F6 key has not been redefined), or by pressing Control-Z, followed by Enter. Either of these will append a Control-Z to the file and close it. In most cases, you may skip the final Enter on the line of text immediately preceding the Control Z. Adding the extra carriage return wastes a bit of time when the batch file is run but otherwise does no harm. For some of the special small files to be created later in this book, the extra carriage return is either mandatory or forbidden, because of how we want DOS to handle the file. In some cases we *want* the carriage return to appear or not appear at certain places. These instances will be clearly pointed out in the text.

One good way to retype a short existing file using COPY CON: is to first display the contents of the existing file with the DOS TYPE command. Then you can create the new file by copying what you see on the screen, using either the same name or, to be on the safe side, a new name. For example, to add a line to your AUTOEXEC.BAT file, you might enter:

```
TYPE AUTOEXEC.BAT
COPY CON:AUTOEXEC.BAK
```

You could copy the lines displayed, change them, or add a new line or two as you prefer. Once you had tested AUTOEXEC.BAK, the old file could be erased and the new one renamed:

```
ERASE AUTOEXEC.BAT
RENAME AUTOEXEC.BAK AUTOEXEC.BAT
```

You can also type just the new lines you want to add to the file and then append the two together. Assume your new lines were in a file created with COPY CON: that you can call AUTOEXEC.NEW. To add them to the old file, type this command:

```
TYPE AUTOEXEC.NEW>>AUTOEXEC.BAT
```

The new file would be typed by DOS, but, instead of being displayed to the screen, would be added to the end of your old AUTOEXEC.BAT file. This technique, which involves *redirection* of DOS, will be explained thoroughly later in this book.

ALTERNATIVE METHODS

Many word processors can also produce simple ASCII text (that is, without complex control codes or print formatting characters.) WordStar 2000, with its "unformatted" option, WordStar, WordPerfect, DisplayWrite, 3 and DisplayWrite 4 all allow directly creating ASCII files, even though their own files are stored in 8-bit binary form. Many other word-processing programs offer an ASCII output option and will also accept input of ASCII files so that you may load a batch file into the word processor and then store it in ASCII form when you are finished editing or revising it.

Other word processors already produce pure ASCII during their typical course of operation. The author used PC-Write to produce some of the modules in this book. This "shareware" program can be obtained from many users' groups or computer bulletin boards. If you find the program of use, you can register it with the program's author for a modest fee and receive a printed manual as well as upgrades as new features are added to the software.

Because word-processing programs allow flexible screen-oriented editing (as opposed to EDLIN's line-at-a-time editing), they are preferable. Test your word processor to see if it has an ASCII (nondocument, some call it) mode. This mode allows reading and writing plain-vanilla text files, which is what batch files. Some WP programs, like WordStar 2000, allow "printing" a document to disk, which places an ASCII image of the file on the disk. When using such a program, however, make sure you'll be able to reload this ASCII file back into the WP for later editing. One way to test for an ASCII file is to TYPE it from the DOS prompt and see if it contains any "garbage," or odd characters produced by the control characters in the file. To do this, type the following line:

```
TYPE filename<ENTER>
```

Substitute for *filename* the name of the text file you want to test for ASCII-ness.

USING EDLIN

Considering its limited capabilities, a surprising number of users rely on ED-LIN. One obvious reason for its popularity may be that it is free; EDLIN comes with DOS. In addition, programmers may be quite comfortable working with line-oriented text editors and see no special reason to learn all the complex syntax of a high-powered word-processing program simply to enter and revise batch files that may range from a line or two to no more than 20 or 30 lines. Because most of the files in this book are short, you may want to learn EDLIN for your batch file entry. It could come in handy sometime when you need to create an ASCII file too long for the COPY CON: method, and no other text editor is available.

Unlike most word-processing programs, EDLIN works only with lines as a text entity. These lines can be created with lengths up to 253 characters per line. During input, line numbers are created and shown on the screen for your reference only. As new lines are inserted, the line numbers following are automatically renumbered to reflect the new scheme. The numbers do not become part of the file, though, and are used only during the creation and editing process.

To create a file using EDLIN, first make sure that the EDLIN program is available on the disk you'll be using, or, if you are using a hard disk, DOS "knows" where to find it through a PATH command. Or, if you know which directory stores EDLIN and you are using DOS 3.0 or later, you may type the full pathname from anywhere to bring up the editor. To start EDLIN, use this syntax:

```
[path1]EDLIN [d:][path2]<filename to edit>[.extension] [/B]
```

Everything on the above line except EDLIN and the filename to edit are optional. *Path1* is the pathname of the directory where EDLIN can be found, and can be used if you are operating with DOS 3.x, which allows running system files by typing the full pathname. *D:* is the drive where the file to be created or edited resides. If the file is present on the currently logged drive, d: is optional. *Path2* is the pathname to the file to be created or edited and is optional if the current directory will be used (those who don't know about paths should be patient; they will be covered shortly.) The filename to edit and its extension, if any, should be entered next on the line. Note that the extension is optional only when creating the file. To edit that file, the extension must be included.

The /B is an option or *switch* that tells EDLIN to continue loading the file even after a Control-Z is encountered. You'll remember that Control-Z marks the end of ASCII files. Therefore, when editing batch files you'll not need to use the /B switch. However, if you should need to load a file likely to contain a Control-Z somewhere in the middle (as a binary file would), this switch will tell EDLIN to load the entire file regardless of any Control-Z's that might be encountered.

Try out EDLIN for youself by typing in this simple batch file following these steps:

1. Type A:EDLIN D.BAT

   If EDLIN is not stored on A:, log over to the disk or directory where EDLIN is stored, and omit the drive specification (A:).

2. EDLIN will display: New File, and an asterisk cursor.

3. Type I to begin entering text.

4. EDLIN will display: 1.

5. Type the following lines as each line number is displayed. Press Enter at the end of each line:

```
1. ECHO OFF
2. DIR A:
3. DIR B:
4. DIR C:
5. <Control C>
```

6. At the EDLIN prompt, enter E to exit. The new file will be written to disk. You can summon this new batch file by typing D at the DOS prompt when you are logged onto the disk containing D.BAT.

For our purposes, EDLIN handles just about any file we care to create or edit. You should know, however, that EDLIN works in memory, and so is limited to files that fit in memory all at one time. In truth, only 75 percent of such a large file will be loaded; you'll need to process very long files in sections.

EDLIN COMMANDS

As you've already seen, the EDLIN prompt is an asterisk. When creating a new file, you'll be faced with the asterisk cursor. To begin entering text, we typed the command I (for Insert) and type and ended each line by pressing Enter.

So far, this looked much like typing files with COPY CON: You may backspace within a line, but previous lines are apparently lost forever. However, you may view and edit those lines using the basic EDLIN commands. Load D.BAT once again by typing EDLIN D.BAT, then try out some of these other commands:

L To list lines, using the line numbers supplied by EDLIN. The format is to type the beginning line number you want to see, followed by the end line number. Use a comma to separate the two. If you want to see the lines displayed from the beginning of the file, you may skip the first line number. For example:

```
25,50L
,30L
```

The first example would display all lines between 25 and 50, inclusive, while the second command would show all lines from the beginning of the file to line 30.

In our example, we could list lines 1–3 by typing:

```
1,3L
or
,3L
```

Try this a few times to become comfortable with listing lines within EDLIN.

I   To insert lines between two existing lines. Type the line number where the insertion is to begin and follow that with the I command. If you don't enter a line number or use a period as the line number, the insertion will begin just before the current line. Line numbers higher than the last line in the file cause the insertion to begin at the end of the file. Press Control-Break to exit Insert mode. Here are some examples:

```
25I
.I
9999I
```

The first example would cause the insert to begin after line 25. All later lines in the file would be renumbered to accommodate the insert. The second example would start insertion after the current line (last line referenced), while the third example would jump to the end of the file and begin the insert there (as long as the file had fewer than 9999 lines, of course).

With D.BAT, try inserting a line between lines 2 and 3:

1. Type 2I.

2. Enter DIR D:

3. Type Control-C to stop inserting.

4. You'll see the asterisk prompt again.

D   Delete lines of text. Syntax is similar to the L command; that is, you type the beginning and last line numbers you want deleted, separated by commas. For example:

```
100,200D
```

This will cause EDLIN to delete all the lines between 100 and 200 inclusive, and renumber the remaining lines to account for the deletion. Leaving off the first number results in the deletion starting with the current line up to the line specified. Omitting the second parameter causes EDLIN to delete only the line shown. Typing D on a line by itself deletes only the current line.

Now, try deleting your new line 3: From the asterisk prompt, type 3D.

Edit a line of text. Just type in the line number to be edited or a period to indicate the current line or just Enter to edit the line *after* the current line. To abort a line edit, press Esc or Control Break instead of Enter, or move the cursor to the beginning of the line and press Enter. To delete the remainder of a line, move the cursor to that point and press Enter.

E To End EDLIN. The file is written to disk.

If you are done working with D.BAT, from the asterisk prompt, just enter E and press ENTER to exit EDLIN. The edited file will be written to disk.

W Writes lines in memory to disk. This command always begins with the first line in memory. Syntax is:

`[n]W`

where *n* is the number of lines to be written. If you leave off *n*, then EDLIN writes lines that take up the equivalent of 25 percent of available memory. This command saves files to disk and helps edit very large files by allowing you to write part of the file to disk to make room for additional lines brought in through the A (append) command.

A Append lines from a disk file to the file currently being edited in memory. These lines are placed at the end of the current lines. This command is the companion to W described above; neither are essential for writing batch files, but are listed for the sake of completeness in this description of EDLIN. Syntax is:

`[n]A`

where *n* is the number of lines to be brought in. If not specified, lines equivalent to 75 percent of the available memory will be loaded.

T Transfers or merges a disk file into the file being edited. You could use this to import one batch file's contents into a new batch file you are editing to reuse (after editing) some of the lines. Syntax is:

`[line]T[d:]filename`

If specified, *line* indicates the line number the file is to be inserted before. If not indicated, the current line will be used.

S Search text. This looks for a specified string of characters in the indicated range of lines. Syntax is as follows:

`[line],[line][?]S[string]`

Both the beginning and ending line numbers to be searched can be indicated, these are optional following the usual line-specification rules already described. If you want a prompt that causes EDLIN to pause after each line is displayed, enter the question mark immediately preceding the S command. The string to be searched follows or, if you do not indicate a string, the last string previously searched (by Search or the Replace command) will be used.

With D.BAT loaded, try typing:

`?SDIR`

R Replace. Similar to Search, except that the first string (to search for) is followed by a Control-Z (F6) and a second string to be used as a replacement for the first place it is found. You may insert the question mark to be queried before each placement. If no second string is specified, the first string will be deleted where it appears. Syntax is as follows:

`[line],[line][?]R[string][<F6>string]`

To test this, type the following lines:

```
RDIR<F6>DUR
,3L
```

You'll be shown the lines 1-3 in D.BAT, with DIR changed to DUR. Type RDUR<F6>DIR to change it back.

M Move a range of lines to the location specified by a third line specified. Syntax is as follows:

`[line],[line],lineM`

Where the first two *line* entries indicate the range, while the third the new location. You can also specify a quantity of lines to be moved:

`100,+30,200M`

This would move 30 lines beginning at line 100 to a location starting at line 200; whereupon all the lines in the file would be renumbered to reflect the change.

Move line 3 ahead of line 2 in D.BAT by typing the following lines:

```
3,1,2M
,3L
```

Notice how the lines have been renumbered? Now, try *copying* some lines with the C command.

C Copy Lines. To produce a duplicate of lines currently in memory, use this syntax.

```
[line],[line],line[count]C
```

Where the first two entries show the range of lines to be copied, the third the location where they are to be copied to and *count* the number of times the operation is to take place. If you had a set of basic lines you wanted to reuse in the file, you could make two, three, four, or more copies of those lines at one step with this command.

Type these lines:

```
3,,2,C
,4L
```

P Display lines (like L), except that the new current line becomes the last line of those displayed by this command.

Q Quit EDLIN. No parameters are necessary, but EDLIN prompts you to be sure that you want to leave the program without saving any of the changes entered. To save those changes, you write the lines to disk first with the W command.

Exit EDLIN now, without saving any changes made in D.BAT by typing Q at the asterisk prompt.

SUMMARY

In this chapter we've learned some basic tools for working with DOS. These include the technique of entering batch files using COPY CON:, more flexible ASCII file entry and editing with a word processor, and DOS' built-in line-oriented editor, EDLIN. We created a practice file using EDLIN and used some of the commands to add, insert, delete, and change lines.

In the next chapter, we'll take our first look at a key DOS concept—hierarchical subdirectories—how they are arranged and how to navigate around within them.

4

Learning About Subdirectories

INTRODUCTION

Without subdirectories, a 100-megabyte hard disk would be a vast jungle of files that we would never be able to access. It might take five or six minutes just to read a directory listing. However, DOS has a solution to this formidable problem—the imposing-sounding hierarchical directory structure. In this chapter, though, you'll discover that subdirectories needn't be difficult to understand or to use.

E Unus Pluribum

From that dubious Latin, we're led to a discussion of how DOS treats a single disk—a floppy or a hard disk—as if it were many different disks by dividing the single disk or diskette into many different subdirectories.

Learning about subdirectories is necessary, because we need to know how to find individual files on a disk. You may be using A: but in a different directory from the one on which your file resides. That is particularly true for hard disk users or those with PC-ATs and their 1.2-megabyte high-density drives or PS/2 computers with their 720K and 1.44-megabyte 3.5-inch disks. These disks can also use subdirectories to divide them into smaller, more easily handled portions.

This type of directory configuration, called "tree-structured," was one of the biggest changes introduced by IBM with DOS 2.0 in 1983 when the PC-XT was unveiled. Subdirectories allow storing large amounts of information on a hard disk, while avoiding the problems associated with single directories that might be hundreds of files long.

Instead, each disk has a main or "root" directory. This directory can contain files. It may also list other directories, which DOS treats as files, except that ERASE won't remove them. You may change to a subdirectory and then list the files there. The files in the higher, or "root" directory become invisible to you (unless you issue the proper DIR command to see them). Each subdirectory may, in turn, have subdirectories of its own. So, a business might store employee records in the following manner:

```
Main directory: EMPLOYE:


Subdirectories:    PAYROLL
                   PROFITS
                   PERSONEL------------------------------I
                                                         I
                   I-------------------------------------I
                   I
                   V
Subdirectories    WEST
of directory      NORTH
PERSONEL          EAST---------------------------------I
                  SOUTH                                I
                                                       I
                  I------------------------------------I
                  I
                  V
Subdirectories    PITT
of directory      CLEV
EAST              PHIL
                  NYC
```

As a disk directory, this arrangement might look something like this:

```
Volume in drive C is EMPLOYE
Directory of  C:\
```

```
COMMAND  COM     22042    8-14-88    8:00a
PAYROLL        <DIR>       9-19-88    5:49p
PERSONEL       <DIR>       9-19-88    5:49p
PROFITS        <DIR>       9-19-88    5:50p
        4 File(s)    2133792 bytes free

Volume in drive C is EMPLOYE
Directory of  C:\PERSONEL

.              <DIR>       9-19-88    5:49p
..             <DIR>       9-19-88    5:49p
WEST           <DIR>       9-19-88    5:51p
NORTH          <DIR>       9-19-88    5:51p
EAST           <DIR>       9-19-88    5:52p
SOUTH          <DIR>       9-19-88    5:52p

        4 File(s)    2133792 bytes free

Volume in drive C is EMPLOYE
Directory of  C:\PERSONEL\EAST

.              <DIR>       9-19-88    5:52p
..             <DIR>       9-19-88    5:52p
PITT           <DIR>       9-19-88    5:53p
CLEVE          <DIR>       9-19-88    5:53p
PHIL           <DIR>       9-19-88    5:55p
NYC            <DIR>       9-19-88    5:55p

        4 File(s)    2133792 bytes free

Volume in drive C is EMPLOYE
Directory of  C:\PERSONEL\EAST\PITT

.              <DIR>       9-19-88    5:51p
..             <DIR>       9-19-88    5:51p
MILLER          3302      7-29-88    5:53p
SMITH           3204      6-11-88    5:53p
JONES           1102      8-09-88    5:55p
JOHNSON         2300      8-06-88    5:55p
BUSCH           9804     10-11-88    4:32p

        5 File(s)    2133792 bytes free
```

Within the main directory, we might find several subdirectories for categories of information files, including one called PERSONEL.

In checking the PERSONEL directory, we might find it further broken down by part of the country, and each of those by plant locations. The breakdown could be as fine as desired, until the final directory would include the actual data files.

This simple explanation shows how a tree-structured directory works. It is like a tree, because each juncture can branch into several subdirectories until there are many that trace back to a single root.

NAVIGATING THE DIRECTORY TREE

How do we climb down this tree? That part is fairly easy. You may change from a current directory to any of the subdirectories listed in that directory simply by typing:

```
CD directory name
```

If you find further directories listed in the subdirectory, you may repeat the process as many times as necessary to get to the final subdirectory you want. There is a faster way of doing this that we will look at shortly.

An important thing to remember that, like a tree or river, each branch stems from a common point of origin. It is always possible to trace back from a subdirectory to the root. Another set of terms that is often applied to tree-structured directories is "parent" and "child." The root directory is the parent of all the subdirectories, which in turn may have their own children. From one parent, many generations of children and grandchildren can derive. Unlike families, no child can have more than one parent. Tracing a tree-structured directory is something like following a family tree back only on your father's and grandfather's side.

CREATING A SUBDIRECTORY

You may create these subdirectories by typing:

```
MD directory name
```

The new directory name you are creating should follow normal file-naming rules; it can have up to eight characters, plus a three-character extension. Directories are usually *not* given extensions, however. Directory names are always followed by <DIR> when they are listed in a higher directory, and they cannot be erased by normal file commands such as ERASE or KILL. Directories will show up as files from BASIC when you use the FILES statement.

Note that it is sometimes necessary to abbreviate filenames because of the eight-character limitation. In the preceding example, the name PERSONEL was selected as a descriptive directory name because PERSONNEL is too long.

REMOVING A SUBDIRECTORY AND MOVING FROM ONE TO ANOTHER

A directory can be removed by typing RD *directory name*, except that the directory must be empty—that is, contain no files or subdirectories of its own. Unless you have one of the utility programs available, deleting a many-branched directory can be tedious. The task can be relieved using a batch file utility, as we will learn.

The route we must take from the main or root directory to a file in a subdirectory is called the "path." Pathnames are constructed using the directory name and a backslash character(\) to separate one directory name from the next. Using our example, if we were working from the root directory and wanted to see if there was a file on someone named MILLER, who worked in the Pittsburgh plant, we might type:

```
DIR B:\PERSONEL\EAST\PITT\MILLER.*
```

DOS would wend through the path to the final subdirectory, PITT, and look there for any files that matched "MILLER.*." Although pathnames may be confusing at first, it is worth your while to learn how to use them. As the trend toward even higher capacity disk drives (some analysts estimate that 80 percent of PC users will have access to a hard disk by 1990), subdirectories will become more useful, or even essential for the average worker.

Logically, you can change to a given subdirectory in one step, using the proper path:

```
CD \PERSONEL\EAST\PITT
```

would switch you to the PITT subdirectory in one step, without the need to type CD repeatedly. In fact, you can embed such a line in a batch file of your choice to go to a frequently visited directory without bothering to remember the correct path. You might call such a file PITT.BAT:

```
ECHO OFF
CD \PERSONEL\EAST\PITT
```

Moving from a subdirectory back to the root can be done in single steps or in one big jump. The first line below will take you from PITT up to EAST, while the second one will move you all the way from PITT (or, actually, as many sub-directories down as you may be) back to the root:

```
CD \EAST
CD \
```

Just as you can't smoothly jump from one branch of a tree to the next—it's better to trace the branches back and then go back down the next—direct jumping from one path to another can't be done; you must type a CD command reaching back at least as far as a common parent directory and include the path back down.

For example, if you were logged onto C:\PERSONEL\EAST\PITT, and wanted to use C:\PERSONEL\SOUTH\MIAMI, you'd need to type the following command:

```
CD ..\..\SOUTH\MIAMI
```

Here, we're using the DOS abbreviation "..", which stands for the parent directory of the current directory. This lets us avoid having to go back to the root directory to type our CD command. The other way to move from the PITT subdirectory to the MIAMI subdirectory would be to type:

```
CD \PERSONNEL\SOUTH\MIAMI
```

Using the double period, you may change from the current subdirectory to the directory immediately above it by typing:

```
CD ..
```

The other abbreviation allowed by DOS is the single period to stand for the current directory. This, too has uses in batch file programming but less than the double period shorthand.

SUMMARY

In this chapter, we've covered the concept of hierarchical directories. We've learned how such directories are set up, how to create and remove subdirectories, and how to move from one directory to another. Subdirectories will be used extensively throughout this book. More on subdirectories, particularly the PATH command, will be covered later.

In the next chapter, we'll cover the use of an important DOS tool, the *installable device driver*, as it can be used to customize the way your computer handles peripherals, including the keyboard and CRT screen. Then, we'll be ready to begin customizing DOS itself with some new commands. The batch files we've typed in and learned from so far have been an introduction to creating some very useful new utilities.

5

Personalizing Your System Prompt

INTRODUCTION

This chapter will introduce our first DOS customized commands, as well as give you a first look at several key concepts. First, we'll look at installable device drivers. Then we'll move into the first of the batch file language commands that will be covered in the book. We'll learn how to use a DOS command, PROMPT, that can be put to work to personalize your system prompt to include any message you wish. Some very sophisticated cursor movement tools will be outlined, along with the first hints of an important DOS feature—the environment—covered in more detail in Chapter 8. We'll start off the chapter with an explanation of installable device drivers.

INSTALLABLE DEVICE DRIVERS

Like many DOS features, device drivers are more intimidating to the new user than they need to be. A device driver is nothing more than a software utility that tells DOS how to handle a new peripheral device. These are almost always supplied with the devices that require them so that the average nonprogrammer user doesn't need to know how or why device drivers work, nor how to create one. However, it will be helpful if you learn how to *use* them.

The "installable device driver" was introduced with DOS 2.0. Before that, DOS had a fixed device driver that couldn't be modified without patching DOS itself, a risky undertaking at best. DOS 1.1, then, could control only those devices, such as disk drives, keyboards, CRT, terminals, printers, and so forth that were provided for in the original operating system.

However, assume that you wanted to interface a new type of device, such as a daisy-wheel printer that requires a software program (or "driver") of its own. If you were locked into DOS' device routines, there would be no way to allow for this new peripheral.

Obviously, since many of today's massive hard-disk drives, low-cost laser printers, optical drives, and other peripherals were barely a gleam in the eye of the most optimistic computer user in 1981, DOS 1.1's device capabilities were severely limited in "modern" terms.

DOS 2.0 opened the door to these peripherals by making it much simpler for anyone with the requisite programming skills to write their own device drivers. Users may install these through a simple command:

```
DEVICE=<driver filename>
```

Because we usually want DOS to boot up with these drivers already installed, DOS has a special file in which these DEVICE commands can be stored, called CONFIG.SYS. This file is actually very similar to a batch file in some ways, specifically AUTOEXEC.BAT.

Like a batch file, CONFIG.SYS is an ASCII text file that has a few lines of commands. It can be created with COPY CON, EDLIN, your word processor, or BATCHED.BAS. DOS checks CONFIG.SYS while booting up, *before* it carries out the commands in AUTOEXEC.BAT. And the allowable commands in CON-FIG.SYS are much more limited. We'll explore some of these later in the book. But the one discussed now for use in this chapter is DEVICE. You may use that command to specify which device drivers DOS will load as it boots.

One common device driver is VDISK.SYS, which is the virtual disk program supplied with DOS 3.0 and upward. This driver will create "RAM" disks in unused portions of your PC's memory. These can be treated as fast (and volatile) disk drives, with the caveat that the information they contain disappears when the computer is turned off. Many memory-expansion boards provide equivalent drivers. If you have these lines in your CONFIG.SYS file:

```
DEVICE=VDISK 100
DEVICE=VDISK 50
```

DOS creates one RAM disk with 100K available for storage and a second one with 50K set aside, assuming you have sufficient memory to spare. If you have two floppy-disk drives in your system, the two RAM disks are defined as Drive C: and Drive D:, respectively. VDISK is a common device driver.

DOS is also supplied with a special device driver file called ANSI.SYS. This driver was written to replace the default screen and keyboard driver built into the operating system and your computer's BIOS.

What ANSI.SYS does is intercept characters received from the keyboard and either pass them on to DOS unchanged, or supply new, redefined characters or strings of characters. This facility would allow redefining the keyboard and, in fact, that will be explored in Chapter 11.

ANSI.SYS also allows control of the display, including the colors shown on the screen, the position of the cursor, and the characters that supply the system prompt itself. One of these capabilities, cursor control, will be explored later in this chapter. Before we can do that, you need to understand a little more about ANSI.SYS and how to activate it for DOS.

You may use any of the ASCII text-entering methods discussed in Chapter 3 to create or edit a CONFIG.SYS file. If you already understand device drivers, you may have previously created a CONFIG.SYS file. Edit that one. Otherwise, create a new one. The simplest way is to type:

```
COPY CON:CONFIG.SYS<ENTER>
DEVICE=ANSI.SYS<F6>
```

For DOS to find it note that your bootup disk must have both CONFIG.SYS and the ANSI.SYS files in the root directory (the main directory of the disk, if you are using subdirectories). If you are using a hard disk, you probably understand subdirectories better than has been explained so far. And if you don't understand subdirectories, they will be explained shortly. If you can already use the PATH command, you may place ANSI.SYS in a subdirectory, but include the proper path in the DEVICE statement:

```
DEVICE=\directoryname\ANSI.SYS
```

In either case, CONFIG.SYS must still be in the root directory. Once this is done, all the pieces are in place. All you need to know are some of the simple rules for batch files that we will incorporate in the first "recipes" in our "cookbook."

USING PROMPT

DOS is supplied with an interesting command called PROMPT. In truth, this command is an abbreviation for a longer command, SET PROMPT. Since

PROMPT is only used in one way, to pass information to the system, DOS allows using it alone without the SET command. The results that derive from the PROMPT command vary, however, depending on the characters or *argument* that you supply with the command.

The syntax for this command is as follows:

SET PROMPT "string"

or

PROMPT "string"

Both commands set the value of a special DOS variable to determine the system prompt. The value is set to the string you type in after the PROMPT command. The variable happens to be called an "environment variable," and the storage area that DOS uses to keep track of this variable, as well as other information, is called the environment. We'll be using the DOS environment extensively in this book and, in fact, all of Chapter 6 is devoted to a more complete discussion of this feature. For now, all you need to know is that PROMPT "string" changes the system prompt to the equivalent of that particular string of characters.

From the DOS prompt, you may change that prompt right now by typing the command and pressing Enter. If you are near your computer now, try it.

You could change your system prompt from A> and B> (as well as C>, and so on) to READY, MASTER! or BY YOUR COMMAND! or any silly phrase you like. Some users *have* modified their prompts in such ways, much to the confusion of other users.

The problem is that you would not know what drive was DOS' current default drive DOS. The old-fashioned standard system prompt *does* have its uses. You can restore the system to the default prompt by typing PROMPT on a line by itself.

Fortunately, the use of PROMPT doesn't end there. You can also include in the DOS command certain "metastrings," which is just a way of saying that you can include characters that aren't displayed literally in the prompt. Instead, DOS interprets them and displays a different string of characters according to certain rules that we will explain to you.

Metastrings all consist of a dollar sign ($) and one other character. If the metastring is a dollar sign, plus any of most of the ASCII characters, the string is considered null and is ignored. For example, "$C" would be a null metastring. Why would you *want* a null string? Well, a group of characters is interpreted by DOS. Some are DOS delimiters, such as semicolons, commas, and blanks. To begin a metastring with one of these, you need to precede it with a null metastring:

`PROMPT :::: HI THERE ! ::::`

would not be accepted because the string begins with a colon. You could, however, enter the following:

`PROMPT $A:::: HI THERE ! ::::`

if you should want to do so for some reason, and DOS would accept the command. Other characters, when used in metastrings, have special meanings.

$t—the time.

$d—the date.

$v—the DOS version number.

$n—the default drive name.

$g—the greater than symbol.

$l—the less than symbol.

$p—current drive and path.

$b—a vertical bar.

$q—the equals sign.

$h—backspace.

$e—ESCAPE.

$_—(The underscore) Go to the next line on the screen.

Please notice that when a lowercase letter is specified, it *must* be used. All the current examples dealing with ANSI.SYS use lowercase letters, but later on we'll find some that require uppercase letters. $H and $h are *not* the same in terms of metastrings. You might think of some of these metastrings as variables, like those used in programs, because the system will substitute the current applicable value for the metastring. When PROMPT$ includes $d, for example, the current system date that you typed in as a response to the start-up DATE prompt (or supplied by your clock board, or the default date if you just pressed Enter) is substituted for "$d."

Other metastrings are actual characters. The $b always appears as a vertical bar, and $g is always be shown as the greater than (>) symbol.

We can use these metastrings, plus strings of our own, to build a customized prompt more useful than the earlier example given. Most often, to avoid the "where am I?" problem, the new prompt includes the standard system prompt as part of it. You might have:

```
PROMPT Ready Master!   $n$g
```

Your prompt would appear, if you were logged onto drive A:, as:

```
Ready Master!   A>
```

You could include "$_", the equivalent of a carriage return, to display the prompt on two different lines: PROMPT Ready Master! $_$n$g would show up as:

```
Ready Master!
A>
```

Your customization of your system prompt is limited only by your imagination. In fact, there are still more sophisticated things that you can do, using some of DOS' built-in screen and cursor control.

USING PROMPT TO COMMUNICATE WITH ANSI.SYS

You probably know that you can clear the screen in DOS by typing CLS. If you do that, the cursor character (and the prompt) appear on the blank screen starting at row 1, column 1. Subsequent characters typed are one space farther to the right, until you reach the right side of the screen, and the line wraps around, or you press Enter, and DOS interprets the line. Each new line begins one line farther down from the last.

That movement is not cast in concrete, though. The cursor can be moved directly. To do that, you have to first install ANSI.SYS as described earlier. The new device driver then looks for special character sequences, which it interpret and use to position the cursor where you indicate on the screen.

The ANSI.SYS sequences all begin with the escape character and a left bracket, which we'll write as "ESC[". Other characters follow the escape and left bracket to tell ANSI.SYS specifically what to do.

Usually, though, you can't just type the sequence from the keyboard, because DOS interprets pressing the Ecape key as a signal to cancel the current line. As soon as you hit Escape, you are back at the beginning of the line and starting over.

If you're sharp, you may already remember that one of the allowable meta-strings was $e, which was defined as the escape character. This metastring was included to allow you to manipulate the cursor while designing your prompts. When you send a PROMPT message to DOS that includes the $e metastring, ANSI.SYS interprets the characters following the ESC as a special command. Certain sequences have special meaning to ANSI.SYS. So, your new prompt string can include any of the cursor movement sequences, as well as other metastrings and strings of your choice.

ANSI.SYS ESCAPE SEQUENCES FOR CURSOR CONTROL

While on the topic of sequences, it seems logical to show what they can do. Here are some of the allowable sequences:

ESC [row;colH—Substitute the row and column you want the cursor to move to for *row* and *col*. If you do not specify row and column, the cursor moves to the home position. To move the cursor to row 4, column 6, type:

```
ESC[4;6H
```

These other examples also include variables that you must provide values for, as well:

ESC [linesA—Moves cursor up *lines* rows.

ESC [linesB—Moves cursor down *lines* rows. In both these cases, the column in which the cursor appears remains unchanged.

ESC [columnsC—Moves cursor *columns* positions forward. Default is one, and this sequence is ignored if the cursor is already at the far right of the screen; in other words there is no wraparound to the next line.

ESC [columnsD—Moves the cursor *columns* positions backward. The default and lack of wraparound is identical to the sequence above.

ESC [row;colf—Same as ESC [row,colH above.

Four other cursor movement sequences allow movement without destroying the current relationship of the cursor. These report the current position of the cursor, save it, and allow restoring the cursor to that position. This is useful if you want to move the cursor around, print something in a new location, and then return the cursor to its old position. Only two of these are within the scope of this book's projects:

ESC[s—saves current cursor position

ESC[u—restores cursor to the value it had when the preceeding sequence was delivered.

So, you might type in the following prompt statement:

```
PROMPT $n$g$e[s$e[1;4H$d$e[u
```

To translate, the first two metastrings, $n and $g, would start off the prompt with the standard system prompt that displays the default drive. Next, the $e[s sequence would store the current cursor position. After that, the $e[1;4H sequence would position the cursor at row 1, column 4. The $d metastring would cause the system date to be printed there, and, finally, $e[u would restore the cursor to its former position.

With this prompt, each time you typed a new line, the standard prompt would seem to appear on its appropriate line, but the system date would be printed each time at the top of the screen (thereby writing over anything that had been written or scrolled up to that point).

You'll recall that the system prompt is stored as a variable in the DOS environment. Since the environment is also used for other information, it is possible that you may attempt to enter a very long prompt definition and encounter a message such as *"Out of environment space."* If this happens, you have used up the default memory assigned to the environment, which can be as little as 44 bytes. Those with DOS 3.0 and later versions can expand the memory allocated to the environment, using methods that will be described later. The possibility is mentioned here only for reference. If you do happen to use up your environment space, jump ahead to Chapter 7 and read how to fix the problem.

USING ANSI.SYS FOR SCREEN CONTROL

Another set of ANSI commands can change the attributes of the video images displayed on your CRT screen. With a color monitor, you may change the colors of the screen (or the prompt), while those using monochrome monitors can alter the screen images to include reverse video, blinking, and other attributes. This function of ANSI.SYS will be covered more completely later. However, for now, we can use it to enhance our system prompts. Several of the recipes included at the end of this chapter use this feature.

Briefly, the screen attribute commands all begin with ESC[followed by a number or numbers and a lowercase *m*. Several of the numbers can be included to put more than one attribute in one command line. The allowable attribute numbers for monochrome monitors are shown in Table 5-1.

With color monitors, it produces different results, because the IBM Color Graphics Adapter doesn't produce underlined characters with the standard character set.

Table 5-1. Allowable Attribute Numbers

Number	Result
0	Normal characters
1	High-intensity characters
4	Underlined characters
5	Blinking characters
7	Reverse video characters
8	Invisible characters

For all monitors; different colors may be displayed in different ways on your monochrome monitor, however (Table 5-2).

Table 5-2. Color Attribute Numbers

Number	Result
30	Black characters
31	Red characters
32	Green characters
33	Yellow characters
34	Blue characters
35	Magenta characters
36	Cyan characters
37	White characters
40	Black background
41	Red background
42	Green background
43	Yellow background
44	Blue background
45	Magenta background
46	Cyan background
47	White background

You could change colors using examples like the following:

```
PROMPT $e[0;1;31
PROMPT $e[5;30;47
```

The first example would produce high-intensity red characters, using the default background color. The second would provide blinking black characters on a white background. Either one of these might be useful to incorporate into our system prompt. Some of the later batch files in this book will show you how to change screen colors from the DOS prompt using a special customizing batch file.

Obviously, you wouldn't want to type long command sequences like those presented in this chapter every time you booted DOS. A better course would be to include the PROMPT command in a batch file that you could call, which could be called as the last command of your AUTOEXEC.BAT file, or which could be included in AUTOEXEC.BAT itself. We're about ready to create some of these batch files for personalizing your system prompt. First you need to know one or two of the most basic batch file language commands, however.

ECHOING TO THE SCREEN

A number of special DOS commands are most useful from batch files. One of these is ECHO. Used with a string, ECHO prints that string to the screen. For example, from DOS command mode, if you type:

```
ECHO  Print this message to the screen<ENTER>
```

DOS prints on the following line:

```
Print this message to the screen
```

That's not especially useful from DOS mode. In a batch file, though, ECHO is extremely useful. All of the commands in a batch file are treated by DOS as if they were typed in at the keyboard. Therefore, they will usually be printed to the screen. This can be distracting or confusing. By entering ECHO OFF as one line of a batch file, the subsequent commands will *not* be printed to the screen, until an ECHO ON statement is encountered:

```
ECHO OFF
DIR A:
ECHO ON
```

With the preceding example, you would see the command ECHO OFF on the screen but would not see the following commands, "DIR A:" or "ECHO ON" displayed. You would see the directory; only the *commands* themselves are suppressed on your screen, not their output. Nor would any message following another ECHO command:

```
ECHO OFF
DIR A:
ECHO  You can see this message.
ECHO ON
ECHO You will see this message twice.
```

If the above lines were in a batch file, your screen display would look something like this:

```
ECHO OFF

Volume in drive A has no label
Directory of  A:\
COMMAND   COM      22042    8-14-85     8:00a
ANSI      SYS       1641    8-14-85     8:00a
FIXIT     BAT        669    1-01-85    12:13a
DOS              <DIR>      8-22-85     6:21p
AUTOEXEC  BAT         96    9-03-85     5:02p
CONFIG    SYS         62    8-31-85     3:40p
PWRUPCLK  COM       1370    5-11-85    11:38a
VDISK     SYS       3080    8-14-85     8:00a
RESULT               0     9-18-85     6:34p
ED        EXE      27136   10-20-85    10:13p
BATED     BAS       4178    9-01-85     6:15p
UTILITY          <DIR>      8-22-85     5:31p
BATCHES          <DIR>      1-01-85    12:07a
        13 File(s)       36864 bytes free

You can see this message.
ECHO You will see this message twice.
You will see this message twice.
```

Because ECHO was back ON, you saw *both* the command, ("ECHO You will see this message twice.") as well as the result ("You will see this message twice."). We use ECHO ON and OFF to simplify the screen display, while using ECHO to display information that we do want the operator to see. Most of the batch files in this book begin with ECHO OFF. The key exception to this rule is that ECHO must be on when we want to use PROMPT to deliver escape sequences to DOS, however. If ECHO is off, then ANSI.SYS has no need to display them to the screen and won't bother to "read" the sequences contained in the PROMPT statement.

A NONSTANDARD REMARK FOR BATCH FILES

The only other special batch command we use in our early batch files is the colon (":") character, and that application may be somewhat controversial. We depart from "good" usage to employ the colon as a replacement for REMARK. There is a special reason for this: clarity.

Many of the batch files in magazines mark a remark at the start of a line with a period—an undocumented feature that gained widespread use. Guess what? With DOS 3.0, this undocumented feature became an undocumented nonfeature. For whatever reason, you cannot use a period to start a remark with DOS 3.0 and, to date, later batch files. REM is the only exact equivalent allowed.

Files full of REMs can be distracting. The eye can be trained to ignore punctuation, such as periods or colons, but resolutely attempts to read words like REM no matter how worthless they are to the functioning of the file. Because this book is intended both as a tutorial and as a reference work, the author wanted all the batch files to be as easy to read as possible. It is not the remarks themselves that make the listing difficult to read, but the letters REM. So, I have taken the liberty of substituting the colon.

This is not an exact equivalent. DOS takes the colon to be a "label" in a batch file, a sort of marker (like the BASIC language's line numbers) which DOS uses as a signpost to jump to when instructed. Batch files can include GOTOs, just like BASIC, except that instead of jumping to a line number, you must GOTO a label starting with a colon.

A label has one to eight characters. If it is longer, the extra is ignored, so labels *can* be longer than eight characters. The ability to use longer strings, and the fact that DOS ignores labels except when looking for places to jump, enables us to use the colon as a replacement for the REM statement. Because we were careful never to label our remarks with the same label that is used as a real label in any of these batch files, this convention works just fine for this book, and makes the listings easier to read. But you should be aware that the practice is nonstandard, and could cause problems for the unwary. The colon does not mean REM. Using a label and a phony label-remark that begin with the same eight characters can cause some unexpected results in your batch file. When DOS encounters a GOTO statement in the batch file, it starts at the beginning of the file and jumps to the first matching label it finds—whether a remark or a real label. Use caution.

One final difference between using the colon and REM to designate REMs is that any remark set off by REM is echoed to the screen if ECHO is ON. A label, or a remark set off by a colon (and therefore a label) will not be echoed to the screen, regardless of whether ECHO is ON or OFF. This enables us to make our remarks truly invisible. REMarks that appear in the middle of an ECHO ON sequence (as when you are using PROMPT) would be printed to the screen.

Such an event is no great annoyance but is unnecessary as long as the colon substitute is available.

BATCH FILE RECIPES FOR CHANGING YOUR PROMPT

We're now ready for our first cookbook recipes. The early ones are short but use a format more useful for later batch files. That is, the listing begins with ECHO OFF (usually), followed by a remark telling the name of the batch file, and a second remark with a short description of its function. Each file has a line number associated with every line, but you *should not type the line numbers in*! Line numbers are included only to describe the function of the lines. They serve no other purpose and would actually prevent the proper functioning of your batch file.

Delete the line numbers as you type in the files. If you *must*, you may also delete the REMARKS that begin with a colon. The disk space saved will be minimal or nonexistent, since DOS always allocates minimal bytes to even the smallest file (this can be as large as 8192 bytes!). The resulting "packed" batch files may be confusing to sort out at some later date. To repeat: The remarks (and, later in this book the HELP messages) are not crucial but should prove useful.

Some users may want to access some of the following routines out of their usual order. So, some of the descriptions include information that has already been presented in previous descriptions. Repeating information makes random access practical.

UTILITIES

PERS.BAT

What it Does: Personalize your system prompt with message of your choice.

Syntax: PERS

Requirements: DOS 2.0 or later, DEVICE=ANSI.SYS command in CONFIG.SYS file.

HOW TO USE IT

Replace "Greetings Master!" in the listing below with a message of your choice. You may construct several versions of this batch file, each with a different message, and give them different names. Change the system prompt to your customized prompt by typing the root name of the batch file, in this case PERS. If you include this listing in your AUTOEXEC.BAT file (only line 4 is needed) your prompt is changed automatically on powerup. If you do this, the line must be the *last* one in the AUTOEXEC.BAT file to use the PROMPT command. That is, if you also include a PROMPT command to redefine a key, that module should appear before this one in any batch file.

Your new prompt will look something like this:

```
Greetings Master!
A>
```

Line-By-Line Description

Line 1:   Turn off screen echoing of commands.

Lines 2–3:   Title remarks.

Line 4:   Change prompt to customized message, then add carriage return, default drive letter, and greater-than symbol.

```
-------------------------------------------------------
1.   ECHO OFF
2.   :        :: PERS.BAT ::
3.   :        *** Message of Your Choice in Prompt ***
4.   PROMPT Greetings Master!$_$n$g
-------------------------------------------------------
```

TIMER.BAT

What it Does: Prints system time on line above the standard prompt.

Syntax: TIMER

Requirements: DOS 2.0 or later, DEVICE=ANSI.SYS command in CONFIG.SYS file.

HOW TO USE IT

Use this as a separate batch file and summon by typing its root name (TIMER), or you may call this batch file as the last line of another batch file by inserting its root name (TIMER) as the last line in that file. You may also insert line 4 into your AUTOEXEC.BAT file so that the prompt is customized each time your computer is turned on. If you do this, any other PROMPT statements must precede this one in the batch file.

Your new prompt will look something like this:

```
12:32
A>
```

Line-By-Line Description

Line 1:   Turn off screen echoing of commands.

Lines 2–3: Title remarks.

Line 4:   Change prompt so that the system time is printed first, followed by six backspaces, to write over the seconds and fraction of a second, leaving only the hours and minutes in the display. Then a carriage return is added and the default drive letter and greater-than symbol.

```
------------------------------------------------------------
1.   ECHO OFF
2.   :         :: TIMER.BAT ::
3.   :         *** Inserts Time on Line above Prompt ***
4.   PROMPT $t$h$h$h$h$h$h$_$n$g
------------------------------------------------------------
```

DATER.BAT

What it Does: Inserts the system date on the line above the standard prompt.

Syntax: DATER

Requirements: DOS 2.0 or later, DEVICE=ANSI.SYS command in CONFIG.SYS file.

HOW TO USE IT

By typing DATER, you can invoke this batch file at any time. It may also be inserted in your AUTOEXEC.BAT file. Only line 4 has to be included. If you use other PROMPT statements in the batch file, this one must be the last to appear for it to take effect. As in the previous module, you should always set the correct system time and date or have a built-in clock card that sets it for you, to have this prompt be of any use.

Your new prompt will look something like this:

```
Mon 01-4-1988
A>
```

Line-By-Line Description

Line 1:   Turn off screen echoing of commands.

Lines 2–3:   Title remarks.

Line 4:   Set system prompt to the current system date, followed by a carriage return, and the default drive letter and greater-than symbol.

```
------------------------------------------------------------
1.    ECHO OFF
2.    :          :: DATER.BAT ::
3.    :            *** Inserts Date on Line Above Prompt ***
4.    PROMPT $d$_$n$g
------------------------------------------------------------
```

CORNER.BAT

What it does: Puts the date and time in the upper righthand corner of the screen.

Syntax: CORNER

Requirements: DOS 2.0 or later, DEVICE=ANSI.SYS command in CONFIG.SYS file.

HOW TO USE IT

By typing CORNER, you may change your prompt at any time. This batch file must be in the default directory you are using or in a subdirectory that DOS has been told to search through the PATH command (this will be explained in an upcoming chapter). Line 4 may also be included in your AUTOEXEC.BAT file, but only if it is the last PROMPT statement in that file. Note that you must have

a CONFIG.SYS file with the line DEVICE=ANSI.SYS on your root directory, and ANSI.SYS must be available to DOS when booting up to use this batch file.
Your new prompt will look something like this:

```
                                   9:54 Mon   1-4-1988
. . .
. . .
A>
```

Line-By-Line Description

Line 1:   Turn off screen echoing of commands.

Lines 2–3: Title remarks.

Line 4:   An escape sequence is sent that first stores the current cursor position, and then moves the cursor to row 1, column 50. Here, the current time is printed, along with six backspaces to erase the seconds and fraction. Then a space is printed and the system date. Next, a final escape sequence restores the cursor to its stored position, and the standard prompt, the default drive letter, and the greater-than symbol, are printed to the screen.

```
------------------------------------------------------------
1.   ECHO OFF
2.   :        :: CORNER.BAT ::
3.   :        *** Puts Date, Time in Upper Right Corner ***
4.   PROMPT $e[s$e[1;50H$t$h$h$h$h$h$h $d$e[u$n$g
------------------------------------------------------------
```

BLINK.BAT

What it does: Produces a blinking system prompt.

Syntax: BLINK

Requirements: DOS 2.0 or later, DEVICE=ANSI.SYS command in CONFIG.SYS file.

HOW TO USE IT

By typing BLINK, you may change your prompt to a blinking version of the default DOS prompt. To be accessed, this batch file must be in the default directory you are using, or located in a subdirectory that DOS can find through a PATH command. Line 4 may also be included in your AUTOEXEC.BAT file but only if it is the last PROMPT statement in that file. Note that you must have a CONFIG.SYS file with the line DE-VICE=ANSI.SYS on your root directory, and ANSI.SYS must be available to DOS when booting up to use this batch file.

Your new prompt looks like the default DOS system prompt but blinks. You can combine this prompt with one of the previous prompt strings in this chapter to cause any or all of those to blink as well.

Line-By-Line Description

Line 1:   Turn off screen echoing of commands.

Lines 2–3:   Title remarks.

Line 4:   Escape sequence tells DOS to use the standard system prompt but to display it in blinking form. Then, the screen attributes are returned to normal to allow conventional display on the CRT.

```
1.    ECHO OFF
2.    :          :: BLINK.BAT ::
3.    :          *** Creates Blinking Prompt ***
4.    PROMPT $e[0;5m$n$g$e[0m
```

RED.BAT

What it does: Produces a high intensity red system prompt with color monitors.

Syntax: BLINK

Requirements: DOS 2.0 or later, DEVICE=ANSI.SYS command in CONFIG.SYS file.

HOW TO USE IT

By typing RED, you may change your prompt to a high-intensity red version of the default DOS prompt. You must include this batch file in the default directory or currently logged disk, or place it in a subdirectory that DOS can find through a PATH command. Line 4 may also be included in your AUTOEXEC.BAT file but only if it is the last PROMPT statement in that file. Note that you must have a CONFIG.SYS file with the line DEVICE=ANSI.SYS on your root directory, and ANSI.SYS must be available to DOS when booting up to use this batch file.

Your new prompt looks like the default DOS system prompt but is a high-intensity red. You may refer to the chart of attributes earlier in this chapter to supply a different color combination. You may also combine this prompt with one of the previous prompt strings in this chapter to cause any or all of those to be displayed in red colors as well.

Line-By-Line Description

Line 1:   Turn off screen echoing of commands.

Lines 2–3:   Title remarks.

Line 4:   Escape sequence tells DOS to use the standard system prompt, but to display it in high intensity red characters. Once the prompt is displayed, the screen attributes are returned to normal to allow conventional display on the CRT.

```
-----------------------------------------------------------
1.    ECHO OFF
2.    :        :: RED.BAT ::
3.    :        *** Creates High Intensity Red Prompt ***
4.    PROMPT $e[0;1;31m$n$g$e[0m
-----------------------------------------------------------
```

SUMMARY

This chapter covered a great deal of territory. The concept of the installable device driver was explained in more detail, and using one such driver supplied with DOS, ANSI.SYS, was covered. Changing the system prompt with the PROMPT command's was also explained. Later, with PROMPT, we passed information to ANSI.SYS to provide control of the cursor on the CRT and the colors displayed with a color monitor. The chapter wound up with six batch file "recipes" of new commands that you can use to customize DOS.

6

Using Parameters
and Conditional
Statements

INTRODUCTION

Now that you've been introduced to simple batch files, we'll proceed to some of the more powerful capabilities these files can exercise. This chapter covers using replaceable parameters in batch files, and conditional statements. Both vary how the batch file operates in different situations. You'll also find out how to change the time and date stored by your computer's system in one step and how to change the colors of the screen background and foreground with a new command that will be created.

A REVIEW OF THE BATCH FILE STATEMENTS SO FAR

So far, we've used just three statements and variations of them in our batch files. Here's a quick review:

ECHO [string]—Displays the text string that follows the ECHO statement.

ECHO OFF—Turns off the display of commands within a batch file as they are carried out.

ECHO ON—Turns on the display of the commands within a batch file.

ECHO—When used alone, ECHO reports the current ECHO status, either ON or OFF.

REM—Remarks are statements inserted in a batch file for informational purposes only. In this book, we substitute the colon, the character that marks labels in batch files, to make the listings easier to read.

PROMPT—PROMPT is not a batch-file language command, but a standard DOS internal command that sets the system prompt with a string of the user's choice. Because PROMPT allows sending an ESC character to ANSI.SYS, it can also transmit extended keyboard control and screen commands.

Note that we've already discovered that there are two distinct types of DOS commands: those that are used both in and out of batch files, and those that only become useful when included in batch files. DOS commands like PROMPT (or COPY or FORMAT) can be used as easily outside a batch file as within. ECHO can be *used* from DOS command mode if you wish but is hardly worth the effort. ECHO, along with other commands we'll learn shortly, is most useful for handling a chore within the batch file, such as turning off the display of commands that are being carried out.

USING PARAMETERS WITH CONDITIONAL STATEMENTS

Batch file language's *conditional* statements supply a means of control over what the batch file does, similar to program branching instructions like GOTO in BASIC. In fact, batch files can include GOTO and IF, which are used much as they are in BASIC. These commands, though, are somewhat limited. There is no ELSE statement (this lack can be overcome with programming techniques, just as in BASIC) and IF can only test for three different types of conditions. Both these control statements hinge around a third feature of batch files, the use of "parameters."

What Is a Parameter?

When applied to DOS and batch commands, a parameter is additional information that you supply on the command line when you type the command. With this information, the command determines how the file acts. When you type:

```
DISKCOPY A: B:
```

or

```
COPY A:*.* B:
```

the data following the external or internal command name are parameters. Each parameter is separated by a space. If you include the wrong number of parameters or enter a parameter with the wrong syntax (say, you typed "COPY A:") an error message results.

When you type the root name of a batch file, you may also follow that name with a series of parameters. Each must be separated by a space. When the batch file is called, DOS substitutes the parameters that you type on the command line for special parameter variable markers that you insert in the batch file. You might compare these parameter markers with variables used in BASIC programs, because they function similarly in one way: DOS substitutes the value that you supply for the variable itself when processing the line.

The variables are typed sequentially on the command line and substituted by DOS in the same order. In the batch file, the variables all start with a percent sign, and are numbered %0, %1, %2, and so on.

The first, %0, is always the filename of the batch file. You cannot enter new information on the command line to substitute for %0. Why would you want a variable to contain the name of the batch file? Assume for a moment that, under certain conditions, you want one portion of the batch file to call itself. You could include the root name of the batch file as a line within the file. When that line is interpreted by DOS, it tries to call the batch file with that name.

For one reason or another, however, the user may have renamed the batch file. Instead of being called SORTER.BAT, the name SORTFILE.BAT may have been applied to avoid confusion with a different batch file with the same name. However, unless the relevant line is edited, SORTFILE.BAT will not call itself but, rather its old name. If you'd used the %0 parameter instead, the correct file would have been called no matter how it was named.

An example of the use of %0 is shown in the next chapter with the utility EDRIVE.BAT. A temporary batch file named E.BAT has as its last line:

```
ERASE %0
```

When that line is called, the batch file erases itself—no matter what it has been called by the user. Since processing is done, we don't care if the file is erased, although DOS becomes a mite upset when it can't find the file anymore. An error message is the only retribution, however. You may safely ignore it.

The other parameters %1 to % 9 are all available for replacement with values you type on the command line with the batch file name. The first parameter on the command line is substituted for %1, while the second will be assigned to %2, and so forth.

Suppose you had created the following batch file, named SHOW.BAT:

```
ECHO OFF
ECHO %1 %2 %3 %4
```

You would then invoke the batch file by typing its root name, SHOW, and follow that with parameters:

```
SHOW DAVID MICHAEL CATHY DENNIS
```

As DOS processes the batch file, it would substitute DAVID for %1, MICHAEL for %2, and continue for as many variables as had matching parameters typed in. We would see on the screen:

```
DAVID MICHAEL CATHY DENNIS
```

If we typed five parameters on the command line, only four would be displayed, because there were only four variables used in the batch file. If we typed just three parameters on the command line, all three would be shown, and no error would be generated, because a null string ("nothing") would be substituted for the variable, and the ECHO command would print the first three parameters, followed by nothing.

Some batch commands are affected by null parameters under certain circumstances. For example, as noted in the beginning of the chapter, if we include ECHO on a line by itself in a batch file, it will *not* simply print nothing. ECHO instead returns the status of the ECHO command, telling us whether echo is ON or OFF. So, if we typed SHOW with no parameters at all, DOS would see the batch file line as ECHO standing by itself and would print the ECHO status.

The batch files in this book take into account the effect of including or of not including parameters on the relevant command line. If you use a parameter in most batch file that do not use them, it is ignored. The exception are complex batch files that include a help screen that can be summoned by typing the file root name, followed by the HELP parameter. For most of the batch files that *do* require a parameter, if you type the root name without any parameter, you automatically are taken to a help screen.

So, keep in mind that when using parameters in your batch files, you may need to keep track of what happens when an operator enters a wrong parameter or no parameter at all.

SOME USES FOR PARAMETERS

DOS allows up to 10 parameters (%0 to %9) but includes a SHIFT command that allows typing more than 10 parameters on a single command line. You might feel that including more than 10 parameters would be unwieldy and that SHIFT therefore is not a useful command. However, while a dozen or more parameters might rarely, if ever, be used, another use for SHIFT makes it extremely valuable indeed. We'll get to that in a moment. Before you get into SHIFTing parameters, you need to gain more experience in using them in their normal state.

A batch file, DAY.BAT, presented in cookbook form at the end of this chapter, demonstrates the use of parameters by allowing you to set the system day and time with a single command line. That in itself is not overwhelmingly useful, but we've included the module because it does make a good teaching tool. The "core" of the file is the following two lines:

```
DATE %1
TIME %2
```

You use the batch file by typing:

```
DAY 12/03/85 12:13:27
```

When you do this, DOS invokes the DATE command, and substitutes the first parameter you have typed for the response needed. The second parameter you type will be substituted for the response required by TIME. That's all there is to it. You have created your first DOS command, DAY, which allows setting date and time with a single command line.

AN EXAMPLE IN HANDLING NULL PARAMETERS

The actual batch file, DAY.BAT, is more complex than the lines shown previously, because we wanted novices to be able to use it. The main part of the file looks like this:

```
1.      IF "%1"=="" GOTO HELP
2.      GOTO SET
3.      :HELP
4.      CLS
5.      ECHO       ENTER MM/DD/YY HH:MM:SS ON A SINGLE LINE
6.      GOTO EXIT
7.      :SET
8.      DATE %1
9.      TIME %2
10.     :EXIT
```

We'll go into this example in a bit of detail. In line 1, the statement tells DOS to compare parameter %1 with a null string ("nothing" or ""), and if they are equal, branch to the portion of the batch file that has been marked with the label HELP.

First note that %1 is enclosed in quotation marks. You often see batch files in magazines where the parameters are *not* in quotation marks. Usually, this works. Here, however, we have a strict interpretation of "nothing." With the quotation marks, if the %1 parameter is not typed in by the user (that is, just DAY is typed on the command line), then DOS translates "%1" as "", which is the null string or a string with a length of zero. Even though the null string contains no characters, it is still a distinct string in its own right. So, if "%1" equals "", then the statement tests as true, and the batch file branches to the line labeled HELP.

If we left off the quotation marks, DOS would substitute nothing for the missing parameter. In this case there would *really* be nothing there, not even the null string. Absolutely nothing does *not* equal "". A syntax error would be generated. So, in this book, the quotation marks included around parameters are usually essential.

The quotation marks are not the only way to accomplish a correct comparison. Any character that appears on both sides of the double equal sign cancels itself out so that no parameter plus the character equals nothing plus the character on the other side. Some users like to use a period or an x on each side of the equal sign:

```
IF .%1==. GOTO HELP
IF %1x==x GOTO HELP
```

Both will work as well as quotation marks and require several less characters to type. Quotation marks are less cryptic, though, so even the neophyte is unlikely to be confused.

Notice that two equal signs are used. The double equal sign commonly differentiates between equals that *assign* a value to a variable and the different equals function that compares two values without changing them. For example, you might type:

```
PROMPT=HELLO THERE
```

This would assign the value "HELLO THERE" to the environment variable PROMPT. To simply compare two variables or a variable and a constant value, DOS requires that a different set of characters, the double equal sign be used.

Because DOS knows when it sees the double equal sign, we mean the comparison operation, we can use single equal signs as part of our strings.

The next section of the line includes the command, GOTO HELP. If the condition is true, DOS does not drop down to the next line. Instead, it tries to send control of the batch file to a line that starts with a colon and the string "HELP,"—in this file, line 3. If a properly labeled line is not found, DOS returns LABEL NOT FOUND and aborts the batch file. If you included ECHO OFF in your file, you may not be aware of this; as a result, install ECHO OFF last, after a new batch file has been debugged.

In this sample file, if "%1" does not equal "", the file drops down to line 2, and branches to the line labeled SET, which is line 7. There, in lines 8 and 9, the proper date and time are set, presuming that parameters %1 and %2 are in the proper format. That is something you have to guard against when building batch files. The parameters typed in must be in the proper format, or else the batch file aborts. If you happen to put them in the wrong order or in the wrong format, the commands will not work.

There are several ways around this. One is to include a HELP message like the one in this file. If users are unsure of syntax, they can skip the parameters and get some help. Another way is to test for every possible acceptable answer and branch to the HELP routine if no correct answer is given.

This can be clumsy. When checking parameters to see if they equal a string, DOS does pay attention to case of the characters entered. So, if you were looking for either an ON or OFF answer you would need to have these lines:

```
IF "%1"=="ON"  GOTO START
IF "%1"=="on"  GOTO START
IF "%1"=="On"  GOTO START
IF "%1"=="oN"  GOTO START
IF "%1"=="OFF" GOTO FINISH
IF "%1"=="off" GOTO FINISH
IF "%1"=="Off" GOTO FINISH
IF "%1"=="OFf" GOTO FINISH
IF "%1"=="OfF" GOTO FINISH
IF "%1"=="oFF" GOTO FINISH
IF "%1"=="ofF" GOTO FINISH
IF "%1"=="oFf" GOTO FINISH
```

• • •

You get the idea. Of course, most users type in an answer either in upper- or lowercase. But some users press the Shift key by mistake, especially as they get to the first character of a new word. To check for every eventuality, you must include many different lines. The last line would be GOTO HELP, because there was no match if the batch file got that far. The alternative would be to send control to whatever label was indicated by the parameter. In such cases, DOS does *not* care about case:

```
IF "%1"=="" GOTO HELP
GOTO %1
```

The preceding syntax is perfectly legal. If %1 is null, the batch file branches to a label marking a section of the file where the user will receive help. If %1 equals OFF or Off or ON or on or any variation, the file proceeds as expected. If the user types something other than those two words, though, the LABEL NOT FOUND message is displayed, and the file aborts.

In this book, whenever the choices are limited, we try to cover every eventuality. When there are more possibilities, we go the more practical route of hoping that the user will either use the file correctly or if unsuccessful because of improper parameters, will check the book to see how to use the batch file. Unlike BASIC programming, batch files can't always trap for every possible user error. In some cases, error trapping must be weighed against making the file so long that no one will bother to type it in.

TWO OTHER USES FOR "IF"

We've covered labels, GOTO, and one application for IF, the comparison of a parameter with another string. IF can also test for two other conditions besides whether one string equals another string. IF can check a program's ERRORLEVEL and see if a file exists. Some programs set an ERRORLEVEL in a special memory register. Unfortunately, few useful DOS functions set an ERRORLEVEL that help us within a batch file. To get around that, we'll give you several utility programs later in this book that *will* set the ERRORLEVEL so that it can be checked by the batch file in a useful way.

The other IF test is to see if a given file exists. This is useful, say, when you want to check for the presence of a file before copying over it with a new file of the same name. We'll use these applications for IF later on in the book.

SHIFTING PARAMETERS

So far, we've also looked at a simple use for parameters that you plug into your command line. Next we'll reveal the true value of SHIFT.

This command causes DOS to move each parameter over one place to the left, with the leftmost "dropping off." If you had 15 parameters on your command line, you could process the first nine (0 is the batch file name, remember) and then have nine SHIFT statements and then continue over again with later parts of the batch file starting with %1, %2 and so forth, and the new parameters.

Bad plan. What user could remember the correct order for 15 parameters? Or what batch file would need 15 different parameters and operate efficiently? We'll look at a command later that *can* use many different parameters (FOR..IN..DO), but even here there are better ways of accomplishing a task.

SHIFT has another purpose, however. If we want to do a task several times, and the parameters are about equal in function, and we don't care in what order DOS carries the statements out, SHIFT can help us. It allows the user to enter parameters in *any* order, and we can process them all as if they were all, say, %1. Look at the following batch file, NAMES.BAT

```
1.   ECHO OFF
2.   GOTO %1
3.   :DAVE
4.   ECHO DAVE WAS HERE!
5.   GOTO NEXT
6.   :CATHY
7.   ECHO CATHY WAS HERE!
8.   GOTO NEXT
9.   :MICHAEL
10.  ECHO MICHAEL WAS HERE!
11.  GOTO NEXT
12.  :DENNIS
13.  ECHO DENNIS WAS HERE!
14.  GOTO NEXT
15.  :NEXT
16.  SHIFT
17.  IF NOT .==.%1 GOTO %1
18.  :EXIT
```

Only one parameter, %1, is used in this file. Even so, you may type as many parameters on the command line as can fit within DOS' line-length restriction. These must consist of the names DAVE, CATHY, MICHAEL, or DENNIS in any order or combination. When DOS begins the batch file, it tries to branch to the label that equals %1. If you've used only the allowable names, the file goes to the proper label and ECHOes a message such as DAVE WAS HERE! Then, the file is directed to the label NEXT, where the SHIFT command is carried out in line 16. All the parameters are shifted one place to the left, so the next name on the command line, which would have been %2, now becomes %1.

In line 17, the file tests to see if %1 is null (a different way from IF "%1"=="" and included to illustrate the operator NOT), and if it is not (because SHIFT has brought a new parameter into position), the file tries to GOTO the next parameter name. The process repeats until all the parameters that were typed in on the command line are "used up." Then, the file drops down to the line labeled EXIT. In this case, nothing happens there, but other batch files we will create have some activity in the file's EXIT portion.

With NAMES.BAT, typing in the four allowable names in any order cause them to be displayed on the screen, in the same order. So, you could type:

NAMES CATHY DAVE

or

NAMES MICHAEL DENNIS CATHY DAVE

or any other combination, to have them displayed on the screen in that order. Of course, this particular example is of little use. But one batch file at the end of this chapter, CHANGE.BAT, uses the technique.

In each of these, we want to make changes in the color of the characters or screen background using escape sequences, similar to those that move the cursor in the last chapter.

As mentioned briefly, different sequences control color and other attributes, such as emphasized characters, underlining, and blinking. (These attributes have different effects depending on whether the monochrome adapter or color graphics adapter is used.) DOS, however, allows us to change the color or the attribute in any order. So, by using SHIFT, the operator can type the command name, and follow with parameters such as YELLOW BRIGHT or BRIGHT YELLOW, without remembering to do it in a certain order. The file branches to one label and sends the proper escape sequence, and then move to the next, if available, until all the parameters have been used.

You may even use "contradictory" parameters, changing the character color from white to yellow and then back to white. There's not much use for this, but SHIFT lets you use batch files that have been set up for multiple interchangeable parameters in this manner.

That's enough explanation for this chapter. Let's move on to the recipes. Study them to see how conditionals and replaceable parameters work in each. By the time you have finished this book, you will be able to alter each of these for additional capabilities and new features in DOS. All the batch files in this book are intended as your models for customizing *your* new utilities. You may combine techniques and tricks presented in these chapters to build advanced DOS commands tailored to your exact requirements.

UTILITIES

DAY.BAT

What it does: Allows setting the day and time from one command line.

Syntax: DAY mm/dd/yy hh:mm:ss

Requirements: DOS 2.0 or later.

HOW TO USE IT

Type the root name, DAY, followed by the date and time (in that order) that you wish to set. You must use the DOS-approved syntax. With DOS 3.0 and higher, you should conform to the order in which your selected country (chosen with SELECT or by including a COUNTRY configuration in your CONFIG.SYS file). For the United States, the date is mm-dd-yy, with either hyphens, a slash, or a period to separate them. That is, 10/12/85, 10-12-85, or 10.12.85 may be entered. You may include leading zeroes, and enter the full year if you wish, for example, 09/09/1985.

Time must include minutes and hours and may include seconds or hundredths of a second. Separate the hours, minutes, and seconds with a colon or period. Depending on the country that you have selected (with DOS 3.0 and higher), either a period or a comma may be required to separate the hundredths of a second. Your screen prompt shows you the old time and clues you in as to which is required, if you don't know.

Note that if you are using an IBM PC-AT, PS/2, or other system with a built-in clock, changing the time does not change the system clock with versions of DOS prior to 3.3. This is also true of most add-on clock boards for the other IBM computers, which use different "addresses" for their clocks. The suppliers of these products offer a special utility program to update the clock board. Refer to your Guide To Operations to see how to change the computer's system clock, which should need to be done only infrequently.

In fact, if you have a clock board, this batch file is useful to you only when you want to "tell" the system a different date, temporarily.

Line-By-Line Description

Line 1:   Turn off screen echoing of commands.

Lines 2–3:   Title remarks.

Line 4:   If parameter is null, go to the HELP module.

Line 5:   Otherwise, go to the time-setting module.

Lines 6–9:   Display help line, then go to EXIT.

Lines 10–12:   Set time, using parameters entered.

Line 13:   End of the file.

```
---------------------------------------------------------
1.    ECHO OFF
2.    :        :: DAY.BAT ::
3.    :           *** Set Day, Time From Single Line ***
4.    IF "%1"=="" GOTO HELP
5.    GOTO SET
6.    :HELP
7.    CLS
8.    ECHO     ENTER MM/DD/YY HH:MM:SS ON A SINGLE LINE
9.    GOTO EXIT
10.   :SET
11.   DATE %1
12.   TIME %2
13.   :EXIT
---------------------------------------------------------
```

SCREEN.BAT

What it does: Changes DOS screen background colors, with the
                color/graphics adapter only.

Syntax: SCREEN color

Requirements: DOS 2.0 or later, color/graphics adapter, ANSI.SYS
                device command in CONFIG.SYS.

HOW TO USE IT

You can choose what colors DOS displays on your screen if you have a color graphics adapter or the monochrome attributes if you have only the mono-chrome display adapter. With this batch file and the one that follows, you can control these from DOS command mode. You may also include these batch files in your AUTOEXEC.BAT file or call them from that file.

Only the colors displayed from DOS are affected. BASIC programs still can use the COLOR statement to print in any color combination available. These modules were written only for the standard color graphics and monochrome monitor adapters supplied for the IBM PC, PC-XT, and PC-AT. The color routines also work with PCjr. They were not written for the new higher resolution EGA or VGA boards for the PC-AT and PS/2 computers.

This batch file, which alters the screen background color, can be used only with the color graphics adapter. If used when the monochrome adapter is activated, nothing happens. It may be invoked by typing its root name, SCREEN, followed by any of these colors: BLACK, RED, GREED, YELLOW, BLUE, MAGENTA, CYAN, or WHITE.

Note that this file does *not* begin with ECHO OFF. For PROMPT to be able to send the escape sequences that change the colors, ECHO must be ON. Your CONFIG.SYS file must contain the line DEVICE=ANSI.SYS. If you do not understand this, consult APPENDIX A.

Line-By-Line Description

Line 1:   If %1 is null, go to HELP.

Line 2:   Otherwise, GOTO line labeled with name the same as %1, which should be an allowable color.

Lines 3–4:   Title remarks.

Lines 5–16:   Display HELP message and then go to EXIT.

Lines 17–39: Send escape sequences to change background.

Lines 40–41: Restore system prompt.

```
1.   IF "%1" =="" GOTO HELP
2.   GOTO %1
3.   :      :: SCREEN.BAT::
```

```
4.    :   *** Changes screen background colors from DOS ***
5.    :HELP
6.    CLS
7.    :
8.    ECHO OFF
9.    ECHO   Type the command name and then any color:
10.   ECHO   Black   Red   Green   Yellow Blue
11.   ECHO   Magenta Cyan   or White
12.   :
13.   :
14.   :
15.   :
16.   GOTO EXIT
17.   :BLACK
18.   PROMPT $e[40m
19.   GOTO EXIT
20.   :RED
21.   PROMPT $e[41m
22.   GOTO EXIT
23.   :GREEN
24.   PROMPT $e[42m
25.   GOTO EXIT
26.   :YELLOW
27.   PROMPT $e[43m
28.   GOTO EXIT
29.   :BLUE
30.   PROMPT $e[44m
31.   GOTO EXIT
32.   :MAGENTA
33.   PROMPT $e[45m
34.   GOTO EXIT
35.   :CYAN
36.   PROMPT $e[46m
37.   GOTO EXIT
38.   :WHITE
39.   PROMPT $e[47m
40.   :EXIT
41.   PROMPT
```

CHANGE.BAT

What it does: Changes the colors or attributes of the screen characters from DOS. For both monochrome and color/graphics displays.

Syntax: CHANGE color attribute

Requirements: DOS 2.0 or later, DEVICE=ANSI.SYS command in
                 CONFIG.SYS.

HOW TO USE IT

This batch file is similar to the last, except that it changes the appearance of the screen characters. With the color graphics adapter, you can adjust the actual color of the characters. With the monochrome adapter, you may change from normal to enhanced, blinking, or underlined characters.

To use the file, type the root name, CHANGE, followed by any of the color parameters:

BLACK, RED, GREEN, YELLOW, BLUE, MAGENTA, CYAN, or WHITE.

With the monochrome adapter, the visible difference in some of the colors is nil; that is, yellow and white characters look the same on the monochrome monitor. Other colors produce a surprising result; BLUE as a parameter changes to underlined characters. BLACK and WHITE are your best choices for character color with the monochrome adapter; any of the parameter colors may be specified with the color graphics adapter board.

You may also put a second parameter on the command line:

NORMAL BRIGHT REVERSE UND BLINK

With the monochrome adapter, BRIGHT causes enhanced letters, and UND produces underlined letters. With color, BRIGHT produces a lighter shade of the existing color, and UND changes the characters to blue. With both adapters, NORMAL changes the characters back to their normal color, REVERSE produces reversed video, and BLINK causes the letters to flash on the screen.

Note that you may include the parameters in any order in your command line. The following lines have the same effect:

CHANGE WHITE BRIGHT
CHANGE BRIGHT WHITE

If applicable, as many parameters as you wish can be included:

CHANGE WHITE REVERSE BLINK

As in the previous file, ECHO OFF is not used. You must have DE-VICE=ANSI.SYS in your CONFIG.SYS file to use this batch file. Check Appendix A if you do not understand this point.

Line-By-Line Description

Lines 1–2:   If %1 is null, go to HELP module.

Lines 3–4:   Title remarks.

Lines 5–14:   Help message.

Lines 15–52: Change color or attribute of character.

Line 53:   Start of Exit module.

Line 54:   SHIFT all parameters over one to the left.

Line 55:   If another parameter is available, branch to that label.

Line 56:   Restore normal system prompt. You can substitute the name of your custom prompt batch file for this line.

```
----------------------------------------------------------
1.    IF "%1" =="" GOTO HELP
2.    GOTO %1
3.    :         *** CHANGE.BAT ***
4.    :              :: Changes character colors from DOS ::
5.    :HELP
6.    ECHO OFF
7.    CLS
8.    ECHO  Type the command name and then any color:
9.    ECHO    Black   Red   Green   Yellow Blue
10.   ECHO    Magenta Cyan   or White
11.   ECHO  You may include the following commands
12.   ECHO  on the same line, in any order:
13.   ECHO  Normal Und Blink Bright Reverse
14.   GOTO EXIT
15.   :BLINK
16.   PROMPT $e[5m
17.   GOTO EXIT
18.   :UND
19.   PROMPT $e[4m
20.   GOTO EXIT
```

```
21.  :NORMAL
22.  PROMPT $e[0m
23.  GOTO EXIT
24.  :BRIGHT
24.  PROMPT $e[1m
26.  GOTO EXIT
27.  :REVERSE
28.  PROMPT $e[7m 29.  GOTO EXIT
30.  :BLACK
31.  PROMPT $e[30m
32.  GOTO EXIT
33.  :RED
34.  PROMPT $e[31m
35.  GOTO EXIT
36.  :GREEN
37.  PROMPT $e[32m
38.  GOTO EXIT
39.  :YELLOW
40.  PROMPT $e[33m
41.  GOTO EXIT
42.  :BLUE
43.  PROMPT $e[34m
44.  GOTO EXIT
45.  :MAGENTA
46.  PROMPT $e[35m
47.  GOTO EXIT
48.  :CYAN
49.  PROMPT $e[36m
50.  GOTO EXIT
51.  :WHITE
52.  PROMPT $e[37m
53.  :EXIT
54.  SHIFT
55.  IF NOT .==.%1 GOTO %1
56.  PROMPT
```

SUMMARY

This chapter introduced two of the most important concepts of batch file programming: parameters and the use of conditional statements like IF. With the parameters, users can type information on the command line to be used by the batch file. This enables you to make a single batch file serve different purposes—performing various tasks or operating on different files each time. The variable information can be passed to the batch file through the parameters.

Conditional statements, like those using IF, allow the batch file to alter how it functions depending on the result of certain tests performed during run time. If a certain parameter is typed on the command line, the batch file can behave one way. If a different parameter is entered, it can act another way. Used with branching statements, such as GOTO, conditionals form the foundation of true batch-file programming.

This chapter looked at how SHIFT can increase the flexibility of batch files and discussed how "null" input can be handled.

7

Using The DOS Environment

INTRODUCTION

In this chapter, we'll learn about the DOS environment, and how to use it effectively in batch files. The environment supplies a way to pass information from one batch file to another, to set up "configuration" information for specific users that can be accessed by your programs and batch files, and to allow a form of subroutine previously unavailable with batch-file programming. The COMMAND command will also be introduced, along with its relationship to the environment.

WHAT IS THE DOS ENVIRONMENT?

The DOS environment is a special area of memory called the master environment block that is set aside to store variables and their values in the form of a string of information. The environment, which can be accessed by batch files as well as any program stores its information in protected form. That is, the data won't change unless altered by the user's program or batch files, and thus the environment can be used to pass information from one place to another in your system.

Environment variables are stored in the following form:

variable=value

where the variable is a name defined by you using the SET command or by DOS as one of its reserved variables. The value is the string that can be assigned using SET. With the DOS-defined environment variables PATH, PROMPT, or COM-SPEC you don't need the SET command. DOS creates COMSPEC and PATH values by default if you don't specify new definitions for them. The normal system prompt won't appear as an environment variable unless you change it.

PROMPT has been covered in Chapter 5, while the PATH variable will be given a complete discussion in the next chapter. It tells DOS which disk drives and directories should be searched for system files ending in .EXE, .COM, and .BAT extensions. COMSPEC tells DOS where to look for COMMAND.COM when it needs to reload the command processor after exiting a memory-hungry program.

For example, you could enter the following commands from the DOS prompt or through the same lines included in a batch file (except you would need to put percent signs on either side of the variables):

```
SET DRIVE=D:
SET MOUSE=YES
SET PASSWORD=HOUSE*MAGNET
PROMPT Hello There!
PATH C:\;C:\BATCHES
COMSPEC D:\
```

From the DOS prompt, you could then type SET on a line by itself, and see a list of the current environment variables and their values.

```
DRIVE=D:
MOUSE=YES
PASSWORD=HOUSE*MAGNET
PROMPT=Hello There!
PATHC:\;C:\BATCHES
COMSPECD:\
```

Note that if you used percent signs in a batch file, they are gone; they are needed only when defining the variable in a batch file to let DOS know that we are working with an environment string.

Whether the environment variables are defined on a DOS command line or through a batch file, you are limited to 123 characters plus the four taken up by

SET and its trailing space. If you are using PATH or PROMPT without SET, a full 127 characters may be used for your string.

An environment variable can hold several *separate* values that may be accessed consecutively by DOS from your batch files. Each value should be separated by a semicolon. For example, the following line would include all the eligible users of a system:

```
USERS=DAVE;BOB;JOE;CAROL;CATHY
```

You would access each of these one at a time. USER.BAT in this chapter is an example of a batch file that would check the replaceable parameter %1 against each of the authorized users listed in the environment, as defined, probably, by an AUTOEXEC.BAT file:

```
:TEST
FOR %%a IN (%USERS%) DO IF "%1"=="%%a" GOTO OKAY
:NOPE
ECHO ACCESS DENIED
GOTO END
:OKAY
ECHO Welcome to the system!
:END
```

The FOR %%a IN (%USERS%) DO... line loop is used extensively in this book. This routine would loop back to keep checking new values for the environment variable until it came to the end. We'll use this feature in a DOS security system presented later in this chapter.

You can *delete* an environment variable by typing SET *variable* = with *nothing* following the equal sign.

ENVIRONMENT LIMITATIONS

One limitation of the environment is that programs don't really work with the environment directly. Each receives a *copy* of the environment. The program can read the variables and make changes, but any changes made will be lost when the program terminates. The original Master Environment Block remains unchanged.

For example, every memory-resident program you load, such as Sidekick, PRINT.COM, or MODE,COM obtains its own complete copy of the environment. This can be costly in terms of memory if you have created a large environment. Since most programs will not alter the environment except for their own use, this limitation should not hinder you much.

One case where this definitely affects you, however, is in using batch files with a second command processor. Because COMMAND.COM is a program like any other, it receives a copy of the environment, and you work this copy when executing your batch files. The same copy of COMMAND.COM usually runs the batch files and other programs you might want to pass values to through variables. So, these all use the same copy of the environment, or will receive a copy of that same environment when they run.

However, DOS allows loading a second copy of COMMAND.COM, which allows batch files to call other batch files during their execution. The reason for this requires a short explanation.

Whenever a *program* is called from a batch file, control returns ordinarily to the batch file when that program ends, because the batch file, in effect, loads a second copy of COMMAND.COM, which then runs the program. When the program terminates, the secondary command processor returns control to the first, which has kept the original batch file on ''hold'' while the program ran. The batch file picks up where it left off.

When a batch file ordinarily calls another batch file, it is using the *same* copy of COMMAND.COM, and COMMAND.COM cannot process two programs at one time (except in the case of memory resident programs that operate in the background by using DOS interrupts to share time with the other programs). So, the first batch file terminates when the second begins, precluding one batch file calling another. This is called ''nesting'' batch files. Examine the following example:

```
ECHO OFF
ECHO Getting ready to run the second batch file now.
PAUSE
BATCH2
ECHO This line will NOT be called when BATCH2 ends.
```

There are several ways around this. DOS 3.3 introduced a CALL command, which does allow one batch file to call another, if sufficient memory is available. Using the COMMAND command accomplishes the same thing with earlier versions of DOS.

The syntax for this is:

```
COMMAND /C command
```

The ''/C'' tells DOS to carry out the command specified, and then return automatically to the original copy of COMMAND.COM. Of course, *command* can be anything, such as DOS commands like DIR, programs, or other batch files.

Example:

```
IF "%1"=="ERASE" COMMAND /C ZAPPER %2
```

In this example, the line would summon a second copy of COMMAND.COM to run the batch file ZAPPER.BAT. That batch file might use INPUT.COM to ask the operator whether that file should really be erased or perform another task. The name of the file is passed along to the second batch file by means of a replaceable parameter, here %2.

COMMAND.COM must be available to DOS, either on your hard disk or a floppy. Invoking a second copy of COMMAND.COM does require an extra 3000 bytes or so of memory (and each additional copy you load does as well). As a result, you may want to avoid nesting too many levels of COM-MAND.COM with your batch files. Given these constraints, there is no reason why batch files can't call other batch files, which call other batch files still.

The big limitation of this method is that, since the second copy of COM-MAND.COM is using a copy of the first batch file's environment, any changes the second batch file makes to the environment will be lost on return. These are ways of "capturing" the new environment and "resetting" your original environment, but they are needlessly complex for most applications. An easier solution is to create *files* to be used as indicators or "flags" that can be tested with IF EXIST.

The other main limitation of the environment is size. DOS 2.x has an environment block limited to 160 bytes and, since a minimum of 29 characters are taken up by the PATH and COMSPEC variables, a maximum of 131 are available for the user.

DOS 3.0 has a number of bugs that limit its usefulness with environment variables. DOS 3.1 and later versions, however, fix those problems and give an easy way of expanding the environment. That method is the SHELL command, to be included in your CONFIG.SYS file. Syntax is as follows:

```
SHELL=COMMAND.COM /P /E:<size>
```

The /P switch tells DOS to load AUTOEXEC.BAT automatically. If you leave it off, AUTOEXEC.BAT *won't* be loaded at all, which might be useful only in a security system where you wanted to fool intruders into thinking that AUTOEXEC.BAT had a function, when it didn't.

The /E switch tells DOS what size environment you would like to set. With DOS 3.1, this must be shown as the number of 16-byte blocks you would like to set aside. That is, if you set the value to 16, your environment would be 256 bytes (16 by 16). A maximum of 992 bytes (62 blocks) can be allocated.

With DOS 3.2 and later versions, things improve considerably. The size of the environment can be set from 160 to 32767 bytes by entering the actual number you would like. Even the most elaborate programming is unlikely to exceed that limitation easily.

CREATING SUBROUTINES WITH ENVIRONMENT VARIABLES

Batch file programming usually has no facility paralleling BASIC-GOSUB...RETURN statements. You may send control of the batch file to a label either through an absolute statement or through a conditional statement:

```
GOTO END
IF "%1""SORT" GOTO SORT
```

The label supplied in either case does *not* have to be explicitly typed in your batch file, however. Instead, you may use an environment variable, which can change as needs dictate. Examine this sample file:

```
1.  ECHO OFF
2.  :FIRST
3.  ECHO The first time we access the subroutine
4.  ECHO the routine will display FILE1.ASC.
5.  SET DISPLAY=FILE1.ASC
6.  SET FROM=1NEXT
7.  GOTO SHOW
8.  :1NEXT
9.  ECHO The subroutine returned to here.
10. :SECOND
11. ECHO The second time we access the subroutine
12. ECHO the routine will display FILE2.ASC.
13. SET DISPLAY=FILE2.ASC
14. SET FROM=2NEXT
15. GOTO SHOW
16. :2NEXT
17. ECHO The subroutine returned to the second point.
18. GOTO END
19. :SHOW
20. TYPE %DISPLAY%
21. GOTO %FROM%
22. :END
```

Line by line, the function of this sample file is as follows:

Line 1:   Turn off echoing of commands.

Line 2:   Label marking first section of the file.

Lines 3–4:   Display comments on function.

Line 5:   Set environment variable DISPLAY with the name of the first file to be TYPEd by the subroutine.

Line 6:   Set environment variable FROM with the label to which we want the subroutine to return after displaying the file.

Line 7:   Branch to the subroutine labeled SHOW.

Line 8:   Label to which the subroutine first returns.

Line 9:   Confirm that the subroutine returned.

Line 10:   Label marking the second section.

Lines 11–12:   Comments on current functions.

Line 13:   Set environment variable DISPLAY with the name of the second file to be TYPEd by the subroutine.

Line 14:   Set environment variable FROM with the label to which we want the subroutine to return after displaying the file.

Line 15:   Branch again to the subroutine labeled SHOW.

Line 16:   Label to which the subroutine next returns.

Line 17:   Confirm that the subroutine returned.

Line 18.   Go to the end of the batch file.

Line 19:   Label marking the subroutine SHOW.

Line 20:   Type the file indicated by environment variable DISPLAY.

Line 21:   Return to the label designated by environment variable FROM.

Line 22:   End of the file.

We'll use the environment to create a microcomputer security system and later the subroutine concept to build a complex menu system. Before we can get into either of those, though, we need to explain a few things about DOS' use of hierarchical directories and "paths."

SUMMARY

This chapter gave an introduction to the DOS environment—a special area of memory that stores strings that can be accessed by batch files and other programs. Limitations of the environment, including how to expand its size, were discussed. The concept of using environment variables to pass values within a batch file to "subroutines" and to designate the label those subroutines are to return "from" was covered.

8

The Path to New
DOS Commands

INTRODUCTION

Earlier, we learned about subdirectories and how they compartmentalize a disk into sections that are easier to keep track of. This chapter explains the concept of *paths*. We'll cover how they are used with hierarchical directory structures, which, you'll recall, allow DOS to store its files in a series of different "file cabinets" that can be nested in logical ways. Even so, we can find any file quickly by using its pathname. DOS can be told where to find certain files, such as .EXE., .COM, and batch files using the PATH command, and given a list of directories to search for other types of files with DOS 3.3's APPEND. This chapter will also give users with hard disk drives eight new command to help them navigate quickly up and down the directory tree.

HELPING DOS FIND OUR NEW DOS COMMANDS

In Chapter 4 we, first created what can be thought of as new DOS commands. That is, from DOS command mode you could type SCREEN WHITE or

CHANGE WHITE and convert your screen to white or the characters on your screen to white automatically. These new commands differ from DOS' internal commands in one important respect. As they are set up now, you can only summon the batch file commands if you happen to be logged onto the directory in which they reside, or if you explicitly type the name of that directory. If you were logged onto B:, and SCREEN.BAT were on A:, you would have to type:

```
A:SCREEN WHITE
```

for DOS to find it. Note that we said you needed to be logged onto the requisite *directory*, not drive. That is because, with DOS 2.0 and higher, you may be using a given drive, and yet DOS will *still* be unable to find a file.

THE SIGNIFICANCE OF PATH

The introduction to paths so far was necessary for you to understand how to use an important DOS customizing tool, the PATH command, which can tell DOS where to look for files if they are not found in the current directory. Consider these points.

For one thing, we can "hide" all our batch files in a subdirectory, so that they won't clutter up our root directory.

For another, we can tell DOS how to find those batch files, no matter where it might be at the time—on another drive or in another directory. To repeat: DOS can be told exactly where to find batch files at any time.

In case the significance of the first point hasn't registered yet, go back and review the first paragraphs of this chapter. The new DOS "commands" that we create are unlike actual internal DOS commands because real internal DOS commands can be accessed from any drive. They are in memory, and DOS doesn't have hunt on disks to find them. So, if we have created SCREEN.BAT and try to use SCREEN from the wrong directory, we are out of luck.

Ah, but not quite. DOS 2.0 and higher's PATH command can be used to tell DOS where to look for any .COM or .EXE or .BAT files (the so-called "system" files) when it can't find them in the root directory. So, we can specify the path DOS should use to find these, and then it will always use that path, until told to do otherwise, or we reboot the system. Once PATH has been used, if you are logged onto Drive B:, or wandering through the remote reaches of some directory and decide to use the SCREEN "command", DOS knows exactly where to look. If you guessed that we would suggest placing an appropriate PATH command in an AUTOEXEC.BAT file so that DOS would boot-up already knowing what to do, chalk up an extra ten points.

While versions of DOS 3.2 and earlier will search only for system files, DOS 3.3 added the APPEND command, which allows you to include other types of files in your PATH searches. In addition, third-party software vendors market various "path extender" utilities that bring this capability to users of the previous versions of DOS.

Like PROMPT, PATH is actually a command that sets an environment variable that stores a list of subdirectories in the order we want them searched. You can view the current path set in your system by typing SET from the DOS prompt. Because PATH is an environment variable, it is possible to construct a path that is too long for the amount of environment space set aside by DOS. While we'll show you how to expand the environment, there are other reasons why long paths are not desirable.

If DOS cannot find a file, it will search through all the directories listed in PATH. That's fine, you say—DOS can therefore have a better chance of locating the needed file. But what if you happen to mistype a command or file name, as when you type C and forget the colon when you want to log over to the C: drive? Such a frequent typo, *any* typo causes DOS to tediously look through all the directories in your long path, and you could be kept waiting for 30 seconds or longer.

Keep in mind that DOS always finds a file in the current directory faster than in any other location, and can locate files placed in the root directory next fastest. Whenever you ask DOS to search through subdirectories, it must read the invisible file containing the names of the files and other subdirectories within a directory. So, if your path points to a subdirectory several levels deep, DOS must search for that directory name through previous directory files before commencing the search for the file that you want.

The moral is to keep your subdirectories relatively shallow where possible and try to limit PATH searches to directories one level down.

PUTTING PATH TO WORK

Savvy PC users who make common typos create batch files with the same names to carry out the commands they wanted in the first place. To speed up their systems, they also minimize the number of directories specified by PATH.

The author's own root directory contains many subdirectories, but only two of them, DOS and BATCHES, are pointed to by the PATH command. Those two, plus the root directory itself, are the only ones included.

Note that you can inadvertently exclude the root directory if you don't include it in a PATH command. That's not a good idea, though, even if you keep no files in the root other than CONFIG.SYS, AUTOEXEC.BAT, and COMMAND.COM. Under certain conditions, DOS cannot function because it needs to reload COMMAND.COM (after it was overwritten in memory by a memory-hungry application).

In the author's case, all DOS external command files, such as FORMAT.COM and MORE.COM are located in the DOS subdirectory and all the batch files in BATCHES.

On powerup, one line in the AUTOEXEC.BAT file reads:

```
PATH C:\BATCHES;C:\DOS;C:\
```

Then DOS first checks C:\BATCHES for any .COM, .EXE, or .BAT files it is looking for. If they are not found, it checks subdirectory DOS, then the root directory.

While you are working with this book, please create a subdirectory on the disk you store the batch files that you type in; call it BATCHES. Create this subdirectory by typing in the following line from the DOS prompt:

```
MD C:\BATCHS<Enter>
```

Then, insert the appropriate PATH command in your AUTOEXEC.BAT file, modeled on the one shown previously. Some of the routines in this book look for a directory explicitly named C:\BATCHES. If you want to use a different name or don't have a hard disk, change the name in the routines to the subdirectory where you *do* store the files, whether it's A:\BATCHES or C:\UTIL or whatever. With that done, you're well on the way to creating your own useful DOS 2.1 and 3.0 commands.

USING PATH WITH APPLICATIONS

Here's another useful tip: Many programs have related data files, overlays, and other files that need to be checked during operation. With hard disks or even with floppy disks, for convenience group all these related files in a subdirectory. You may create a batch file that changes directories for you, calls up the program you want, and then changes back to the root directory, or another directory of your choice.

You see, when a batch file calls up a program, the file is *still* active when you exit the program—and any other batch commands available are completed. DOS remembers where the batch file was so that even if you have changed directories in the meantime, the batch file is located. If you have removed the disk containing the batch file in the meantime, DOS tells you to insert the disk containing the batch file.

For example, the author frequently uses PC-Talk III, which uses files such as PC-TALK.DEF, PC-TALK.DIR, and PC-TALK.KEY to store configuration, function key definitions, and dialup data. These are all stored in a separate subdirectory, COMM, within another subdirectory, PROGRAMS. A batch file named COMM.BAT looks like this:

```
ECHO OFF
CD \PROGRAMS\COMM
PC-TALK
CD \
```

If you do not change the directory before calling PC-Talk, the program doesn't know where to find its own data files. Note that the last line changes the directory back to the root once we exit PC-Talk. A warning, however: some programs, especially those introduced before DOS 2.0, do *not* know how to accept paths as part of filenames. Their authors cunningly built in error traps to filter out invalid filenames and didn't know, at the time, about paths or that they would become such an important part of PC use. So, if you store a given program in a subdirectory and want to access a text file or other data in another directory, you may not be able to do it. Even later versions of PC-Talk allow transmitting only files that reside on a currently logged drive and directory. Some older word processing programs, such as unpatched versions of WordStar work the same way; you must copy all the files you wish to use into their directory.

More recent offerings, such as IBM's DisplayWrite 4, allow you to use pathnames or even to change directories from within the program.

SOME BATCH-FILE UTILITIES

This chapter offers interesting new batch-file commands to implement. Four of them streamline moving from one subdirectory to another—with a twist. If you use one of these commands to go to another subdirectory, by typing RE-TURN you can go back to your subdirectory of origin. Another command allows adding paths to your PATH variable at any time. We've also included a utility that lets you log the current directory as your HOME directory and then return to that directory at any time by typing HOME. Finally, for users of DOS 3.1 or later, we supply EDRIVE, which substitutes the currently logged drive for drive specification E: You may then access that path for most DOS commands (LABEL and BACKUP are exceptions) using the shorter syntax: DIR E:, COPY A:*.* E:, and so on.

Although there are explanations given with each batch file, some of the techniques used are common to more than one and so can be explained here. Examine this "core" listing of the code used in several of the files:

```
1.   CLS
2.   ECHO Leaving subdirectory:
3.   CD
4.   CD >CD.$$$
5.   COPY C:\BATCHES\CD.ASC+CD.$$$ C:\BATCHES\RETURN.BAT >NUL
6.   ERASE CD.$$$ >NUL
7.   CD ..
8.   ECHO Now in subdirectory :
9.   CD
10.  ECHO OFF
11.  ECHO Type RETURN to return.
```

When the command (in this case UP) is typed, the first thing the batch file does is erase the screen, in Line 1. Next, a line is ECHOed to the screen telling users that they are leaving the current subdirectory. Line 3 shows how CD, when used without an argument, instead ECHOs to the screen the currently logged directory pathname.

Line 4 begins our trickery. The CD command is again used "alone" except that its output is *redirected* (using the > sign) to a file called CD.$$$, which contains nothing but the name of the currently logged directory.

To use this batch file, you need to create a file containing nothing but the characters "CD" *without* a carriage return at the end. The batch file looks for this file, CD.ASC in C:\BATCHES. So, if you store it somewhere else, change the batch file appropriately.

Create CD.ASC with COPY CON:

```
COPY CON:CD.ASC<Enter>
ECHO OFF<Enter>
CD <F6><Enter>
```

Note that you *must* press F6 when the cursor is on the same line as "CD" to avoid embedding a carriage return in the file. Note that you should put a space between the CD and <F6> on the last line.

Next, in Line 5, we use DOS' COPY command to concatenate or add together several files to produce a new file, called RETURN.BAT, which is automatically deposited in the C:\BATCHES subdirectory, out of sight but ready to use.

ADD *path* where *path* is the new path you would like added. Note that this command doesn't work in DOS 3.0 owing to a bug fixed in later versions.

This command introduces a sneaky trick that is necessary to get around one shortcoming of batch-file language. To use it, you need to create for your C:\BATCHES subdirectory a file called PATH.ASC. Follow these directions:

```
COPY CON:PATH.ASC<Enter>
ECHO OFF<Enter>
```

```
PATH <F6> <Enter>
```

Be sure and press Enter *only* where shown. The inner workings of ADD.BAT are as follows:

```
1. ECHO %PATH% | MORE >PATH.$$$
2. COPY C:\BATCHES\PATH.ASC + PATH.$$$
   C:\BATCHES\OLDPATH.BAT
3. ERASE PATH.$$$
4. PATH=%PATH%;%1
```

The environment variable %PATH% stores the current path settings and can be accessed by a batch file simply by including its name in the operation we want to carry out. However, if you try to ECHO the path setting to the screen, and then to redirect it to a file, DOS ignores the redirection symbol (">") and instead includes it as part of the string to display on the screen.

DOS is set up, though, so that the MORE filter ("more" on that in a later chapter) is *not* ignored, even if it is found on a line containing ECHO. As a result, we can follow the text we want echoed with the vertical bar symbol (which directs output to MORE.COM). MORE actually displays ASCII text in pages on the screen. Since %PATH% is never long enough to activate MORE, the contents of the variable will be passed right through to the redirection symbol on the other side, where it can then be sent to the temporary file, PATH.$$$.

Line 2 builds a new file, called OLDPATH.BAT, which contains the commands "ECHO OFF and PATH=", found in an ASCII file PATH.ASC, which you must create and store in C:\BATCHES. OLDPATH.BAT also has the original path information. When called, that batch file restores the original path settings.

You can use ADD.BAT to temporarily add a path while running an application. If you wish, you can automatically perform this by embedding the commands in a batch file that calls the application and then restores the OLDPATH by placing that command in same file for use after the application has returned to DOS (and the calling batch file is automatically reactivated).

Actually changing the path couldn't be simpler; just specify PATH= and follow that, as in Line 4, with the original path as stored in %PATH%, plus the new path entered by the user as parameter %1.

One more useful trick we used in these batch files you can use in creating your own DOS commands is the facility to enable temporary batch files to erase themselves when finished. First, create an ASCII file called KILLER.ASC:

```
COPY CON:KILLER.ASC:<Enter>
ERASE %0<Enter>
<F6><Enter>
```

Then, when combining files to create a new batch file (as for most of the files in this chapter), if you want the file to erase itself when finished, add KILLER.ASC as the last part of the file. When the temporary batch file reaches that point, it erases itself (%0 being the name of the current file, remember). DOS, of course, will be frustrated in trying to continue processing the batch file, even though there were no actual commands left. So, ignore the error message.

While all the following batch files will prove most useful to those with hard disks, they also work with floppy disks, Bernoulli drives, and high-capacity disks set up with subdirectories. Some of the descriptive material is repetitious to allow each of the batch files to stand alone. You should find these utilities to be very useful in navigating around in your directory structure. All are much easier to remember than the equivalent DOS commands, and automatically give the ability to *return* to your previous directory by typing the RETURN command.

UTILITIES

OVER.BAT

What it does: Moves over to parallel directory path.

Syntax: OVER directory

Requirements: DOS 2.0 or later, hard disk. See also notes.

HOW TO USE IT

This command allows you to move directly from one subdirectory to another subdirectory on the same level beneath a common parent directory or one below that level beneath a parallel directory. You would type OVER, followed by the name of the directory desired.

For example, if you are logged into a subdirectory called LETTERS and want to move to MEMOS, which is also a child directory of the same root or another directory, you could type OVER MEMOS. The batch file would move up one level, then down one level to MEMOS.

You could also move to a directory below MEMOS by typing its path, as well:

```
OVER MEMOS\86
```

However, you may not move to a subdirectory that is not beneath the parent of the current directory. In such cases, it is simpler just to type CD and the pathname.

You must have a file called C:\BATCHES\CD.ASC. Create it by typing:

```
COPY CON:C:\BATCHES\CD.ASC<Enter>
ECHO OFF<Enter>
CD <F6><Enter>
```

Note that a space must be placed between the CD and the <F6> on the second line.

Line-By-Line Description

Line 1:   Turn off screen echoing of commands.

Lines 2–3:   Title remarks.

Line 4:   Check for parameter. If none, show HELP.

Lines 5–22:   Help display. Enter the blank line in Line 21 by holding down the Alt key will typing "255" on the numeric keypad (not the top row of numbers on the keyboard).

Line 23:   Label marking start of processing.

Line 24:   Clear the screen.

Line 25:   Notify user of departure from current subdirectory.

Line 26:   Display current subdirectory on screen.

Line 27:   Redirect the name of current subdirectory to a temporary file called CD.$$$.

Line 28:   Concatenate a new file, RETURN.BAT, containing the original subdirectory name and commands contained in CD.ASC (ECHO OFF and CD).

Line 29:   ERASE the temporary file CD.$$$.

Line 30:   Change the subdirectory up one level, then down to the level specified in %1.

Lines 31–32:   Show user new current subdirectory.

Line 33:   Turn ECHO OFF again.

Line 34:   Remind of RETURN option.

Line 35:   END label file jumps to if no parameter entered.

```
------------------------------------------------------------
1.  ECHO OFF
2.  :    :: OVER.BAT ::
3.  :    *** Moves to Parallel Directory ***
4.  IF NOT '%1'=='' GOTO START
5.  :HELP
6.  ECHO   You must enter a directory name
7.  ECHO   that is on the same level as the
8.  ECHO   current one within the same parent
9.  ECHO   subdirectory.  For example, if you
10. ECHO   are logged into subdirectory LETTERS
11. ECHO   you may move to MEMOS by typing
12. ECHO   OVER MEMOS
13. ECHO             Root Directory
14. ECHO                  :
15. ECHO             ____:____
16. ECHO             :    '
17. ECHO             WP
18. ECHO         ____:____
19. ECHO         :        :
20. ECHO         MEMOS  LETTERS
21. ECHO  <Alt-255>
22. GOTO END
23. :START
24. CLS
25. ECHO Leaving subdirectory:
26. CD
27. CD >CD.$$$
28. COPY C:\BATCHES\CD.ASC+CD.$$$ C:\BATCHES\RETURN.BAT >NUL
29. ERASE CD.$$$ >NUL
30. CD ..\%1
31. ECHO Now in subdirectory :
32. CD
33. ECHO OFF
34. ECHO Type RETURN to return.
35. :END
------------------------------------------------------------
```

DOWN.BAT

What it does: Moves to specified directory below current directory.

Syntax: DOWN subdirectory

Requirements: DOS 2.0 or later, hard disk. See also notes.

HOW TO USE IT

This command moves to the directory specified by the parameter typed in when the file is invoked. The directory must be one below the currently logged directory.

You must have a file called C:\BATCHES\CD.ASC. Create it by typing:

```
COPY CON:C:\BATCHES\CD.ASC<Enter>
ECHO OFF<Enter>
CD <F6><Enter>
```

Note that a space must separate CD and the <F6> on the second line.

Line-By-Line Description

Line 1:	Turn off screen echoing of commands.
Lines 2–3:	Title remarks.
Line 4:	Check for parameter. If none, show HELP.
Lines 5–7:	Help display.
Line 8:	Label marking start of processing.
Line 9:	Clear the screen.
Line 10:	Notify user of departure from current subdirectory.
Line 11:	Display current subdirectory on screen.
Line 12:	Redirect the name of current subdirectory to a temporary file called CD.$$$.
Line 13:	Concatenate a new file, RETURN.BAT, containing the original subdirectory name and commands contained in CD.ASC (ECHO OFF and CD).
Line 14:	ERASE the temporary file CD.$$$.

Line 15:   Change the subdirectory to one a level below, as
                  specified in %1.

Lines 16–17:   Show user new current subdirectory.

Line 18:   Turn ECHO OFF again

Line 19:   Remind of RETURN option.

Line 20:   END label file jumps to if no parameter entered.

```
-----------------------------------------------------------
1.  ECHO OFF
2.  :      :: DOWN.BAT ::
3.  :      *** Moves Down to Specified Directory ***
4.  IF NOT "%1"=="" GOTO START
5.  :HELP
6.  ECHO    You must enter a directory name
7.  GOTO END
8.  :START
9.  CLS
10. ECHO Leaving subdirectory:
11. CD
12. CD >CD.$$$
13. COPY C:\BATCHES\CD.ASC+CD.$$$ C:\BATCHES\RETURN.BAT >NUL
14. ERASE CD.$$$ >NUL
15. CD %1
16. ECHO Now in subdirectory :
17. CD
18. ECHO OFF
19. ECHO Type RETURN to return.
20. :END
-----------------------------------------------------------
```

UP.BAT

What it does: Moves up one level to next highest directory.

Syntax: UP

Requirements: DOS 2.0 or later; hard disk.

HOW TO USE IT

Simply type UP. There are no arguments required. Repeat as required to move up further steps. If you are already in the root directory, nothing happens. You may return to the directory of origin by typing RETURN. Keep in mind that the command CD .. also takes you up one directory level; where this differs is in adding the ability to *return* to your previous directory by typing the RETURN command.

You must have a file called C:\BATCHES\CD.ASC. Create it by typing:

```
COPY CON:C:\BATCHES\CD.ASC<Enter>
ECHO OFF<Enter>
CD <F6><Enter>
```

Note that a space must be placed between the CD and the <F6> on the second line.

Line-By-Line Description

Line 1:	Turn off screen echoing of commands.
Lines 2–3:	Title remarks.
Line 4:	Clear the screen.
Line 5:	Notify user of departure from current subdirectory.
Line 6:	Display current subdirectory on screen.
Line 7:	Redirect the name of current subdirectory to a temporary file called CD.$$$.
Line 8:	Concatenate a new file, RETURN.BAT, containing the original subdirectory name and commands contained in CD.ASC (ECHO OFF and CD).
Line 9:	ERASE the temporary file CD.$$$.
Line 10:	Change the subdirectory to one level above.
Lines 11–12:	Show user new current subdirectory.

Line 13:   Turn ECHO OFF again.

Line 14:   Remind of RETURN option.

```
------------------------------------------------------
1.  ECHO OFF
2.  :    :: UP.BAT ::
3.  :    *** Moves Up One Level ***
4.  CLS
5.  ECHO Leaving subdirectory:
6.  CD
7.  CD >CD.$$$
8.  COPY C:\BATCHES\CD.ASC+CD.$$$ C:\BATCHES\RETURN.BAT >NUL
9.  ERASE CD.$$$ >NUL
10. CD ..
11. ECHO Now in subdirectory :
12. CD
13. ECHO OFF
14. ECHO Type RETURN to return.
------------------------------------------------------
```

ROOT.BAT

What it does: Changes to root directory, with option to RETURN to current directory.

Syntax: ROOT

Requirements: DOS 2.0 or later; hard disk.

HOW TO USE IT

Unlike the CD \ command, ROOT remembers where you were and allows you to return by typing RETURN. No arguments are needed; simply type ROOT from any subdirectory on the disk and you are taken to the root directory of the current disk. You must have a file called C:\BATCHES\CD.ASC. Create it by typing:

```
COPY CON:C:\BATCHES\CD.ASC<Enter>
ECHO OFF<Enter>
CD <F6><Enter>
```

Note that a space must separate CD and <F6> on the second line.

Line-By-Line Description

Line 1:	Turn off screen echoing of commands.
Lines 2–3:	Title remarks.
Line 4:	Clear the screen.
Line 5:	Notify user of departure from current subdirectory.
Line 6:	Display current subdirectory on screen.
Line 7:	Redirect the name of current subdirectory to a temporary file called CD.$$$.
Line 8:	Concatenate a new file, RETURN.BAT, containing the original subdirectory name and commands contained in CD.ASC (ECHO OFF and CD).
Line 9:	ERASE the temporary file CD.$$$.
Line 10:	Change the subdirectory to the root directory.
Lines 11–12:	Show user new current subdirectory.
Line 13:	Turn ECHO OFF again.
Line 14:	Remind of RETURN option.

```
-----------------------------------------------------------
1.  ECHO OFF
2.  :    :: ROOT.BAT ::
3.  :    *** Moves To Root Directory ***
4.  CLS
5.  ECHO Leaving subdirectory:
6.  CD
7.  CD >CD.$$$
8.  COPY C:\BATCHES\CD.ASC+CD.$$$ C:\BATCHES\RETURN.BAT >NUL
9.  ERASE CD.$$$ >NUL
10. CD \
11. ECHO Now in Root Directory:
12. CD
13. ECHO OFF
14. ECHO Type RETURN to return.
-----------------------------------------------------------
```

ADD.BAT

What it does: Adds paths to the PATH environment variable.

Syntax: ADD newpath

Requirements: DOS 2.0 or later; hard disk. See also notes.

HOW TO USE IT

Type ADD, followed by the new path you want to add. You can include such lines in the following batch file in special batch files that load application programs consisting of various .COM or .EXE programs. Then, your application knows how to find the files it uses. The original PATH setting is stored in OLDPATH.BAT and can be restored by typing OLDPATH when finished.

You may do this manually or create a batch file that calls your application, changes the path, and restores it automatically.

Line-By-Line Description

Line 1:   Turn off screen echoing of commands.

Lines 2–3:   Title remarks.

Line 4:   Clear the screen.

Line 5:   If parameter entered, jump to START and begin processing.

Lines 6–10:   Display HELP.

Line 11:   Start processing.

Line 12:   Redirect output of PATH to OLDPATH.BAT.

Line 13:   Change PATH to existing value, plus %1.

Line 14:   Label where the file jumps to after HELP display.

```
1.  ECHO OFF
2.  :    :: ADD.BAT ::
```

```
3.  :       *** Adds Path to Environment ***
4.  CLS
5.  IF NOT "%1"=="" GOTO START
6.  :HELP
7.  ECHO  Include a pathname to be added.
8.  ECHO  To restore original PATH settings,
9.  ECHO  Type OLDPATH.
10. GOTO END
11. :START
12. PATH >C:\BATCHES\OLDPATH.BAT
13. PATH=%PATH%;%1
14. :END
```

LOG.BAT/HOME.BAT

What it does: Logs the current directory as the HOME directory.

Syntax: LOG (To log current directory)

Syntax: HOME (To return to logged directory)

Requirements: DOS 2.0 or later; hard disk.

HOW TO USE IT

Log onto the directory that you wish to log as your home directory and type LOG. To return to that directory at any time, type HOME. You must have a file called C:\BATCHES\CD.ASC. Create it by typing:

```
COPY CON:C:\BATCHES\CD.ASC<Enter>
ECHO OFF<Enter>
CD <F6><Enter>
```

Note that a space must separate CD and <F6> on the second line. This utility assumes that you are already logged onto the hard disk where the home directory resides. That is, typing HOME while logged onto A: or B: does *not* return you to a directory logged on C: The command *does* change the current directory of the drive that was logged to the home directory. Example:

You were logged onto A:\ when you typed LOG. If you are now logged onto A:\FILES, typing HOME logs you back onto A:\. However, if you are logged onto B:, typing HOME changes the current directory of A: to A:\ (if necessary), but you will remain logged onto B:

Line-By-Line Description

Line 1:	Turn off screen echoing of commands.
Lines 2–3:	Title remarks.
Line 4:	Clear the screen.
Line 5:	Redirect current PATH setting to a temporary file called LOG.$$$.
Line 6:	Build new batch file HOME.BAT from file CD.ASC and LOG.$$$.
Line 7:	Erase temporary file LOG.$$$.

```
-----------------------------------------------------
1.  ECHO OFF
2.  :    :: LOG.BAT ::
3.  :    *** Logs Current Path to HOME.BAT ***
4.  CLS
5.  CD >LOG.$$$
6.  COPY C:\BATCHES\CD.ASC + LOG.$$$
C:\BATCHES\HOME.BAT
7.  ERASE LOG.$$$
-----------------------------------------------------
```

EDRIVE.BAT

What it does:	Assigns currently logged directory to DOS Drive E: specification, so user may type DIR E:, CD E:, and so on to access that directory as if it were a separate drive.
Requirements:	DOS 3.1 or later, hard disk. See also notes.
Syntax:	EDRIVE—To substitute current directory.

HOW TO USE IT

Assign current directory path to Drive E: with the DOS SUBST command. You must not already have a RAM disk or hard disk assigned to Drive E:. If so, insert a LASTDRIVE=x line in your CONFIG.SYS file, where x equals the last drive you are using beyond E: A file must be created called EDRIVE.ASC in your subdirectory C:\BATCHES. Create the file by typing the following:

```
COPY CON:C:\BATCHES\EDRIVE.ASC<Enter>
ECHO OFF<Enter>
SUBST E: <Enter>
```

If you are using a drive specification other than E:, change the line in the preceding file to reflect that.

You also need a file called KILLER.ASC. Create it by typing the following:

```
COPY CON:C:\BATCHES\KILLER.ASC<Enter>
ERASE %0<Enter>
<F6><Enter>
```

This ASCII file, when appended to the end of the file that activates the substitution, E.BAT, erases E.BAT. Ignore the error message produced when a batch file erases itself during processing.

To use the command, log onto the directory you want to use as Drive E: and type EDRIVE. Thereafter, you may access that path as Drive E: until you invoke the EDRIVE command again.

Line-By-Line Description

Line 1: Turn off screen echoing of commands.

Lines 2–3: Title remarks.

Line 4: Clear the screen.

Line 5: Redirect current PATH setting to a temporary file called TEMP.$$$.

Line 6: Build new batch file E.BAT from file EDRIVE.ASC and TEMP.$$$.

Line 7: Erase temporary file TEMP.$$$.

Line 8: Invoke batch file E.BAT.

Note: E.BAT erases itself when finished.

```
-----------------------------------------------------------
1.  ECHO OFF
2.  :     :: EDRIVE.BAT ::
3.  :     *** Substitutes Current Path for Drive E: ***
4.  CLS
5.  CD > TEMP.$$$
6.  COPY C:\BATCHES\EDRIVE.ASC + TEMP.$$$ + KILLER.ASC E.BAT
7.  ERASE TEMP.$$$
8.  E

-----------------------------------------------------------
```

SUMMARY

This chapter introduced the important concept of using PATH with hierarchical directories and explained how the PATH command could tell DOS where to find system files. Techniques were explained for navigating the directory tree. The batch files in this chapter supply tools for moving up, down, over, or back to the root directory. Also given are routines that let you log the current directory, return to a designated HOME directory, and define a given directory as Drive E:

9

Using the
Environment To
Create a
"Security" System

INTRODUCTION

In this chapter, we'll apply some of the tools introduced so far to build a computer "security" system. Since the DOS environment is so little used, even by relatively knowledgeable users, we'll take advantage of that obscurity to hide passwords and other information that could be easily read out of a batch file. To make things really interesting, we'll investigate some ways to make "visible" files that are invisible to prying eyes—unless they know the secret. Some readers will find the security tips useful. Others will find them less practical because of their particular working environment. However, all should enjoy the tricks and techniques—unavailable from any other source—presented for the first time.

THE MYTH OF MICROCOMPUTER SECURITY

It's difficult to provide foolproof security for a microcomputer. Password systems can be broken by any knowledgeable user. If the system is equipped with a lock on the front, the entire computer can be stolen and broken into at the thief's leisure.

If you want to keep your computer, its programs, and its data safe from the *average* computer use, though, the following system has some new tricks that offer a measure of security. The accompanying utilities are also a fun way to learn some interesting ways to use the environment.

One of the key tricks to this system involves the invisible character invoked by holding down the Alt key and typing 255 on the numeric keypad of your computer. DOS accepts this character as part of environment strings, directory names and filenames. Alt 255 *won't* show up on your screen, though. Unless an intruder has read this book or is very sharp, he won't suspect the presence of the odd character.

For example, you may create a file called TEST<Alt 255>. Try it now, using COPY CON:

```
COPY CON:TEST<Alt 255><Enter>
This is my test file<F6><Enter>
```

Now if you do a directory, sure enough, a file called TEST exists. However, if you try to list the file by entering TYPE TEST, DOS reports FILE NOT FOUND. Intruders cannot see the contents of that file. Or, if it is a batch file or program, they cannot execute it unless they know about the sneaky extra invisible character. Of course, an expert who *knows* that DOS can't not find a file that clearly shows up in a directory might suspect that a space or another invisible character has been embedded in the filename. This expert wouldn't need to know what the invisible character was, since simply typing:

```
RENAME TEST*.* NEW.TXT
```

would copy the file to a new name that *could* be accessed quite easily.

Calling a file by the name <Alt 255> would work and the whole filename would be invisible. However, the file size and creation date in the directory would surely tip off the knowledgeable user.

As you may know, DOS has a provision to make a file *really* invisible—to hide special files used by copy protection schemes when installing a program on a hard disk. The user is unaware of the invisible file, but the protected software knows to look for it before running. Invisible files are also used by the operating system itself. The key point is that the user never needs to access these invisible files from the DOS prompt and as a result, doesn't need to know or remember the filenames. For our security system, we want to be able to list the "invisible" files without keeping a separate catalog of those filenames. For our purposes, the "purloined letter" technique makes the filename *seem* innocent yet erects some obstacles to casual access by intruders.

PROTECTED SUBDIRECTORIES

We can make things a little more difficult. DOS allows you to create a subdirectory with invisible characters. Choose an innocent-sounding name, such as UTILITY or BIN or another that you currently don't use. Make sure the name is no more than seven characters long. Create the subdirectory in the usual manner, with two tiny changes:

```
MD UTILITY<Alt 255>.<Alt 255>
```

You've just created a subdirectory that *looks* as if it is called UTILITY on your disk; however, it is followed by the invisible character Alt 255; *plus* it has an invisible extension, which is also Alt 255. Since extensions are so rarely used with subdirectory names, it takes an exceptional user to wade through this thicket. Intruders cannot get a directory of your secret directory or log onto it. (Before you get too excited, keep in mind that TREE and CHKDSK produce a listing of all the files and subdirectories on your disk. The determined expert will at least try these to look at the files within the secret directories, if nothing else.)

A note for the truly sneaky: DOS won't allow you to create a subdirectory called "..<Alt 255>" or any other permutation involving periods, which DOS, of course, uses to signify the current directory and parent directory within subdirectories. If you create within a subdirectory another subdirectory called <Alt 255> as the first file in that subdirectory, it appears immediately below the . and .. listings, and *might* be overlooked by the less than eagle-eyed intruder. It's worth a try. Of course, there are ways to use DEBUG and other tools to make directories truly invisible like the other invisible files such as IBMBIOS.COM, but we leave off here.

If you store your sensitive programs and data files in these hidden subdirectories, they are reasonably secure. Even those who can get past the password system to follow may not be able to load and run your programs if they can't even find them.

Note that: Some applications "choke" on weird filenames and directory names. Check out your own programs. If you get a directory error message even though your batch file or your keyboard entry has the right name, there may be a conflict. Some programs still get confused even if you log onto the weird directory before running them.

You'll want to hide batch files that run your programs in the secret directories. Let's assume that the batch file that runs your key application is called UN-LOCK.BAT, and it is hidden in a secret subdirectory called C:\UTILITY<Alt 255>.<Alt 255>. UNLOCK could also just change directories for you to your hidden directory so that you can access files as usual. UNLOCK may itself also contain a hidden character like Alt 255 so that intruders have a hard time accessing it.

You also have deposited in the secret subdirectory two utilities called SETPASS.BAT and SETUSER.BAT. Set up a PATH command to show DOS how to find these batch files. For extra security, if you are using DOS 3.x, you may explicitly type the pathname to the batch file to invoke it. By taking that extra measure, you can avoid listing the secret directory path at all in the environment.

HIDING USER LISTS AND PASSWORDS IN THE ENVIRONMENT

Since we also store our passwords there, however, it probably makes little sense to disguise our PATH as well.

To activate the batch file UNLOCK.BAT, you must type from the DOS prompt this command:

```
PASSWORD username password
```

The username is a valid name stored in the DOS environment as variable USERS, and the password is stored there as variable PASSWORD. Why wouldn't an intruder check the environment using SET to find out the password and list of user names? There are several obstacles in the way.

First, the intruder must know that a password and username are required and in what order they must be entered to be valid. The intruder must also know that these are stored in the DOS environment. Finally, we can make things difficult even if those two facts are known because we can embed the invisible character Alt 255 in the password. It won't show up with the SET command, but the user must type it in anyway.

Finding out what is going on by examining the batch file PASSWORD.BAT won't be easy. First, PASSWORD.BAT is hidden in our secret directory. Second, the key lines have been hidden from view even if the intruder manages to type the file. Another character, Alt 13, is embedded in the middle of the key lines. This carriage return (without linefeed) moves the cursor back to the beginning of the line without dropping down a line. We follow the Alt 13 in the key lines with a REMark that overwrites the important part of the line.

You cannot enter Alt 13 using COPY CON. You'll need to use a word-processing program that lets you enter Alt characters from the keyboard, such as PC-WRITE. Since the separate lines that call the password and the UNLOCK.BAT file are disguised, the intruder can't learn about the use of the environment to store the password or the existence of the UNLOCK.BAT file—at least from that source. Before you are lulled into a false sense of security, remember that once someone has found PASSWORD.BAT, it can be loaded into a word processor that accepts ASCII files and examined that way.

As written, when the user types PASSWORD without following it with a correct username and the password, the computer goes into an endless loop of beeping. Control-C takes you out of this loop. If you suspect legitimate users may enter a typo from time to time, substitute for the GOTO BELL line, ECHO Try Again and let them try again.

If you wanted to be fairly nasty, you could substitute CTTY NUL for the ECHO <Alt 7> line. That would redirect output of the computer to the NUL device, effectively locking it up and forcing a reboot. In practice, this is hardly worthwhile, since the savvy user does not fall for the same trick twice. This security system should slow down intruders enough to protect you from casual or even fairly concerted efforts.

Since your files are hidden in a hard-to-access subdirectory, booting from a floppy disk instead of the hard disk is of no help. Potential intruders have to learn your password, make a guess about the environment—including the invisible characters—or figure out how to use the invisible characters to log onto your secret directories. Without one of these breaks, your system is secure.

DELETING USERS

The only thing missing from this security system is a way to delete users. Unfortunately, there is no easy way to *remove* part of an environment variable, even though the variable can be parsed using the batch file command FOR..IN..DO. The file SETUSER.BAT adds to a file called STARTUP.BAT a list of current users. STARTUP.BAT can be hidden in your secret directory and called from AUTOEXEC.BAT each time you turn on the computer. To *delete* users, you need to edit STARTUP.BAT with the same ASCII word-processor tool, or EDLIN, that you use to create or revise your AUTOEXEC.BAT file.

The main purpose of these files is to teach you some tricks about using the environment. If real microcomputer security is needed, examine some of the third-party encrypting tools and other professional protection schemes. The utilities that follow can offer some security when one computer is shared among a group of users, some of whom use general files, while others need access to private files. You can have both types of users on the system; the "general" users can use the computer as always and don't even need to know about the passwords and other hidden features.

CUSTOMIZING YOUR CUSTOMIZATION

To minimize the amount of typing that you are faced with, most of the routines in this book offer basic features that can be tailored further by the advanced DOS user. From time to time we'll offer suggestions, but you can undertake many of these on your own. For example, the security routines in this chapter can be augmented by several techniques and tricks based on what we have learned already.

Say that your security needs are casual; you would like to *know* when someone tries to access your system and would like them to know you know. Locking up the computer as suggested is one answer. A series of beeps produced by embedding Control-G (Alt 7) in a batch file is another.

Why not consider making your screen begin *blinking* maddeningly, since most intruders won't know how to make it stop without rebooting the computer? Two simple lines in any batch file do the trick when those lines are called:

```
ECHO ON
PROMPT=$e[5m
```

When activated, the characters printed on the screen henceforth will blink, until the following lines are called:

```
ECHO ON
PROMPT=$e[0m
```

You could also place these in separate batch files, BLINKER.BAT and UNBLINK.BAT for calling by other batch files or from DOS command mode. Or you might call BLINKER.BAT by the name PASSWORD.BAT and see if the unwary intruder activates it by mistake.

If you have an ASCII word-processing facility that lets you enter ESC directly (or by typing Alt 27), you can put the blink/unblink commands in your batch files as ECHO commands:

```
ECHO <Alt 27>[5m
```

works just as well as the PROMPT command. You can include any of the screen control commands discussed in Chapter 5 in this way, moving the cursor to one part of the screen to another, erasing part of the screen, changing colors of the text and background, and so on. Simply put the commands you want in the batch files using your ASCII word processor. The batch files in this chapter, as well as those later in this book can be dressed up with these sophisticated tools. Because such dressing makes the listings harder to read and really adds little functionality to a batch file, most of the routines to follow in this book rarely use them. Fancy colors, flashing prompt lines, and other touches do make for more professional-looking batch files. Experiment with these features if you wish.

Another customization feature for batch files is applying the PC's built-in character graphics to draw boxes and lines around menus and so forth in your batch files. Character graphics are special characters built into the PC's 256-character set that can be used to draw boxes and other figures. For example, a double-line box can be drawn with the commands shown below:

```
ECHO   <Alt 201><Alt 205><Alt 205><Alt 187>
ECHO   <Alt 186><Alt 32><Alt 32><Alt 186>
ECHO   <Alt 186><Alt 32><Alt 32><Alt 186>
ECHO   <Alt 200><Alt 205><Alt 205><Alt 188>
```

Note that Alt 32, which is simply the space character, may also be entered by pressing the space bar. The resulting box would be four characters on a side and thus has only a small amount of room inside (replacing the spaces) for text. To make a larger box, simply add the number of Alt 205 characters at both top and bottom to increase the width or the number of Alt 186 characters at the sides to increase the height. You may also use these characters to produce odd-sided figures, which do not necessarily have to be rectangles or squares, but which must, of course, be constructed only from right-angled graphics characters.

UTILITIES

PASSWORD.BAT

What it does: Allows user to run UNLOCK.BAT by entering a valid username and current password.

Syntax: PASSWORD username password

Requirements: DOS 2.0 or later.

HOW TO USE IT

Type PASSWORD followed by your username and password. If you enter correct strings, the batch file UNLOCK.BAT is invoked. You should hide UN-

LOCK.BAT in your secret directory and write it so that it either starts your application program or logs onto the hidden directory. PASSWORD.BAT also stores in environment variable NOW the username of the current user. Your other batch files can access this as required, for example, to grant or deny further levels of access.

If you want to provide a way for users to log out of the secure system, simply write a batch file called LOGOUT.BAT that contains the line CD \, which logs the user onto the root directory, from where PASSWORD.BAT must be run again to gain access to the secret directory.

Line-By-Line Description

Line 1:   Turn off echoing of commands.

Lines 2–3:   Title remarks.

Line 4:   If no username entered, go to DENIED.

Line 5:   If second parameter does not equal PASSWORD, go to denied. Optional <Alt 13> plus remark keeps intruders from reading this key line if they manage to TYPE the file.

Line 6:   Compare each name in USERS with name entered.

Line 7:   If no match, go to DENIED.

Line 8:   Begin unlock module.

Line 9:   Set NOW variable to current username.

Line 10:   Access UNLOCK batch file.

Line 11:   Begin DENIED section of file.

Line 12:   Echo ACCESS DENIED to screen.

Lines 13–14: Sound Beep.

Line 15:   Loop back.

```
------------------------------------------------------------
1.   ECHO OFF
2.   :  :: PASSWORD.BAT ::
3.   :  *** Locks Up System Without Password ***
4.   IF "%1"=="" GOTO DENIED
```

```
 5.  IF NOT "%2"=="%PASSWORD%' GOTO DENIED<Alt 13>REM
     ****** Password Protection Module *****
 6.  FOR %%a IN (%USERS%) DO IF %%a==%1 GOTO UNLOCK
 7.  GOTO DENIED
 8.  :UNLOCK
 9.  SET NOW=%1
10.  UNLOCK <Alt 13> REM Enter Password
11.  :DENIED
12.  ECHO ACCESS DENIED
13.  :BELL
14.  ECHO <Alt 7>
15.  GOTO BELL
```

SETPASS.BAT

What it does: Allows setting a new password.

Syntax: SETPASS oldpassword newpassword

Requirements: DOS 2.0 or later. See also notes.

HOW TO USE IT

Type SETPASS followed by the existing password, a space, and the new pass-word. The system administrator should either use this utility to set a password each day when the system is turned on or create a batch file that sets the password automatically. If no password has been set, PASSWORD.BAT allows a blank password entry to match.

Because embedding your password in AUTOEXEC.BAT is not a good idea and AUTOEXEC.BAT must be in your root directory, instead you can have AUTOEXEC.BAT call another batch file that *is* located in your hidden directory. This file assumes that you have called your hidden directory C:\UTILITY<Alt 255> and that the second startup batch file is called C:\UTILITY<Alt 255>\STARTUP.BAT.

Make the last line in your AUTOEXEC.BAT file read C:\STARTUP.BAT if you have DOS 3.x or later. If you have DOS 2.x, you need to first change the current directory to C:\UTILITY<Alt 255> with the CD command before starting STARTUP.BAT.

SETPASS appends a line to STARTUP.BAT that sets the environment variable PASSWORD to the new value. If you run this program often, eventually STARTUP.BAT will include a group of new password defining lines; however, only the last one will be in effect when you first see the DOS prompt. If untidiness offends you, occasionally edit STARTUP.BAT with your ASCII editing tool, such as EDLIN, to remove the extra lines.

To use this file, you need a file called C:\BATCHES\SETPASS.ASC which contains the words "SET PASSWORD=" with no carriage return. You may create it by typing:

```
COPY CON:C:\BATCHES\SETPASS.ASC<Enter>
SET PASSWORD=<F6><Enter>
```

Line-By-Line Description

Line 1:   Turn off screen echoing of commands.

Lines 2–3:   Label remarks.

Line 4:   If no password currently exists, go to NEWPASS.

Line 5:   See if %1 matches existing password.

Lines 6–9:   If not, display HELP.

Lines 10–12:   Set password to value supplied by %2.

Lines 13–14:   Replace existing password with value stored in %2.

Line 15:   Begin final routine.

Line 16:   Redirect echoing of password variable to temporary file, TEMP.$$$.

Line 17:   Add to STARTUP.BAT a line consisting of SET PASSWORD= (from SETPASS.ASC) and the new password (from TEMP.$$$).

Line 18:   Erase the temporary file.

```
1.  ECHO OFF
2.  :    :: SETPASS.BAT ::
3.  :    *** Sets System Password ***
4.  IF "%PASSWORD%"=="" GOTO NEWPASS
5.  IF "%1"=="%PASSWORD%" GOTO ENTER
6.  :HELP
```

```
 7.  ECHO  Type SETPASS oldpassword newpassword
 8.  ECHO  If no password exists, just type new one.
 9.  GOTO END
10. :NEWPASS
11. SET PASSWORD=%1
12. GOTO END
13. :ENTER
14. SET PASSWORD=%2
15. :END
16: ECHO %PASSWORD%>TEMP.$$$
17: COPY C:\UTILITY<Alt 255>\STARTUP.BAT
    +C:\BATCHES\SETPASS.ASC+TEMP.$$$
    C:\UTILITY<Alt 255>\STARTUP.BAT
18. ERASE TEMP.$$$
```

SETUSER.BAT

What it does: Adds authorized user to your user list.

Syntax: SETUSER password newuser

Requirements: DOS 2.0 or later. See also notes.

HOW TO USE IT

With this utility, you can add a new user to your user list and create a batch file that can be called from your AUTOEXEC.BAT file on bootup to install the list each time your computer is powered on.

To use it, type SETUSER followed by the current password and the user's name. You may have no more than 123 characters' worth of usernames in your list. This file adds a line to STARTUP.BAT, which should be called by your AUTOEXEC.BAT file as its last step. STARTUP.BAT is hidden in your "special" directory, for example, C:\UTILITY<Alt 255>.

Make the last line in your AUTOEXEC.BAT file read C:\UTILITY<Alt 255>\STARTUP.BAT if you have DOS 3.x or later. If you have DOS 2.x, you need to first change the current directory to C:\UTILITY<Alt 255> with the CD command before starting STARTUP.BAT.

SETUSER appends a line to STARTUP.BAT that sets the environment variable USERS to the new value on bootup. If you run this program often, eventually STARTUP.BAT includes a group of such lines; however, only the last one is in effect when you first see the DOS prompt. If untidiness offends you, occasionally edit STARTUP.BAT with your ASCII editing tool, such as EDLIN, to remove the extra lines.

To use this file, you need a file called C:\BATCHES\SETUSER.ASC, which contains the words "SET USERS=" with no carriage return. You may create it by typing:

```
COPY CON:C:\BATCHES\SETUSER.ASC<Enter>
SET USERS=<F6><Enter>
```

Line-By-Line Description

Line 1:   Turn off ECHO.

Lines 2–3:   Title remarks.

Line 4:   Check to see if first parameter equals password.

Lines 5–9:   If not, show help.

Line 10:   Start processing.

Line 11:   If no current USERS variable, jump to NEW.

Line 12:   SET USERS to equal old value, plus new.

Line 13:   Jump to END.

Lines 15–15:   SET USERS to new value.

Line 16:   Start END routine.

Line 17:   Redirect echoing of USERS variable to temporary file, TEMP.$$$.

Line 18:   Add to STARTUP.BAT a line created from SETUSER.ASC, and contents of TEMP.$$$ (current USERS value).

Line 19.   ERASE the temporary file, TEMP.$$$.

```
1.   ECHO OFF
2.   :   :: SETUSER.BAT ::
3.   :   *** Adds New User ***
4.   IF "%1"=="%PASSWORD%" GOTO ENTER
5.   :HELP
```

```
 6.  ECHO   Type SETUSER password newuser
 7.  ECHO   Only 123 characters of usernames
 8.  ECHO   may be included.
 9.  GOTO END
10.  :ENTER
11.  IF "%USERS%"=="" GOTO NEW
12.  SET USERS=%USERS%;%2
13.  GOTO END
14.  :NEW
15.  SET USERS=%2
16.  :END
17.  ECHO %USERS%>TEMP.$$$
18: COPY C:\UTILITY<Alt 255>\STARTUP.BAT
    +C:\BATCHES\SETUSER.ASC+TEMP.$$$
    C:\UTILITY<Alt 255>\STARTUP.BAT
19.  ERASE TEMP.$$$
```

SUMMARY

In this chapter we've set up a microcomputer security system using the environment to hide user lists and variables. Also, we've "protected" filenames and subdirectories created by embedding the invisible character Alt 255 in them. Ways to lock up the computer using the CTTY command were explained, along with suggestions for getting the most from your protected microcomputer. Most important, ways to get around this system were shown, demonstrating that no microcomputer can truly be protected from sophisticated intruders.

10

New Directory
Commands—Part 1

INTRODUCTION

This chapter will use one of the simplest of all DOS commands, DIR, to demonstrate several important DOS concepts: redirection and the use of filters like SORT. We'll prepare some new DOS commands that perform simple functions—such as displaying a directory of A: or B: when you type A or B or sorted directories that can be output to a file or shown on the screen. Also included is a utility that creates a whole clutch of batch files that take you to every directory on your hard disk simply by typing the last portion of the directory name.

NEW DIR-ECTIONS

The DIR command found in DOS is already extremely flexible. We can type DIR /W or DIR /P to get a listing of available programs displayed in a wide format or conveniently paged. Wildcards can be used to look only for certain file specifications: DIR *.BAS would show only BASIC programs. DIR, of course, also accepts pathnames, so that it is possible to look at subdirectories by specifying the correct path. And you may not be aware of some slightly lesser-known capabilities of DOS. Did you know you can capture an image of the directory in an ASCII text file simply by typing DIR > filename?

DOS' ability to redirect output, used off and on previously in this book, will be put to work extensively in this chapter and others to follow. We'll learn how to sort directories, print them out for permanent record, and even clean up a disk directory automatically. There will even be a utility to automatically create a couple dozen—or hundred—batch files for you to help you navigate more easily among your directories.

But first quickly review of DOS' input/output redirection capabilities. You may have seen the terms "standard input" and "standard output" in the DOS manual. The novice probably finds those terms confusing, because they usually refer to the keyboard and screen, respectively. The reason that standard input device and standard output device are used instead is that DOS allows changing the definition of these devices so that DOS looks for its input from a source other than the keyboard or sends output to a peripheral other than the screen. Although a printer and a video screen are very different to human users, to DOS the difference is rather transparent. DOS merely sends characters to one or the other. The device drivers built into DOS and your application software take care of controlling the video or printer in terms of how much to show/print on a line, and so forth.

Once information has been directed to one or the other, the hardware handles the interchange differently, but up until that point, one is no different than the other.

Three symbols are used for redirection. The greater-than sign (>), also called the right angle bracket, redirects output from the source on the left of the sign to the new output device on the right of the sign:

```
DIR>PRN
DIR>COM1
DIR>FILE
```

The first would send the output of the directory command to the printer, rather than to the screen. The second example would send it to the serial port, while the third would direct it to an ASCII file named FILE.

The less-than sign, also called the left angle bracket (<), tells a program on the left side of the symbol to look for its input from a file on the right of the sign, instead of from the keyboard:

```
DATABASE<DATAFILE
```

One additional symbol may be used—a double greater than sign (> >), which redirects output to an existing file, and appends it to the end of that file. The single > starts the designated file anew, erasing any previous one by that name that might exist on the disk.

DOS FILTERS

Redirection is useful when you need a disk file of information that would normally appear on the screen. It can also be used in combination with "piping"—another UNIX-like feature introduced with DOS 2.0. A pipe connects two programs so that the output from one program becomes the input for the second. Most frequently, pipes work with several of DOS' built in "filters," such as MORE, SORT, and FIND, to take the characters from a file or from program output (when they are piped to the filter) and perform some manipulation.

MORE takes the characters and displays one screenful at a time, pausing with a—More—message to give you time to read the screen. The next page can be displayed by pressing a key. MORE is useful for displaying ASCII files, such as batch files, one screenful at a time.

SORT takes the same stream of characters and sorts the information according to certain rules we'll look at shortly. SORT can be accessed from BASIC through the SHELL command, as well as used with DOS, and is a very fast sort routine for lists of typical length, so you'll find it extremely useful.

FIND searches through the character stream for a string of characters that you specify and displays all the lines that contain that string, or that do *not* contain that string. You can also ask for a count of the number of lines containing the string and ask FIND to display a relative line number in front of each line. You can redirect FIND's output to a file to save a copy of the results.

FIND's syntax is as follows:

```
FIND [/V] [/C] [N] "string to search for" [drive] [path]
```

The /V switch tells FIND to display only those lines not containing the specified string. The /C switch is the command to print only the count of how many lines contain a match. The /N switch precedes the lines with their relative line number. If you want to search for a string that contains quotation marks, you must type double quotation marks around the string.

Pipes are created using the vertical bar symbol (|), which tells DOS to pipe the output of one program or command to the filter. For example, if you wanted to use MORE instead of DIR /P to see a paged disk directory, you could type:

```
DIR | MORE
```

Because of the temporary files being created and the fact that MORE is an external program, using this method would be a great deal slower than an internal DOS command, like DIR /P. Filters can also be used with redirection:

```
MORE<FILE.TXT
```

That line would direct the text file, FILE.TXT to MORE, with the result that the file would be printed to the screen one page at a time. This is a convenient way of looking at ASCII files without needing to load a word-processing or text-editing program. A batch file at the end of this chapter performs this task for you.

SORT is very useful, because sorted lists are so handy to have. Four of the files in this chapter sort directories for you, each by a different parameter. The directory can be sorted by file root name, by extension, by date created, by time created (or updated) or by file size.

SORT's syntax is as follows:

```
SORT [drive][pathname][/R][/+n]
```

The *drive* and *pathname* refer to the file to be sorted, while the /R switch reverses the sort, starting from Z to A, rather than A to Z. If you use the /+n switch, substitute for *n* the column on each line that you want SORT to sort by. Otherwise it sorts starting with the first character, or column one. In our batch files, we sort by different columns in the directory by specifying as *n* the column where that directory attribute starts.

That is, no /+ switch sorts by the file's root name. The /+9 switch starts the sort at the file extension; /+14 at the size in bytes; /+23 at the date; +/32 at the time the file was created. Note that SORT follows a strict alphabetic sort, rather than numeric so that 10.BAT appears before 1.BAT in a sorted list.

Here are some examples of directories sorted by various parameters:

For a directory sorted by extension, type:

```
C>DIR | SORT /+9
```

```
LIST                  632      8-12-86    11:10a
FN                   4096      8-11-86     5:55p
BATCHES       <DIR>           8-12-86     2:02p
DOS           <DIR>           8-12-86     2:02p
FMC      ASN         4096      4-10-86     9:05a
SORTER   BAT           24      8-12-86     2:03p
TEST     BAT           45      8-12-86    11:10a
KODA     CAP        44544      8-11-86     5:31p
BOB      MEM         4096      8-12-86    11:49a
MCI      MON         7552      8-11-86     4:41p
PAPER    TXT        10240      8-04-86    10:55a
```

```
FCC       TXT     11264     8-12-86   11:04a
BBS       TXT     12800     8-06-86    4:42p
SCANNER   TXT     22016     8-08-86   11:43a
```

For a directory sorted by size, type:

```
C>DIR | SORT /+14
```

```
SORTER    BAT        24     8-12-86    2:03p
TEST      BAT        45     8-12-86   11:10a
LIST                632     8-12-86   11:10a
RESULT              796     8-12-86    2:04p
FMC       ASN      4096     4-10-86    9:05a
FN                 4096     8-11-86    5:55p
BOB       MEM      4096     8-12-86   11:49a
MCI       MON      7552     8-11-86    4:41p
PAPER     TXT     10240     8-04-86   10:55a
FCC       TXT     11264     8-12-86   11:04a
BBS       TXT     12800     8-06-86    4:42p
SCANNER   TXT     22016     8-08-86   11:43a
KODA      CAP     44544     8-11-86    5:31p
```

For a directory sorted by date, type:

```
C>DIR | SORT /+23
```

```
FMC       ASN      4096     4-10-86    9:05a
PAPER     TXT     10240     8-04-86   10:55a
BBS       TXT     12800     8-06-86    4:42p
SCANNER   TXT     22016     8-08-86   11:43a
MCI       MON      7552     8-11-86    4:41p
KODA      CAP     44544     8-11-86    5:31p
FN                 4096     8-11-86    5:55p
BATCHES          <DIR>      8-12-86    2:02p
DOS              <DIR>      8-12-86    2:02p
SORTER    BAT        24     8-12-86    2:03p
RESULT             1633     8-12-86    2:04p
FCC       TXT     11264     8-12-86   11:04a
TEST      BAT        45     8-12-86   11:10a
LIST                632     8-12-86   11:10a
BOB       MEM      4096     8-12-86   11:49a
```

For a directory sorted by time, type:

```
C>DIR | SORT /+32
```

```
BATCHES         <DIR>        8-12-86     2:02p
DOS             <DIR>        8-12-86     2:02p
SORTER    BAT        24      8-12-86     2:03p
RESULT           2470        8-12-86     2:05p
MCI       MON      7552      8-11-86     4:41p
BBS       TXT     12800      8-06-86     4:42p
KODA      CAP     44544      8-11-86     5:31p
FN                4096       8-11-86     5:55p
FMC       ASN      4096      4-10-86     9:05a
PAPER     TXT     10240      8-04-86    10:55a
FCC       TXT     11264      8-12-86    11:04a
TEST      BAT        45      8-12-86    11:10a
LIST               632       8-12-86    11:10a
SCANNER   TXT     22016      8-08-86    11:43a
BOB       MEM      4096      8-12-86    11:49a
```

For a directory sorted by root file name, type:

```
C>DIR | SORT /+32
```

```
BATCHES         <DIR>        8-12-86     2:02p
BBS       TXT     12800      8-06-86     4:42p
BOB       MEM      4096      8-12-86    11:49a
DOS             <DIR>        8-12-86     2:02p
FCC       TXT     11264      8-12-86    11:04a
FMC       ASN      4096      4-10-86     9:05a
FN                4096       8-11-86     5:55p
KODA      CAP     44544      8-11-86     5:31p
LIST               632       8-12-86    11:10a
MCI       MON      7552      8-11-86     4:41p
PAPER     TXT     10240      8-04-86    10:55a
RESULT           3307        8-12-86     2:05p
SCANNER   TXT     22016      8-08-86    11:43a
SORTER    BAT        24      8-12-86     2:03p
TEST      BAT        45      8-12-86    11:10a
```

As you know, you can log onto any particular subdirectory by typing CD followed by that subdirectory name. To take yourself to C:\WP\LETTERS, you would type:

```
CD C:\WP\LETTERS
```

You could, of course, write a batch file called LETTERS.BAT so that you could go to that subdirectory just by typing the last part of its name. If you have many subdirectories, though, this chore would be somewhat tedious. One of the utilities in this chapter is a file and BASIC program that compiles a list of the directories on your hard disk and creates batch files for you.

UTILITIES

A.BAT, B.BAT

What it does: Allows summoning a directory of drive A: or drive B:
                 by keying only the letters A or B at the keyboard.

Syntax: A

Syntax: B

Requirements: DOS 2.0

HOW TO USE IT

The simplest batch files in this book, these two are presented for the nontechnical computer user who may be extracting various modules from this book for personal use without reading the explanatory material. Those who have been reading along should be able to accomplish the same result without reading any further.

When the following batch files are available, the user may summon a directory of drive A: or drive B: simply by typing letter A or B. If you want this command to be available regardless of what directory is logged, the PATH command (explained in Appendix A) must be used first.

You may customize either file. Substitute another drive letter if you have a hard disk (drive C:) or other drives. The files are set up to display the directory wide (A.BAT) or one page at a time (B.BAT). Simply exchange the "/W" or "/P" in your batch file if you want the other result.

Line-By-Line Description

Line 1:   Turn off screen echoing of commands.

Lines 2–3:   Title remarks.

Line 4:   Carry out DIR command.

```
-------------------------------------------------------
1.   ECHO OFF
2.   :    :: A.BAT ::
3.   :       *** Display Directory A: Wide ***
4.   DIR A: /W
-------------------------------------------------------
-------------------------------------------------------
1.   ECHO OFF
2.   :    :: B.BAT ::
3.   :       *** Display Directory B: Paged ***
4.   DIR B: /P
-------------------------------------------------------
```

D.BAT

What it does: Allows obtaining a directory of default drive, either displayed wide, paged, or normally, with minimal keystrokes.

Syntax: D.BAT allows for a variety of different syntaxes.

Requirements: DOS 2.0, SORT.EXE, and MORE.COM

Table 10-1. Summary of D.BAT

Entry	Result
D	Normal directory of default drive.
D P	Paged directory of default drive.
D W	Wide directory of default drive.
D A or D B	Normal directory of specified drive. (Other drive letters, if available, also may be used.)
D A W	Wide directory of drive A: (B or C may also be substituted.)
D A P	Paged directory of drive A: (B or C may also be substituted.)

Lowercase letters may be used in all cases.

Line-By-Line Description

Line 1:   Turn off screen echoing of commands.

Lines 2–3:   Title remarks.

Line 4: If no parameter, go to SAME label.

Lines 5–8: If "W" or "P" is first parameter, go to module that provides directories of default drive, either wide or paged.

Lines 9–12: If "W" or "P" is second parameter, go to module that provides directories, wide or paged of drive specified by %1.

Lines 13–14: Provide normal directory of drive specified by %1, then go to EXIT.

Lines 15–22: Provide directories as specified.

Lines 23–24: Exit routine.

```
-------------------------------------------------------
1.     ECHO OFF
2.     :      :: D.BAT ::
3.     :      ****** DIRECTORY WIDE OR PAGED ******
4.     IF "%1"=="" GOTO SAME
5.     IF "%1"=="W" GOTO WIDE
6.     IF "%1"=="w" GOTO WIDE
7.     IF "%1"=="P" GOTO WIDE
8.     IF "%1"=="p" GOTO WIDE
9.     IF "%2"=="W" GOTO DIR
10.     IF"%2"=="w" GOTO DIR
11.     IF"%2"=="P" GOTO DIR
12.     IF"%2"=="P" GOTO DIR
13.     DIR %1:
14.     GOTO EXIT
15.     :SAME
16.     DIR
17.     GOTO EXIT
18.     :WIDE
19.     DIR /%1
20.     GOTO EXIT
21.     :DIR
22.     DIR %1: /%2
23.     :EXIT
24.     ECHO ON
-------------------------------------------------------
```

DSORT.BAT

What it does: Provides sorted directory, which may be listed to the screen or saved on a file, with sort by any parameter.

Syntax: DSORT "drive letter" "param" [SAVE or PRINT]

Requirements: DOS 2.0, SORT.EXE.

HOW TO USE IT

DSORT.BAT allows sorting your disk directory by file root name, extension, size, date, and time. If date is used, the sort is only by month. The syntax for the command is as follows:

```
DSORT "drive letter" "param" [SAVE or PRINT]
```

Drive letter may be A, B, C, or another legal drive. You cannot enter a file specification as with the DIR command (for example, DSORT A:*.BAS). The second parameter, "param," may be one of the following:

NAME to sort by file root name

EXT to sort by extension

SIZE to sort by file size

DATE to sort by date

TIME to sort by time

FILE to send unsorted directory to file LIST

The third parameter, which is optional, may be either SAVE, FILE, or PRINT. Note that FILE can either be the second or third parameter used. If used as the third, the sorted file is saved to disk (as long as the second parameter was not also FILE). If PRINT is used, the file LIST is directed to your printer. FILE causes the unsorted directory, as it usually appears, to be directed to a file called LIST. SAVE causes the sorted file to be stored in LIST. Parameters can be in all upper- or lowercase but not mixed.
Example:

DSORT A DATE—Sorts directory of A: by DATE, and displays on screen
without making permanent disk file.

DSORT A SIZE SAVE—Sorts directory of A: by Size, displays on the screen,
and saves in file LIST.

DSORT B NAME PRINT—Sorts directory of B: by file root name and directs to screen and printer.

Line-By-Line Description

Line 1:   Turn off screen echoing of commands.

Lines 2–3:   Title remarks.

Line 4:   If no parameters entered, provide HELP.

Line 5:   If only one parameter listed, then go to FILE and save an
               unsorted directory to disk.

Line 6:   Otherwise go to label specified by %2.

Lines 7–22:   Provide HELP message.

Lines 23–27:   Print directory.

Lines 28–45:   Sort by specified field.

Line 46:   Show directory file.

Lines 47–52:   If third parameter used, either print or skip ''erase file''
               module.

Line 53:   Erase file LIST if SAVE or FILE not used as third parameter.

Line 53:   Exit file.

```
------------------------------------------------------
 1. ECHO OFF
 2. :       :: DSORT.BAT ::
 3. :       *** Sorts directory by desired attribute ***
 4. IF "%1"=="" GOTO HELP
 5. IF "%2"=="" GOTO FILE
 6. GOTO %2
 7. :HELP
 8. CLS
 9. :
10. ECHO  You may type :
11. ECHO   DSORT "drive letter" "param" [SAVE,PRINT]
```

```
12. ECHO    where "param" is
13. ECHO      NAME  to sort by file root name
14. ECHO      EXT   to sort by extension
15. ECHO      SIZE  to sort by file size
16. ECHO      DATE  to sort by date
17. ECHO      TIME  to sort by time
18. ECHO      FILE  to send unsort directory to file LIST
19. ECHO    For example:  DSORT A EXT
20. ECHO    If FILE,PRINT or SAVE specified, file LIST
21. ECHO      is created.
22. GOTO DONE
23. :PRINT
24. ECHO  Make sure printer is on and ready
25. PAUSE
26. PRINT LIST
27. GOTO DONE
28. :FILE
29. DIR %1:>LIST
30. GOTO DONE
31. :NAME
32. DIR %1:|SORT>LIST
33. GOTO EXIT
34. :EXT
35. DIR %1: |SORT /+9>LIST
36. GOTO EXIT
37. :SIZE
38. DIR %1: |SORT /+14>LIST
39. GOTO EXIT
40. :DATE
41. DIR %1: |SORT /+23>LIST
42. GOTO EXIT
43. :TIME
44. DIR %1: |SORT /32>LIST
45. :EXIT
46. MORE<LIST
47. IF "%3"=="SAVE" GOTO DONE
48. IF "%3"=="save" GOTO DONE
49. IF "%3"=="PRINT" GOTO PRINT
50. IF "%3"=="print" GOTO PRINT
51. IF "%3"=="FILE"  GOTO DONE
52. IF "%3"=="file"  GOTO DONE
53. ERASE LIST
54. :DONE
```

SUBMAKE.BAT

What it does: Produces a series of batch files that allow changing to a desired subdirectory by typing the last portion of the directory's name.

Syntax: SUBMAKE

Requirements: DOS 2.0 or later; hard disk. See also notes.

HOW TO USE IT

This utility and accompanying BASIC program will make a series of batch files for you to allow logging onto a specific directory just by typing the last part of the directory pathname. For example, to log onto C:\WP, you would type WP. The batch file WP.BAT is created by these routines.

Note, you must have BASICA on your disk in a directory that can be found by your PATH statement. If you have more than one directory with the same "last" name (not a good idea), such as C:\86\LETTERS and C:\87\LETTERS, only the last one encountered by SUBMAKE.BAS is accessible through this technique. Because each file on your hard disk occupies a minimum number of bytes (from 2048 to 8192, depending on the number of sectors assigned as a unit by your particular version of DOS), storing several dozen or a hundred of these files can consume a lot of disk space. You may kill those accessing subdirectories you seldom use. If you have many such subdirectories, though, why not combine files and remove them to free up more disk space?

Line-By-Line Description: SUBMAKE.BAT

Line 1:   Turn off screen echoing of commands.

Lines 2–3:   Title remarks.

Line 4:   Use CHKDSK's /V option to list all file and directory names on the disk, then filter that through FIND to redirect only those containing the string "Directory" to the temporary file, FILE.$$$.

Line 5:   Go to BASICA and run MAKEBAT.BAS.

Line 6:   On return, erase the temporary file.

```
---------------------------------------------------------
1.  ECHO OFF
2.  :    :: SUBMAKE.BAT ::
3.  :    *** Makes Subdirectory Batch Files ***
4.  CHKDSK /V | FIND "Directory" >FILE.$$$
5.  BASICA C:\BATCHES\MAKEBAT.BAS
6.  ERASE FILE.$$$
---------------------------------------------------------
1 ' **********************
2 ' *                    *
3 ' *     MAKEBAT.BAS     *
4 ' *                    *
5 ' **********************
10 ' *** Makes Subdirectory Batch Files ***
20 CLS
30 OPEN "FILE.$$$" FOR INPUT AS 1
40 LINE INPUT 1,A$
50 D$=MID$(A$,INSTR(A$,CHR$(32))+1)
60 A$=MID$(A$,INSTR(A$,"\")+1)
70 IF INSTR(A$,"\")<>0 GOTO 60
80 IF A$="" GOTO 40
90 F$=A$+".BAT"
100 OPEN F$ FOR OUTPUT AS 2
110 PRINT 2,"ECHO OFF"+CHR$(10)+CHR$(13)+"CD "+D$+CHR$(13)
120 CLOSE 2
130 IF EOF(1) GOTO 150
140 GOTO 40
150 SYSTEM
```

SUMMARY

DOS allows redirecting output to another device, such as a printer, instead of the standard output device, the CRT screen. DOS also lets programs accept input from a source such as a disk file, other than the standard input device, the keyboard. Along the way, these data can be filtered through special DOS utilities such as MORE, SORT, and FIND.

In this chapter, we have had an assortment of new commands, ranging from the ridiculously simple to the not-so-easy, using these facilities. New directory commands come up in Chapter 11, where we'll also learn how to redefine any key on the keyboard to give us a new definition from DOS.

Along the way, we'll learn some new tricks with ANSI.SYS, and, in the next chapter, ways to build interactivity into your batch files two different ways—by using BASIC and through two easy-to-type machine language utilities.

11

"Interactive" Batch
Files the Easy Way

INTRODUCTION

Batch-file programming's weakness is how difficult it is for users to interact
with the batch file after it has already begun processing. Certainly, you can type
in parameters on the command line, and interrupt the file with Control-C (or
more gracefully by inserting PAUSEs within the file to allow the user to stop
processing). What is really required, though, is a way for a user to enter information that can be used by the batch file before continuing.

In this chapter, we'll offer several ways of producing interactive batch files.
These methods include interfacing BASIC with our batch files, using the environment, and two machine language utilities, INPUT.COM and YESNO.COM,
which allow you to enter choices at the keyboard while the batch file is
operating.

Use of DEBUG is entirely optional for readers of this book; any short machine
language programs supply to enhance your batch files can be created through
the use of BASIC loader programs, which perform the task for you automatically.
Even BASIC is optional if you choose not to use the utility programs. DEBUG is

a useful tool, however, even for those who don't understand machine language, since you can enter and modify short programs directly.

One way and probably the clumsiest method of adding interactivity to batch files is to use BASIC to handle our interaction. BASIC, though, also happens to be the most flexible tool. You can use the language not only to enter information that can be interpreted by the batch file, but you may also perform other tasks that are difficult or impossible to carry out from batch files at all.

Resorting to BASIC every time we want to get some simple information into a batch file isn't necessary, though. Later in this chapter you'll see two machine language utilities that are actually *new* batch-file language commands. INPUT functions much like INPUT in BASIC, allowing you to print a prompt on the screen and request that the user press a single key. That key can be interpreted by the batch file and used to determine the next step to be carried out.

The second machine language utility gives you a YESNO command. This fast command doesn't require entering a prompt; it displays an "Enter (Y)es or (N)o:" message automatically and *only* accepts either an uppercase or lowercase Y or N.

BATCH FILE INTERACTION—WHY?

Since the original version of this book, many other books and magazines have published versions of a batch-file routine called, variously, MOVE.BAT or MOVER.BAT. It usually looks something like this:

```
ECHO OFF
COPY %1 %2
ERASE %1
```

As written, this file copies any files that you list from one drive to another and then DELETEs the old files from the source disk. MOVE.BAT is useful in transferring data disk files to a hard disk for permanent storage while they are active or in transit. The problem stems from the fact that DOS does not check to see if a file already exists on a target diskette before it copies over it with a new file with the same name.

If you type COPY A:MYFILE.TXT B:, and a file on B: already exists called MYFILE.TXT the contents of the old file will be lost, and the new one replaces it. DOS is nice enough to keep us from RENAMing a file over an old file, but it doesn't mind COPYing. Because MOVE.BAT uses DOS' COPY command, it suffers from the same weakness.

The IF EXIST test doesn't help much, because it is somewhat tricky to write a batch file that checks for various combinations of copying syntax, including the wildcards that might be included. We can apply IF EXIST to MOVE.BAT in its simplest form. We could change the file to look like this:

```
ECHO OFF
IF EXIST %2 GOTO EXIT
COPY %1 %2
ERASE %1
:EXIT
```

Here, to use the command, we must explicitly type the name of the destination file. If we typed:

```
MOVE A:FILE1.TXT B:FILE1.TXT
```

MOVE.BAT would first check to see that %2 did not already exist. If it did, then the file would skip over the copy-and-erase step and proceed to the label :EXIT. The big problem with this method is that we must always explicitly name the destination file with MOVE.BAT. We cannot simply type:

```
MOVE A:FILE1.TXT B:
```

With the original version of MOVE.BAT you *could* do that, for much added flexibility. Rather than cripple MOVE.BAT by removing its wildcard and ambiguous filename capabilities, one of the other solutions is recommended, including one not covered in this chapter—using the FOR..IN..DO command and the COMMAND command to load a secondary command processor. Those capabilities deserve a chapter of their own. For now, we'll explore other options, including BASIC/DOS interfacing.

And, in any case, the preceding solution would also *prevent* copying over files that we do want to overwrite. What is really needed is a way for the batch file to present each file and prompt us for the correct action.

XCOPY AND REPLACE WITH DOS 3.2 AND LATER VERSIONS

DOS 3.2 and later versions provide a partial solution with the XCOPY command. This file copying utility allows adding a "/P" switch to the command line:

```
XCOPY A:*.* B: /P
```

Here, you would be prompted for a Y/N answer before each file is copied to the destination. XCOPY allows several other switches that you may find useful:

- /A copies only source files that have their "archive" bit set. When you make changes to a file, the invisible archive bit associated with that filename in the directory is set, indicating that no copy of that version has been made. When DOS copies a file (as for backup) it resets the bit. This switch ensures copying only files not previously backed up since their most recent change.

- /D*date* allows specifying a date that DOS uses to determine if a file should be copied. Only files modified after that date are copied.

- /S tells DOS to copy any files and directories beneath the one specified, unless they are empty.

- /E is used *with* /S to instruct DOS to copy subdirectories beneath the one specified even if they are empty.

- /V asks DOS to verify each file as it is written to the destination disk to ensure that the files are identical.

- The /W switch causes DOS to pause until you press a key before copying any files. Without this switch, the command goes to work immediately. This switch allows the opportunity to access the REPLACE command from one disk, then to remove that disk and to insert a second disk in the drive for the source and/or for the destination. Users of dual floppy-disk systems will find this feature of most use.

DOS 3.2 and up also has a REPLACE command that can be used for copying. It *replaces* files in the destination directory with files having the same name in the source drive/directory, and you may use wild cards.

REPLACE also can add files that reside on the source disk/directory but are not found in the target directory, when a switch, /A is used.

Syntax for REPLACE is as follows:

REPLACE [drive]path [drive] [/A][/P][/R][/S][/W]

- The /D switch tells DOS to replace files in the destination directory *only* if the system date associated with the file on the source disk is later than the file on the destination disk. This would keep you from inadvertently copying over a newer version of a file with one created earlier.

- The /P switch provides prompting, like XCOPY, so that DOS asks you whether or not each file to be overwritten should, in fact, be replaced.

- The /R switch causes DOS to replace files that are marked as "read only" with ATTRIB.

- The /S switch tells DOS to search through all the subdirectories below the destination directory and replace matching files. There is no way to ask REPLACE to perform a similar search on the source disk/directory.

- Since the /A switch adds files rather than replaces existing files, it may not be used with the /D or /S switches.

- /W switch tells DOS to wait until you press a key before starting. It works like the /W switch with XCOPY.

Many PC users still have DOS 3.1 or earlier. Since this will remain true for several more years, our search for solutions first concentrates on those tools readily available to all DOS computer users.

SOLUTION 1: INTERACTIVITY WITH SUPPLEMENTAL BATCH FILES

Can we enter Yes/No responses into a batch file? The exact answer YES/NO. That is, DOS doesn't usually allow putting questions of that sort in batch files, as is possible with BASIC programming. There is no exact equivalent of INPUT for batch files. DOS' only concession to this need is to allow PAUSE to be embedded in a batch file.

Glance over the following batch file:

```
::MENU.BAT::
ECHO OFF
ECHO                    ==== Enter your choice ===
ECHO <Alt 255>
ECHO            1.   Word Processing
ECHO            2.   Spread sheet program
ECHO            3.   Database Manager
ECHO            4.   Copy all files from A: to B:
ECHO            5.   Format Disk in A:
ECHO            6.   Park Hard Disk
```

Note that a blank line is entered into a batch file by following ECHO with a null character (earlier versions of DOS allowed entering a space, but this doesn't work with DOS 3.0 or later versions). Enter the ASCII 255 character by holding down the Alt key and typing 255 on the numeric keypad (not the top row of numbers on your keyboard).

To use this menu, you would press 1, 2, 3, or another key of your choice to activate the program or function desired. How is this accomplished? Simply write batch files to carry out the chore and give them names like 1.BAT, 2.BAT, 3.BAT, and so on. DOS searches for 1.BAT when the 1 key and Enter are pressed and carries out the commands therein. In this case, 1.BAT might look like this:

```
::1.BAT::
ECHO OFF
C:
CD C:\WP
WS
CD \
MENU
```

1.BAT would change directories to the hard disk and subdirectory WP (where the word-processing program and its files are stored), then call up WS, the actual program. When exiting the word processor, the directory would be changed back to the root. Then, MENU.BAT is summoned again to keep the user from seeing the dreaded DOS prompt.

For the other options on the menu, simply create appropriate batch files. You are not limited to 10 menu entries (0 to 9). You may number choices as A... Z and AA to ZZ if you can fit that many columns of options on the screen. The big problem with this method is that if a key is pressed for which no menu choice is presented (a number larger than six in the preceding example or any letter or punctuation key), the easy-to-use menu system dumps the user back at the DOS prompt.

The other limitation of this method is that you can have only *one* menu using a given set of choices, unless you resort to some fancy directory or path shenani-gans. In other words, if 1.BAT loads your word-processing program, you may not have another set of menus asking the user to press 1 to activate another function. One alternative would be to have two different menu systems, such as 1, 2, 3, 4, and A,B,C,D. Beyond two menus, having an X, Y, Z, and so on, list of choices would look somewhat bizarre.

You could go through some contortions to allow reusing the 1.BAT, 2.BAT, etc. choices. Your batch file would need lines like this:

```
ECHO %PATH% >OLDPATH.$$$
SET PATH =C:\MENU1;C:\DOS;C:\BATCHES;C:\
COPY C:\BATCHES\PATH.ASC+OLDPATH.$$$
C:\BATCHES\OLDPATH.BAT
ERASE OLDPATH.$$$
    . . .
    . . .
```

You would store *each* set of menu choices, that is, all the duplicate 1.BAT, 2.BAT, and so on files in separate subdirectories called MENU1, MENU2, and so forth. Then, when calling up each menu, you would copy the existing PATH to a temporary file, OLDPATH.$$$, and add that to PATH.ASC (which would contain ECHO OFF, plus PATH followed by no carriage return). The system path would be reset so that the desired MENU subdirectory was the first directory to be searched.

Your batch file would then continue. A big problem with this solution, other than its sheer clumsiness, is the need to reset the path to its old value after the menu system is finished. It could be left as-is, except that DOS would needlessly search through the MENU subdirectory first for its system files.

SOLUTION 2: A REFINEMENT USING PAUSE AND REDIRECTION

As you know, PAUSE may be embedded within a file. When PAUSE is encountered, the file displays the message "Strike a key when ready . . ." You may either press a key to continue with the batch file or else press Control-C to end the whole batch file. So, batch-file programmers may choose to offer the opportunity to abort the whole file at some point but not to enter a yes/no or other response.

You can take advantage of DOS' ability to redirect input and output to achieve a limited degree of interactivity. While PAUSE waits for you to press any key, DOS generally ignores the keypress. You can, however, redirect the "output" of PAUSE to a file and then use that information in your batch file:

```
PAUSE>NEXT.BAT
NEXT
```

In this case, when the batch file reaches the first line, it displays the message "Strike a key when ready . . ." When you press the key, that keypress is *not* displayed on the screen. Instead, it is redirected to a new batch file called NEXT.BAT. That is, if you pressed A, B, or C, then NEXT.BAT contains only the single character A, B, or C. The lines before PAUSE>NEXT.BAT might display:

```
ECHO   A. Word Processing
ECHO   B. Spreadsheet
ECHO   C. Database
ECHO      Enter choice:
```

Then, when you press A, B, or C and that character was stored in NEXT.BAT, the next line in the batch file calls up the new file. Of course, since only A, B, or C is in that file, DOS immediately tries to run A.BAT, B.BAT, or C.BAT (assuming you don't have any files called A.EXE, A.COM and so on).

As before, all you need to do is prepare your own A.BAT and so forth in advance to call up the program you want. It seems complicated but is actually quite clever. You could bypass the redirection, as the user could press A plus <ENTER> to do exactly the same thing, but this method doesn't require pressing the Return key.

SOLUTION 3: BASIC INTERACTION

Now, let's look at how BASIC can provide batch file interaction. By using both BASIC and DOS, we can take advantage of their strengths while minimizing their weaknesses.

For example, creating our own DOS commands is convenient because we can call them anytime we are in DOS command mode. Many programs have a feature that allows you to temporarily call up DOS and perform tasks—including those involving special batch files.

BASIC, on the other hand, is not quite as convenient to use, because we have to load BASIC and the program and then exit to DOS. BASIC is much more flexible in the things it can do, though, compared to the relatively skimpy commands available for batch-file programming.

Examine this batch file, which uses the concept of redirection:

```
:: MOVER.BAT ::
ECHO OFF
ECHO %1>A:DRIVES
ECHO %2>>A:DRIVES
BASICA B:MOVER.BAS
```

To use a batch file to trigger the process we need to be able to pass parameters to the BASIC program. MOVER.BAT demonstrates how to do that. To use it, type *MOVER sourcedrive targetdrive*, as:

```
MOVER A: B:
```

This tells MOVER which drive we wish to "move" files from and the destination drive. The second line of the batch file echoes the first parameter, %1 but instead of printing it to the screen, it is *redirected*, using the right angle bracket (greater than sign) to a file called A:DRIVES. If you have a hard disk, you can change this specification to C:DRIVES if you want to use the hard disk as a temporary storage place. That is not strictly necessary, however, since MOVER has been taught to "ignore" the file called DRIVES when it moves files from one drive to another.

The second line places the second parameter, %2, in the same file, DRIVES, using the double-angle bracket symbol, which tells DOS to APPEND the new information onto the end of the old file without erasing its present contents. If we had used a single-angle bracket in this line, only the second parameter would appear in the file DRIVES.

The last line tells DOS to load BASIC and RUN a program called MOVER.BAS, which is stored on B: Again, if you have a computer with a hard disk, you can change this specification to the disk and subdirectory where you permanently store your batch files or BASIC programs.

MOVER.BAS follows. You might find interesting some of the program's techniques to interface DOS with BASIC.

Listing 11-1. MOVER.BAS Program

```
1 ' ***************
2 ' *             *
3 ' *  MOVER.BAS  *
4 ' *             *
5 ' ***************
10 CLS
20 DIM S$(25)
30 ' ** Define filenames to store drives and directory ***
40 DIRFILE$="A:\DIRFILE"
50 DRIVES$="A:\DRIVES"
60 ' ** Read names of drives **
70 OPEN DRIVES$ FOR INPUT AS 1
80 LINE INPUT #1,D1$
90 LINE INPUT #1,D2$
100 CLOSE 1
110 ' ** Read Directory of Source Disk to file **
120 CMD$="DIR"+CHR$(32)+D1$+">"+DIRFILE$
130 SHELL CMD$
140 ' ** Display Directory on Screen **
150 LOCATE 2,1
160 CMD$="DIR "+D2$+" /w"+">"+"A:TEMP.FIL"
170 SHELL CMD$
180 OPEN "A:TEMP.FIL" FOR INPUT AS 1
190 L=L+1
200 LINE INPUT #1,S$(L)
```

Listing 11-1. Continued

```
210 PRINT S$(L)
220 IF EOF(1) GOTO 240
230 GOTO 190
240 CLOSE 1
250 KILL "A:TEMP.FIL"
260 ' ** Open Directory File **
270 OPEN DIRFILE$ FOR INPUT AS 1
280 FOR N=1 TO 4:LINE INPUT #1,A$:NEXT N
290 ' ** Read directory entry, see if is subdirectory **
300 LINE INPUT #1,A$
310 IF INSTR(A$,"<DIR>") GOTO 570
320 IF ASC(A$)=32 GOTO 610
330 ' *** Extract filename and extension **
340 ROOT$=LEFT$(A$,8)
350 EXTENSION$=MID$(A$,10,3)
360 FILENAME$=LEFT$(ROOT$,(INSTR(A$,CHR$(32))-1))
370 IF ASC(EXTENSION$)=32 THEN GOTO 400
380 FILENAME$=FILENAME$+"."+EXTENSION$
390 ' ** Skip working files, if present **
400 IF FILENAME$=MID$(DRIVES$,(INSTR(DRIVES$,"\")+1))
    OR FILENAME$=MID$(DIRFILE$,(INSTR(DIRFILE$,"\")+1))
    THEN GOTO 570
410 ' ** Print filename, ask if move it **
420 LOCATE 25,1:PRINT STRING$(32,50);:LOCATE 25,1
430 PRINT FILENAME$;TAB(20)"MOVE IT? (y/n/q)";
440 B$=INKEY$:IF B$="" GOTO 440
450 IF B$="Q" OR B$="q" THEN GOTO 610
460 IF B$="y" OR B$="Y" GOTO 480 ELSE GOTO 570
470 ' ** If yes, then move it, delete old **
480 Z$="COPY "+D1$+FILENAME$+CHR$(32)+D2$
490 SHELL Z$
500 Z$=D1$+FILENAME$:KILL Z$
510 CLS
520 LOCATE 1,1
530 FOR N=1 TO L
540 PRINT S$(N)
550 NEXT N
560 ' ** If not end, loop back for more **
570 IF EOF(1) GOTO 610
580 GOTO 300
590 ' ** Close and kill working files **
600 GOTO 300
610 CLOSE
620 KILL DIRFILE$
630 KILL DRIVES$
640 ' ** Return to DOS **
650 SYSTEM
```

How it Works

Lines 40 and 50 define the filenames used by the program to store a record of the disk directory of the source disk (we call it A:\DIRFILE) as well as the file that stores our choice of source and target drives (called A:\DRIVES). These filenames are defined here rather than using constants because users may easily change the names in this one place if they decide to put them on C:.

Lines 70–100 simply open the file where the batch file has stored the names of the source and target drives and put the values found in D1$ and D2$.

In Line 120, the program assembles a string that looks something like this:

```
'DIR A:>DIRFILE'
```

In the following line this string operates with the SHELL command, which allows us to load a secondary command processor from DOS and thus to carry out some DOS commands from BASIC. The directory of our source drive is stored in a disk file named DIRFILE.

We could have used the same trick to display the directory of the target disk (so that we can check for files we don't want to overwrite). With some versions of DOS, however, the screen is cleared every time SHELL is called (this happened with DOS 2.11; it didn't with DOS 3.x during our tests). As a result, instead, the directory is read into a temporary file (cleverly called TEMP.FIL) and then loaded into a string array, S$(L) from which the directory information can be recalled and displayed again following each SHELL statement.

In experimenting with SHELL, keep in mind that this command became documented only with later versions of DOS, and there are some limitations (for example, you cannot call BASIC from BASIC).

As the next step, the program OPENs DIRFILE for input and ignores the first four lines of the file (Line 280), which are always descriptive information and not directory entries.

When we get to the "real" directory entries, MOVER.BAS ignores those that are subdirectories (line 310). The file root name and extension are extracted (lines 340–380) and blank extensions cut off at the period.

Line 400 ignores our working files. Then, any remaining filenames are printed to the screen, and we are offered the choice of moving it, quitting entirely, or going on to the next filename. If we decide to move it, SHELL once again COPYs the file from one drive to the other.

When all the files are moved, the program KILLs the working files and returns us to the system. The only hitch with this program is that you must check the directory of the target disk and make sure there is no file about to be overwritten.

SOLUTION 4: MACHINE LANGUAGE AND ERRORLEVEL

While the BASIC solution just described is appealing for some applications, the machine language solution that follows will be more palatable. The two files that follow, YESNO.COM and INPUT.COM, *add* capabilities to batch-file language. Neither one allows entering more than one character (unlike BASIC), but for many uses, such as menus, one character is plenty.

When some functions finish operation, they write a value called the ERRORLEVEL to a register in memory that can be accessed by batch files. If the batch file calls that DOS function, it may immediately read the ERRORLEVEL to determine whether the function was carried out successfully.

Unfortunately, most DOS functions don't report an ERRORLEVEL. The two that do which are of the most use to us are the REPLACE and XCOPY commands of DOS 3.2 and later. For example, examine the sample lines below:

```
ECHO OFF
:    ::ERRDEMO.BAT ::
:    *** Demonstrates Errorlevel ***
XCOPY %1 %2 %3
IF ERRORLEVEL 0 IF NOT ERRORLEVEL 1 GOTO 0
IF ERRORLEVEL 1 IF NOT ERRORLEVEL 2 GOTO 1
IF ERRORLEVEL 2 IF NOT ERRORLEVEL 3 GOTO 2
IF ERRORLEVEL 4 IF NOT ERRORLEVEL 5 GOTO 4
IF ERRORLEVEL 5 IF NOT ERRORLEVEL 6 GOTO 5
:0
ECHO == No Errors Occurred ==
GOTO END
:1
ECHO No files were found to copy.
GOTO END
:2
ECHO User terminated with Control-C.
GOTO END
:4
ECHO There is not enough memory for the function,
ECHO or an invalid drive specification was entered,
ECHO or the file or path were not found, or there
ECHO was a syntax error.
GOTO END
:5
ECHO Disk read/write error
:END
```

This batch file could substitute for XCOPY and would check following the copy function for one of the indicated errors. The batch file could then branch to the label spelling out the error.

Note that ERRORLEVEL reports the *error level*, not a fixed error *number*. That is, if ERRORLEVEL equals 2, we know that the true value is 2 or *higher*; therefore, it is not 1 but could be anything from 2 up to 255. To test to see what the exact value is, we need *two* IFs. The first checks to see if the level is at *least* the number we are checking for. The second checks to see if the number is equal to or higher than the number immediately following. That is, if the ERRORLEVEL is 1 but is not 2 then we know it is exactly 1. This extra bit of logic checks for specific ERRORLEVELS in all the batch files using this technique in the book.

If you happen to be checking for consecutive ERRORLEVELS, it is not necessary to perform the double IF in every line, if your first line filters out all the codes higher than those searched for in the checks that follow. For example:

```
:INPUT
INPUT
IF ERRORLEVEL 61 GOTO INPUT
IF ERRORLEVEL 60 GOTO 60
IF ERRORLEVEL 59 GOTO 59
IF ERRORLEVEL 58 GOTO 58
IF ERRORLEVEL 57 GOTO 57
...
```

By placing the *highest* ERRORLEVEL check first, we can determine that the true ERRORLEVEL is no higher than the value being checked for. Therefore, each of the other lines can be written to assume that if, for example, ERRORLEVEL is 59, it doesn't equal 60 because branching would already have taken place. Keep this fact in mind when constructing your own batch files to reduce the amount of your typing.

Since only a few DOS functions report ERRORLEVEL, we'll have to create several new ones that *do*: INPUT.COM and YESNO.COM. Each waits for the user to press a single key and then sets the ERRORLEVEL to a value relating to the key pressed.

DOS reports a special code number for each individual key on the keyboard. The standard alphanumeric keys all deliver a code consisting of one number. The special keys, such as the function keys, keypad keys, and keys pressed in combination with the Alt and Control keys, respond with a two-part code called an extended key code. The first number is always a 0, while the second number relates to the special key pressed. (Note that at present, F11 and F12 can't readily be accessed from DOS.)

Because the special keys aren't essential to menus and other batch-file operations, INPUT.COM and YESNO.COM report only on the codes for the conventional keys. As a result, a special key that shares its second number with another key causes the same ERRORLEVEL to be reported. Few users will find this a nuisance. The codes shown in Table 11-1 are duplicated in Appendix B so that you can reference them quickly without hunting for these pages in the book.

Table 11-1. ASCII Codes for the IBM PC

Key	Code	Shift	Control	Alt
A	97	65	1	0;30
B	98	66	2	0;48
C	99	67	3	0;46
D	100	68	4	0;32
E	101	69	5	0;18
F	102	70	6	0;33
G	103	71	7	0;34
H	104	72	8	0;35
I	105	73	9	0;23
J	106	74	10	0;36
K	107	75	11	0;37
L	108	76	12	0;38
M	109	77	13	0;50
N	110	78	14	0;49
O	111	79	15	0;24
P	112	80	16	0;25
Q	113	81	17	0;16
R	114	82	18	0;19
S	115	83	19	0;31
T	116	84	20	0;20
U	117	85	21	0;22
V	118	86	22	0;47
W	119	87	23	0;17
X	120	88	24	0;45
Y	121	89	25	0;22
Z	122	90	26	0;44
1	49	33		0;120
2	50	64		0;121
3	51	35		0;122
4	52	36		0;123
5	53	37		0;124
6	54	94		0;125
7	55	38		0;126
8	56	42		0;127
9	57	40		0;128
0	48	41		0;129
-	45	95		0;130
=	61	43		0;131
TAB	9	0;15		
SPACE	57			

Table 11-2. Extended ASCII Codes for Numeric Keypad and Function Keys

Key	Code	Shift	Control	Alt
F1	0;59	0;84	0;94	0;104
F2	0;60	0;85	0;95	0;105
F3	0;61	0;86	0;96	0;106
F4	0;62	0;87	0;97	0;107
F5	0;63	0;88	0;98	0;108
F6	0;64	0;89	0;99	0;109
F7	0;65	0;90	0;100	0;110
F8	0;66	0;91	0;101	0;111
F9	0;67	0;92	0;102	0;112
F10	0;68	0;93	0;103	0;113
F11	0;133			
F12	0;134			
Home	0;71	55	0;119	
Crs-Up	0;72	56		
Pg Up	0;73	57	0;132	
Crs-Lf	0;75	52	0;115	
Crs-Rt	0;77	54	0;116	
End	0;79	49	0;117	
Crs-Dn	0;80	50		
Pg Dn	0;81	51	0;118	
Ins	0;82	48		
Del	0;83	46		
PrtSc			0;114	

Note that these codes can vary from computer to computer with different clones, especially for function keys F11 and F12. To be on the safe side, find the chart supplied with your particular model and use that if you experience problems with any of the routines in this book. Generally, only the special keys such as function keys differ from machine to machine.

CREATING INPUT.COM AND YESNO.COM

There are several ways to create these programs. The simplest way is to type in the BASIC loader shown in the accompanying listing. To save keying, the same program can be used for both machine language routines. However (and this is *important*) you must make several changes between the two. For IN-PUT.COM, use *only* Line 7. Delete Line 8. In addition, you must type in *only* the DATA lines shown for INPUT.COM. To create YESNO.COM, use Line 8 and *not* Line 9 and be sure and type in only the DATA lines shown for YESNO.COM.

You may type in the program to create one of the two first, then SAVE it, and make the changes necessary to switch it to the other mode. Then save *that* under a different name to have two copies. RUN them when you are ready to create the programs.

A routine that adds up the values on each DATA line and checks them against the final value (or checksum) shown on that DATA line gives *some* measure of protection against typos in the DATA lines (only). The data values must add up to the value in the checksum, or the program halts and alerts you as to which line has the typo. Keep in mind, however, that two errors in a line that cancel each other out (that is, producing the same final sum) are not flagged. In addition, you must type in the checksum value correctly for it to catch errors. In the worst case, you might have errors in data that happen to add up correctly to an incorrectly entered checksum. At the very least, double-check the checksum numbers before running the program. Odds are at least fairly remote against canceling errors, since most typos of this sort come from leaving a number out or transposing two digits within one number.

You may also enter the programs using DEBUG, in one of two ways. We'll need to examine DEBUG first and learn some of its simpler commands.

USING DEBUG

Like EDLIN, DEBUG is an editing program. While EDLIN is line-oriented, DEBUG treats files as a series of bytes that can be entered or modified as we wish. As you might guess, DEBUG most often manipulates individual bytes in program or data files.

If you find the thought of using DEBUG intimidating, note that you don't have to master it to use this book. Read the following command description, however. You'll probably find that DEBUG is easier to use than you thought. Knowing how to load or create files and modify bytes with DEBUG is a useful skill in the world of DOS customization.

Unfortunately, IBM in its wisdom has made DEBUG something of an exotic animal for those using DOS 3.3. This version, the first upgrade prepared entirely in-house by IBM (Microsoft then adapted IBM's changes for its own version of DOS 3.3), lacks a description of DEBUG.COM in the DOS system manual, although the program is included on the DOS Supplementary disk. At least for PC-DOS, DEBUG is henceforth considered a supplementary program fully explained only in the optional IBM DOS Technical Manuals.

To use DEBUG, first make a copy of a file that you would like to practice with:

```
COPY MYFILE.TXT MYFILE.BAK
```

Then, making sure that DEBUG is available on the disk or directory you are using, type:

DEBUG MYFILE.BAK

You may also enter DEBUG without accessing a particular file to start "fresh," as when you are creating a new file rather than editing an existing file.

After DEBUG has loaded, all you'll see is a hyphen cursor that is even more cryptic than EDLIN's asterisk. DEBUG is ready for a command. If you have loaded a file into DEBUG, you can display or *dump* a portion of the file now in memory using the D command:

    -d

displays the first 128 bytes of the file on eight lines that look something like this:

```
         DEBUG Dump
xxxx:0100 54 68 69 73 20 66 69 6C 65 20 69 73 20 6E 73 61  This file is nea
xxxx:0110 72 69 79 20 73 6D 70 79 2D 0E 0A 00 00 00 00 00  rly empty.......
xxxx:0120 00 00 00 00 00 00 00 00 00 00 00 00 00 00 00 00  ................
xxxx:0130 00 00 00 00 00 00 00 00 00 00 00 00 00 00 00 00  ................
xxxx:0140 00 00 00 00 00 00 00 00 00 00 00 00 00 00 00 00  ................
xxxx:0150 00 00 00 00 00 00 00 00 00 00 00 00 00 00 00 00  ................
xxxx:0160 00 00 00 00 00 00 00 00 00 00 00 00 00 00 00 00  ................
xxxx:0170 00 00 00 00 00 00 00 00 00 00 00 00 00 00 00 00  ................
```

The display won't look exactly like this. The column of xxxx's to the left of the colon contain different values depending on the memory address where DEBUG loaded your program. That group of four numbers contains the address of the first of the sixteen bytes displayed on that line. For the purposes of this book, you can ignore that part of the address entirely. The second four digits gives the relative position of the bytes within the file. As before, the grouping shows the address of the first byte in the line. In the example above, 0100 is the starting address of the first byte, while 0101 is the address of the second byte, and so forth. DEBUG uses hexadecimal notation (numbering from 0 to 15 as 0,1,2,3,4,5,6,7,8,9,A,B,C,D,E,F), so that the last byte in the first line would be 010F and the first byte in the second line 0110. This section on DEBUG is the only part of this book to even mention hexadecimal, so you don't need to learn more if you are not already familiar with the numbering system.

The pairs of 16 numbers on each line represent consecutive bytes in memory and can have a value of 00 to FF (0 to 255). Next to that listing are 16 characters that represent the ASCII value, if any, of the bytes. You'll note that since this is an ASCII file, each of the hexadecimal numbers can be represented by appropriate characters. The exceptions are the last two of the file, hex 0D (13 decimal), which is the carriage return at the end of the line, and hex 0A (10 decimal), which is the linefeed character. Characters that cannot be translated into alphanumerics are shown as periods.

Because DEBUG displays memory in neat pages, you will probably find that some bytes beyond the end of the file are shown. Here, we've included zeros. Any characters, though—probably a mixed collection of random "garbage"—may result.

Most files you examine with DEBUG are longer than the 128 initial bytes shown by simply typing D at the prompt. You can see the next 128 bytes after whatever "page" was just shown by typing D again. You may also dump specific areas of memory by typing in the addresses:

-D 200–210

shows you the bytes in the range 200 to 210 (hexadecimal).

For this book, you need to know how to load DEBUG, either enter or "assemble" a program from bytes that you type in, and to save the bytes to disk.

ENTERING BYTES

You enter values using DEBUG when you already know the machine language codes that will be used. You might do that if you have a listing of unassembled machine language code and want simply to type in the hex values shown. You may enter bytes with the following syntax:

e <address to change> <byte to enter>

For example, if you wanted to enter the file shown in our example, you would type:

```
-e 100 54 68 69 73 20 66 68 6C 65 20 69 73 20 6E 73 61
        72 69 79 20 73 6D 70 79 2D 0E 0A
```

Or since the information is an ASCII string, you could type the string and enclose it in quotation marks to tell DEBUG to translate the string into the ASCII equivalent:

-e "This file is nearly empty."

The Enter command can be used to *change* the values found in memory. You could use this command to edit an ASCII file (or a program file, too—use caution). The changes would exist only in memory, of course, until you write them back to disk.

To enter our machine language utilities, we'll have you use the related *assemble* command, a more convenient way of entering bytes that make up a machine language program instead of simple ASCII text. Machine language programmers find it convenient not to constantly look up the hexadecimal values of the instructions they write for the computer. Instead, they use DEBUG's assemble command (or, if a program is more than just a few lines long, an assembler). It isn't necessary to type in the bytes corresponding to the machine language instructions. You may type *mnemonic* abbreviations that DEBUG translates into the correct values when the bytes are assembled. Consider the following example, which needn't mean much to you (now or in the future).

```
-a 100
xxxx:0100 MOV AH,0
xxxx:0102 INT 21
xxxx:0104 CMP AH,0
xxxx:0106 <enter>
```

The first line tells DEBUG to begin assembling code at relative memory location 100. When you press Enter, DEBUG responds with:

```
xxxx:0100
```

You then respond with the mnemonics, "MOV AH,0" and press Enter again. DEBUG supplies the next memory location and you continue with INT 21. Respond with nothing but Enter when finished. The "program" you have typed in is assembled in memory, ready to be written to disk. To check on it, you can either *dump* the memory locations (you would type d 100 104) or you can *unassemble* the locations with:

```
-u 100 106
```

In the latter case, DEBUG responds with a display something like this:

```
xxxx:0100 B400    MOV AH,0
xxxx:0102 CD21    INT 21
xxxx:0104 3D00    CMP AX,0
```

You must be sure to *write* your file to disk before exiting DEBUG. The Write command can be typed alone or followed by the number of bytes that should be written from memory to disk:

```
-w
-w 108
```

With the first example, DEBUG defaults to a start address of 100. In the second case, DEBUG starts writing to disk the data starting at memory location 108. The information is written to a file with the same name as the one you typed when you entered DEBUG (if you are *editing* an existing file) or one that you enter by using the N command:

```
-N <filename>
```

Once that command has been entered, DEBUG responds to any Write (W) commands using that filename as the new default.

DEBUG determines how many bytes of memory to include in the file by looking at a special memory location, called a register. This register, CX, is loaded with the length of the file when you access a particular file through DEBUG. If you add to the file's length or if you are creating a new file, you must change the value in CX before trying to save the file. That can be done using the DEBUG register command:

```
-r cx
CX 00
:1A
```

For our 26-byte long example shown earlier, we would type the first line to see the contents of the CX register. DEBUG would respond with the current value, supply a colon, and pause while we entered a new value. In this case, the figure would be 1A hex or 26 decimal.

To summarize, creating a file with debug consists of the following steps:

1. Type DEBUG at the DOS prompt.

2. Begin to Enter or Assemble the program starting at relative memory location 100 by typing either E 100 or A 100 at the prompt.

3. If using Enter, type in the hexadecimal numbers. With Assemble, enter the mnemonics. To quit, press Enter on a line by itself.

4. Provide a name for the file with the N command.

5. Tell the CX register how many bytes long the file will be.

6. Write the file to disk using the W command.

7. Quit DEBUG with the Q command.

Such a session would look like this:

```
C>DEBUG<enter>
-a 100
-xxxx:0100 MOV AH,0
-xxxx:0102 INT 21
```

```
-xxxx:0104 CMP AX,0
-<enter>
-n JUNK.COM
-r cx
CX 00
:6
-w
-q
```

USING A DEBUG SCRIPT

Now that you have found how easy DEBUG is to use, even for the neophyte who doesn't understand machine language, you'll want to type in many of the utility programs found in books and PC-oriented magazines. You should know that it isn't necessary to type everything while within the DEBUG program itself. That's needless work and inconvenient when errors are typed in.

You may instead type in all the commands you will be entering in the form of a DEBUG script—nothing more than an ASCII file with the commands in the order that they are typed. You could use your word processor to create a script that would create the same JUNK.COM file given in the example above. It might look something like this:

```
a 100
MOV AH,0
INT 21
AX,0
<enter>
n JUNK.COM
r cx
6
w
q
```

Note that this looks a lot like the session shown previously, only the "-" prompts and DEBUG's responses are not shown. The <enter> shown should consist of a blank line in your script file that includes only the carriage return.

To use the script, you would store it on your disk under a name like JUNK.SCR, then type:

```
DEBUG<JUNK.SCR
```

This would cause DEBUG to use the ASCII file JUNK.SCR for its input, using DOS' redirection feature. Redirection will be covered in more detail later in this book.

This is basically all you need to know to use DEBUG successfully. If this explanation hasn't eased your fears, you may still enter the programs that follow using BASIC.

ENTERING YESNO.COM AND INPUT.COM WITH DEBUG

You may assemble these utilities following the guidelines just covered or write a DEBUG script. Sample DEBUG sessions are shown for each. You'll need to call up DEBUG, of course, from the DOS prompt (as shown) and start assembling at relative address 100. DEBUG displays the memory addresses as indicated, except that "xxxx" is replaced by a value that you can ignore. You must type in *only* the codes and numbers shown, following each line entry with Enter. DEBUG automatically counts the number of bytes in the line and supplies the next set of memory addresses. When finished, press Enter (as shown), then respond to the - prompt with the commands listed to name the file and write it to disk.

You may also enter *only* the commands (starting with a 100) into an ASCII text file. *Leave out* the memory addresses and hyphen prompts and be sure and put an extra carriage return before the R CX command. The advantage of this method is you may proofread your entries carefully before actually using DEBUG. Call the files YESNO.SCR and INPUT.SCR respectively, and then create the COM files by redirecting their output to DEBUG:

```
DEBUG<INPUT.SCR<Enter>
DEBUG<YESNO.SCR<Enter>
```

Using scripts of this sort is a popular way to simplify "canned" DEBUG sessions that you should learn.

USING INPUT.COM AND YESNO.COM

Plenty of batch files appearing later in this book use these routines. To incorporate them in your own utilities, simply list the command on a line by itself, or, for INPUT.COM, followed by a short prompt. Quotation marks are not required around the prompt. Don't use a dollar sign in your prompt, because machine language routines use the dollar sign to indicate the end of the string being printed to the screen.

The utility waits for the user to press a key and then stores the code in the ERRORLEVEL. YESNO.COM automatically delivers its own prompt, "Enter (Y)es or (N)o:" so that you don't have to do this. Since both routines change lower-case alpha characters to uppercase (but won't change numbers), you don't have to check for both types.

The next line in your batch file should check to see what the ERRORLEVEL is and act appropriately. For example:

```
ECHO OFF
ECHO    A.   LOAD LOTUS
ECHO    B.   GOTO DOS
:INPUT
INPUT Which do you want ? (A/B)
IF ERRORLEVEL 67 GOTO INPUT
IF ERRORLEVEL 66 GOTO B
IF ERRORLEVEL 65 GOTO A
GOTO INPUT
:A
LOTUS
:B
```

Note that in this example, if neither A nor B are pressed, the batch file returns to INPUT to wait until the user presses the correct key. If BREAK is ON, the user may abort by pressing Control-C or Control-Break. Also, we put the test for B *first* so that the test for A could be shorter.

You can check for the user pressing a function key just as easily as for alpha-numeric keys. Use the *unshifted* value for the function keys, as INPUT.COM only changes alpha characters to uppercase. Try these lines:

```
:INPUT
INPUT Press a Function Key F1-F10
IF ERRORLEVEL 69 GOTO INPUT
IF ERRORLEVEL 68 GOTO F10
IF ERRORLEVEL 67 GOTO F9
IF ERRORLEVEL 66 GOTO F8
IF ERRORLEVEL 65 GOTO F7
IF ERRORLEVEL 64 GOTO F6
IF ERRORLEVEL 63 GOTO F5
IF ERRORLEVEL 62 GOTO F4
IF ERRORLEVEL 61 GOTO F3
IF ERRORLEVEL 60 GOTO F2
IF ERRORLEVEL 59 GOTO F1
GOTO INPUT
:F1
ECHO F1 PRESSED
GOTO END
```

```
:F2
ECHO F2 PRESSED
...
...
:END
```

INPUT.COM is best when you want to give your own prompt and may need a broad range of responses. However, you need to write longer routines to sort through the different ERRORLEVELS. You'll find that DOS is somewhat slow in processing each of the lines in the batch file, so that it's not practical, say, to check for every letter of the alphabet. YESNO.COM is faster to use, since it supplies its own prompt. If a yes or no response is needed, you can reuse the same YES/NO code in your batch files over and over:

```
:YESNO
YESNO
IF ERRORLEVEL 89 IF NOT ERRORLEVEL 90 GOTO YES
IF ERRORLEVEL 78 IF NOT ERRORLEVEL 79 GOTO NO
GOTO YESNO
```

In later chapters, you'll pick up additional tips on using these two utilities.

SUMMARY

In this chapter we've learned four ways of providing batch file interaction. BASIC is the most flexible, yet at the same time the clumsiest method. Using special batch files, called by the user when a single-character choice is entered, is easy to learn and use but makes it difficult to have more than one menu with the same numbering or lettering system. Two machine language programs, IN-PUT.COM and YESNO.COM, let the user enter single-character responses that can be interpreted by the batch file and further provide prompts to indicate the correct action.

Listing 11-2. Basic Loader, INPUT.COM, and YESNO.COM Programs

```
1 ' ******************
2 ' *                *
3 ' *  BASIC LOADER  *
4 ' *                *
5 ' ******************

6 ' *** Use ONE of these lines with correct DATA lines ***
```

Listing 11-2. Continued

```
7 F$="INPUT.COM":L=55: 'Use this line with INPUT.COM DATA
8 F$="YESNO.COM":L=60: 'Use this line with YESNO.COM DATA


10 OPEN F$ AS #1 LEN = 1
20 FIELD #1,1 AS A$


25 ' *** Read Bytes From DATA ***


30 WHILE N<L
40 N=N+1
50 C=N MOD 9
60 IF C=0 GOTO 150
70 READ B
80 CU=CU+B
90 LSET A$ = CHR$(B)
100 PUT #1
110 WEND


115 ' *** Test Checksum Last Group ***


120 READ CHECK
130 N=N+6
140 IF CHECK=CU THEN GOTO 180 ELSE GOTO 170


145 ' *** Test Checksum Individual Groups ***


150 READ CHECK
160 IF CHECK=CU THEN CU=0:GOTO 30


165 ' *** Error Found ***


170 PRINT "Error in line ";INT(N/9)*10+180
180 CLOSE
------------------------------------------------------
185 ' *** Program Data For INPUT.COM ***


190 DATA 190,128,0,138,28,128,251,0,863
200 DATA 116,19,48,255,198,135,129,0,900
210 DATA 32,198,135,130,0,36,186,129,846
220 DATA 0,180,9,205,33,180,8,205,820
230 DATA 33,60,65,126,2,36,223,60,605
240 DATA 0,117,2,205,33,180,76,205,818
250 DATA 33,33
```

Listing 11-2. Continued

```
-----------------------------------------------------
185 ' *** Program Data For YESNO.COM ***

190 DATA 180,9,186,31,1,205,33,180,825
200 DATA 8,205,33,60,0,117,2,205,630
210 DATA 33,36,223,60,89,116,4,60,621
220 DATA 78,117,236,180,76,205,33,69,994
230 DATA 110,116,101,114,32,40,89,41,643
240 DATA 101,115,32,111,114,32,40,78,623
250 DATA 41,111,32,58,32,36,310
-----------------------------------------------------
```

INPUT.COM

```
C>DEBUG
-a 100
xxxx:0100 MOV SI,080
xxxx:0103 MOV BL,[SI]
xxxx:0105 CMP BL,0
xxxx:0108 JZ 11D
xxxx:010A XOR BH,BH
xxxx:010C MOV BYTE PTR [BX+081],20
xxxx:0111 MOV BYTE PTR [BX+082],24
xxxx:0116 MOV DX,081
xxxx:0119 MOV AH,09
xxxx:011B INT 21
xxxx:011D MOV AH,08
xxxx:011F INT 21
xxxx:0121 CMP AL,41
xxxx:0123 JLE 127
xxxx:0125 AND AL,DF
xxxx:0127 CMP AL,0
xxxx:0129 JNZ 12D
xxxx:012B INT 21
xxxx:012D MOV AH,4C
xxxx:012F INT 21
xxxx:0131 <Enter>
-r CX
CX 0000
:31
-n INPUT.COM
-w
Writing 0031 Bytes
```

YESNO.COM

Listing 11-2. Continued

```
C>DEBUG
-a 100
xxxx:0100 MOV AH,9
xxxx:0102 MOV DX,011F
xxxx:0105 INT 21
xxxx:0107 MOV AH,8
xxxx:0109 INT 21
xxxx:010B CMP AL,0
xxxx:010D JNZ 111
xxxx:010F INT 21
xxxx:0111 AND AL,DF
xxxx:0113 CMP AL,59
xxxx:0115 JZ 11B
xxxx:0117 CMP AL,4E
xxxx:0119 JNZ 107
xxxx:011B MOV AH,4C
xxxx:011D INT 21
xxxx:011F DB 'Enter (Y)es or (N)o : $'
xxxx:0136 <Enter>
-r CX
CX 0000
:36
-n YESNO.COM
-w
Writing 0036 Bytes
```

12

New Directory
Commands—Part 2

INTRODUCTION

In this chapter we're going to see how to redefine almost any key on the keyboard to a string of our choosing as well as to explore ways of having batch files call other batch files. We'll also make use of the INPUT.COM utility introduced in the last chapter.

Redefining keys has been much discussed in magazines, but we'll cover it again here for the sake of completeness. Keys can be redefined by taking advantage another aspect of the installed device driver, ANSI.SYS. As before, ANSI.SYS must be on your startup disk's directory, and DEVICE=ANSI.SYS should be included in your CONFIG.SYS file.

REDEFINING KEYS

You may love or hate your PC keyboard, but nevertheless it is an intelligent little devil, with a lot going on from the time you press a key until the PC's microprocessor interprets the character that you "sent." As described in the last chapter, though, a character was not sent nor necessarily even that character's ASCII code.

The code—recorded as an ERRORLEVEL by INPUT.COM and YESNO.COM—generally is passed on to COMMAND.COM by ANSI.SYS. The PC knows which key is pressed by examining the code. If the code is preceded by the code for the control, Alt, or one of the shift keys, the computer also notes this and knows whether we wanted Shift-C or Control-C by that means.

If the DOS keyboard driver ANSI.SYS gives a *different* translation at our direction, we can substitute a *new* set of definitions for any key or key combination. Since they are all distinct keys to the driver, we can designate one definition for Alt-A, Control-A, Shift-A, or any other keys we want.

You might think of a "table" of definitions built into the driver. When ANSI.SYS receives a scan code of 65 from the keyboard, it checks the table. If no key redefinition has been done, then key 65 equals its default value, "A", and an "A" is sent on to DOS. If we happened to substitute a new definition in the table, say, "Hey! This is an A!!" then that string is sent instead.

There does not have to be a one-to-one correspondence between the key pressed and the string sent; we can translate one character into another or send an entire sentence if we wish. Now, there's not much use in redefining keys that we will need (such as the normal alphanumerics) to use DOS. It would be quite difficult to get a directory of drive 'Hey! This is an A!!' But many other keys, such as the function keys not used for DOS editing and Alt key combinations, can be usefully redefined. Remember that you can use each combination as a different key, so that you may have a separate definition for F10, Shift F10, Alt-F10, or Control F10, as you wish.

Actually, this is not exactly true for the novice. When DOS loads ANSI.SYS, it sets aside about 200 bytes for your new key definitions. If you use more, the adjacent COMMAND.COM, is written over, and the computer locks up. The solutions are to modify ANSI.SYS and other messy tasks beyond the scope of this book.

To keep you from danger, we confine ourselves to showing you how to redefine only the function keys F1 to F10 and Alt key combinations. If you remember to keep your definitions to a total of about 190 characters, you'll stay out of trouble.

DOS can be told about the new definitions we want by sending escape sequences, similar to how we moved the cursor in Chapter 4. Although DEBUG and some other tools can create these escape sequences, we'll use PROMPT, as before, to do all the work.

The chore is actually very simple, even though it may look a bit tricky. The syntax is as follows:

```
PROMPT $e[0;(scan code);"new string"p
```

If you'd like the new key definition to end with a carriage return, substitute "13p" for "p" in the preceding line. We'll make this procedure a bit clearer with some examples. The scan codes for the function keys F1 through F10 are 59 through 68. So, we could change F1, F2, and F3 to produce "DIR A:<ENTER>", "DIR B:<ENTER>" and "DIR C: /P<ENTER>" by the following lines:

```
PROMPT $e[0;59;"DIR A:";13p
PROMPT $e[0;60;"DIR B:";13p
PROMPT $e[0;61;"DIR C: /P";13p
```

The initial zero in the preceding lines tells the driver that we are defining a function or Alt key. The second number is the scan code of the key to be redefined. Next, we have the actual string, and, in this case, a carriage return signified by the final "13."

You may change a key back to its normal definition at any time by replacing the new string with the old scan code for the key involved:

```
PROMPT $e[0;59;0;59p
```

would return F1 to normal. This technique is used in KDIR.BAT, a module presented in this chapter. It allows you to define Alt-A, Alt-B, Alt-C, and Alt-D so that the directories of those drives can be summoned by pressing the appropriate Alt key combination. We think you'll find this method even more convenient than the new DOS directory commands created in Chapter 8. Since ANSI.SYS resides in memory, the whole process works much faster than one using batch files.

Notice that, unlike INPUT.COM, we are *not* ignoring the initial zero value. So keys like F7 (0;65) are *not* considered the same key as A (65), even though they share *part* of the same scan code. INPUT.COM may see both keys as the same, but ANSI.SYS does not.

MORE USES FOR FILTERS

FIND was mentioned in Chapter 10, but hasn't been used extensively in this book so far. As described, FIND operates something like SORT. Instead of rearranging a file, FIND extracts from the ASCII file strings that we specify. The syntax is as follows:

```
FIND [switch] "string" "filename(s)"
```

Without a switch, FIND looks through "filename," or multiple files listed after the first filename and finds all occurrences of "string." The lines containing the string are displayed. You may not use a global filename so that you may have:

```
FIND "IBM PC" INDEX1.TXT  INDEX2.TXT INDEX3.TXT
```

but not:

```
FIND "IBM PC" *.TXT
```

A batch file in this chapter, SUPERFIND.BAT, *does* allow for wildcards. You'll want to use it in these situations.

The case of the characters counts, so "Ibm Pc" would *not* be located by the first line above. FIND's "/V," "/C," and "/N" switches alter the way the search is conducted. If /V is used, only the lines that do *not* contain the string being searched for would be displayed. So, if you wanted to strip all the lines with REM in them out of a BASIC program, you would first store the program in ASCII form:

```
SAVE "FILENAME.BAS",A
```

Then, from DOS you could type:

```
FIND /V " REM " FILENAME.BAS>NEWFILE.BAS
```

This line would send any line in program FILENAME.BAS that does not contain REM to a new program, NEWFILE.BAS. Note that we have included a space on either side of REM in the quotes—that is " REM ", not "REM". That way, FIND searches for stand-alone appearances of REM and does not delete lines that happen to have words with REM in them, such as REMEMBER. Notice, also, that any line that had REM following a valid statement would be deleted:

```
10 GOTO 100 : REM SAVE TO DISK
```

So this particular technique would work only on programs in which REM was always used on a line with no other statement. More often, however, FIND is used with text files.

Another switch for FIND is /C, which tells the program to display a count of the number of lines containing the string. /C cannot be used with /V or /N, or, in any case, not successfully. This switch overrides the other two, and they are ignored. So, you cannot obtain a count of the number of lines that do *not* contain a string.

The last switch, /N, tells FIND to display a line number of each matching line ahead of the line from the file. This line number exists only on your screen and has not been added to the file's line numbers. The line number is relative to the other lines in the file—that is, if FIND locates a string in lines 4, 6, and 8 of a file, those line numbers are displayed.

As you get more involved with filters and piping, you'll want to combine FIND and SORT to find and rearrange lists for you.

So far we've covered several aspects of batch files that make them very like BASIC programs in some ways. The control structures, such as IF and GOTO, let us alter the functions of the batch file, based on our input.

INPUT.COM and YESNO.COM give us one way to do this. You can *store* these responses for later reference in one of several ways. One way would be to use an environment variable to hold a value corresponding to the response. This method has one serious drawback. When you load a second command processor, it makes a *copy* of the environment and any changes entered aren't passed along to the original COMMAND.COM environment on your return. However, since both copies share a single set of disk files, any files that are created as flags *are* accessible to both. For example, supposing the user answered YES, NO, YES, YES to questions 1, 2, 3, and 4. The program could create the following files on the disk:

```
B:YES1.FLG
B:NO2.FLG
B:YES3.FLG
B:YES4.FLG
```

When control returned to the batch file, it could test for the existence of these flags, using another condition that IF allows but which we have not covered yet. That condition is EXIST. It tests to see if a file exists or not:

```
:1
IF EXIST YES1.FLG ECHO "|Answer was YES"
IF EXIST YES1.FLG GOTO 2
IF EXIST NO1.FLG ECHO "|Answer was NO"
:2
IF EXIST YES2.FLG ECHO "|Answer was YES"
IF EXIST YES2.FLG GOTO 3
IF EXIST NO2.FLG ECHO "|Answer was NO"
...
...
:END
ERASE *.FLG
```

You get the idea. While this technique is a bit clumsy, it is an interesting way of passing information to an active batch file. You don't need to create the "flag" files from BASIC; they can be created by another batch file. In fact, in this chapter that is exactly what is done with REMOVE.BAT. A temporary file is created when the user enters a "Q" (Quit) command. The existence of that file cancels further processing.

You may be unfamiliar with DOS' CHKDSK command, which can provide a list of all files in all subdirectories on a disk by including the /V switch. DIRS.BAT takes advantage of this capability, with the added feature of redirecting CHKDSK's output to a file, where we can use FIND and SORT to give us a sorted list of all the files in all the directories on a given disk—even a fixed disk.

UTILITIES

KDIR.BAT

What it Does: Redefines Alt-A through Alt-D to deliver DIR

Syntax: KDIR

Requirements: DOS 2.0 or later.

HOW TO USE IT

You must have DEVICE=ANSI.SYS in your CONFIG.SYS file (Appendix A explains this), and ANSI.SYS must reside on the root directory of the disk you boot up DOS with.

KDIR.BAT can be incorporated in your AUTOEXEC.BAT file, so that your new key definitions are in place as soon as you are powered up. To use, simply hit Alt-A, Alt-B, Alt-C, or Alt-D. No carriage return is required. If you have fewer drives, you may delete an unneeded line, but keep in mind that DOS 3.0 and above makes it especially easy to set aside extra RAM (like the huge quantities available for the PC-AT) for virtual disks. You may want to use these as drive C: and drive D: if you do not have a hard disk.

Line-By-Line Description

Line 1:   Turn screen echoing of commands off.

Lines 2–3: Title remarks.

Line 4:   Turn ECHO back on so that PROMPT will operate properly.

Lines 5–8: Redefine keys.

Line 9:   Restore system prompt. You may substitute a line producing your favorite personalized prompt (Chapter 3) if you wish.

```
--------------------------------------------------------
1.    ECHO OFF
2.    :      :: KDIR.BAT ::
3.    :      *** Redefines ALT keys to provide Directory ***
4.    ECHO ON
5.    PROMPT=$e[0;30;"DIR A:";13p
6.    PROMPT=$e[0;48;"DIR B:";13p
7.    PROMPT=$e[0;46;"DIR C:";13p
8.    PROMPT=$e[0;32;"DIR D:";13p
9.    PROMPT
--------------------------------------------------------
```

REMOVE.BAT

What it Does: Provides prompted file deletion.

Syntax: REMOVE filename

Requirements: DOS 2.0 or later; hard disk.

HOW TO USE IT

The two files involved, REMOVE.BAT and REMOVER.BAT, must be available. Type REMOVE "filename.ext" to initiate the process. You may use wildcards in the file name, if you wish:

REMOVE B:*.BAS

would initiate removal of BASIC files on B: only. You will be shown each filename and asked to enter "Y", "N," or "Q." If you enter "N" (upper or lowercase is acceptable) or any other character, the program assumes you want to keep the file. You must explicitly enter "Y" to kill a file and then press Enter when asked, as a double fail-safe. Entering "Q" ends the removal process.

Line-By-Line Description: REMOVE.BAT

Line 1:	Turn off echoing of commands.
Lines 2–3:	Title remarks.
Line 4:	If no parameter entered, show help.
Line 5:	If the temporary file C:\TEMP.$$$ exists, erase it.
Line 6:	For each of the file specifications pointed to by %1, repeat these steps: If C:\TEMP.$$$ does not exist, call a second copy of COMMAND.COM and run the batch file REMOVER, using %%a as the first parameter on the command line.
Line 7:	Go to the end.
Lines 8–15:	Display help.
Lines 16–17:	End of the routine.

Line-By-Line Description: REMOVER.BAT

Line 1:	Turn off echoing of commands.
Lines 2–3:	Title remarks.
Line 4:	ECHO the file being processed to screen.
Lines 5–6:	Ask if it should be removed.
Line 7:	If Y entered, go to REMOVEIT.
Line 8:	If Q entered, go to QUIT.
Line 9:	If N entered, return without erasing.
Line 10:	No match, so go back for another keypress.
Lines 11–14:	Erase the file.

Lines 15–16:   Create TEMP.$$$ as flag to Quit.

Line 17:   End of file. Control returns to original command
                processor and REMOVE.BAT for next filename.

```
-----------------------------------------------------
1.  ECHO OFF
2.  :    :: REMOVE.BAT ::
3.  : *** Prompted file removal ***
4.  IF "%1"=="" GOTO HELP
5.  IF EXIST C:\TEMP.$$$ ERASE C:\TEMP.$$$
6.  FOR %%a IN (%1) DO IF NOT EXIST C:\TEMP.$$$ COMMAND /C
    REMOVER %%a
7.  GOTO END
8.  :HELP
9.  ECHO     Syntax:
10. ECHO           REMOVE [d:][filename.ext]
11. ECHO       You are asked if you want to delete the
12. ECHO       file or individual files that meet the
13. ECHO       specification.  Wildcards are permitted.
14. ECHO       Substitute drive specification for [d:]
15. ECHO <Alt 255>
16. :END
17. CLS
-----------------------------------------------------
```

```
-----------------------------------------------------
1.  ECHO OFF
2.  :       ::: REMOVER.BAT :::
3.  : *** File Remover ***
4.  ECHO %1
5.  :INPUT
6.  INPUT Remove this file (Y/N/Q)?
7.  IF ERRORLEVEL 89 IF NOT ERRORLEVEL 90 GOTO REMOVEIT
8.  IF ERRORLEVEL 81 IF NOT ERRORLEVEL 82 GOTO QUIT
9.  IF ERRORLEVEL 78 IF NOT ERRORLEVEL 79 GOTO RETURN
10. GOTO INPUT
11. :REMOVEIT
12. ERASE %1
13. ECHO Removing %1
14. GOTO RETURN
15. :QUIT
16. ECHO DONE>C:\TEMP.$$$
17. :RETURN
-----------------------------------------------------
```

SUB.BAT

What it does: Shows desired subdirectory automatically.

Syntax: SUB

Requirements: DOS 2.0 or later versions, hard disk.

HOW TO USE IT

You should substitute the PATH name of your desired subdirectory. We assume that if you need this command, you know about paths, and can make the desired substitution. This routine is a manual method of producing subdirectory-accessing batch files. SUBMAKE.BAT, in Chapter 10, does this for an entire hard disk automatically. If you don't know how to do this, you probably should not be using this feature yet. Read your DOS manual or Chapter 4 for more information.

You may create several similar batch files, each with a different name, so you can look at many different directories without remembering the pathname. Choose batch filenames that you can easily connect with the directory desired, such as: UTILITY, WORDSTAR, dBASE, and so on.

Line-By-Line Description

Line 1:   Turn off screen echoing of commands.

Lines 2–3: Title remarks.

Line 4:   Display desired directory.

```
----------------------------------------------------------
1.   ECHO OFF
2.   :      :: SUB.BAT ::
3.   :      *** Shows Subdirectory Automatically ***
4.   DIR C:\COMMANDS\DOS
----------------------------------------------------------
```

RDIR.BAT

What it does: Provides a "reverse" directory, that is, all the filenames
                 that do *not* contain the specified string.

Syntax: RDIR string to avoid

Requirements: DOS 2.0 or later versions; hard disk.

HOW TO USE IT

Type RDIR "filename." You will be shown a list of all files without that string. For example:

RDIR BAS

would display all files without the .BAS extension. It also does not show files that include BAS anywhere in their name, such as BASIC.COM; so use it with care. Your strings should only include the characters A–Z. If numbers or punctuation are included, valid filenames are not shown, because FIND locates the numbers in the file size, date, and time fields of the directory entries.

Line-By-Line Description

Lines 1–2:   Title remarks.

Line 3:   Turn off screen echoing of commands.

Line 4:   If parameter %1 is null, display HELP message.

Line 5:   Otherwise, go to FIND.

Lines 6–14:   Display HELP message.

Lines 15–16:   FIND filenames without the string.

17:             End of file.

```
------------------------------------------------------
1.  :      :: RDIR.BAT ::
2.  : *** Finds files WITHOUT specified string in name ***
3.  ECHO OFF
4.  IF "%1" == "" GOTO HELP
5.  GOTO FIND
6.  :HELP
7.  ECHO        Reverse Directory-type string,
8.  ECHO        and display will show all files
9.  ECHO        on directory of currently logged drive
10. ECHO        that do not have that string in
```

```
12.   ECHO        their name.  Case of the string DOES count.
12.   ECHO        "bas" is not the same as "BAS."
13.   ECHO     <Alt 255>
14.   GOTO EXIT
15.   :FIND
16.   DIR | FIND /V "%1"
17.   :EXIT
```

NOSUB.BAT

What it does: Displays only the files in a directory, omitting
                subdirectories.

Syntax: NOSUB

Requirements: DOS 2.0 or later versions; hard disk.

HOW TO USE IT

Type NOSUB when you are logged onto the directory that you wish to view
without any of the subdirectories cluttering up the screen.

Line-By-Line Description

Line 1:   Turn off screen echoing of commands.

Lines 2–3:   Title remarks.

Line 4:   Display directory files only.

```
1.   ECHO OFF
2.   :      :: NOSUB.BAT ::
3.   :      *** DIR excluding Subdirectories ***
4.   DIR - FIND /V "<DIR>"
```

SD.BAT

What it does: Shows only the subdirectories of the logged directory.

Syntax: SD

Requirements: DOS 2.0 or later versions, hard disk.

HOW TO USE IT

Type SD when logged onto the directory that you wish to see only subdirectory entries for. Does not show subdirectories of the subdirectories themselves. For that, use DIRS.BAT, which follows.

Line-By-Line Description

Line 1:   Turn off screen echoing of commands.

Lines 2–3: Title remarks.

Line 4:   Display only the subdirectories of the logged drive.

```
------------------------------------------------------------
1.   ECHO OFF
2.   :      :: SD.BAT ::
3.   :         *** Shows Subdirectories Only ***
4.   DIR %1 - FIND "<DIR>"
------------------------------------------------------------
```

DIRS.BAT

What it does: Gives a list of files in all directories.

Syntax: DIRS drive letter

Requirements: DOS 2.0 or later versions; hard disk.

HOW TO USE IT

Type DIRS [drive letter]
The colon following the drive letter is not required, or allowed. If you enter no drive letter, the default drive is used. If you are not using a fixed disk, prepare to insert the disk you wish to check when asked.

Line-By-Line Description

Line 1:   Turn off screen echoing of commands.

Lines 2–3:   Title remarks.

Lines 4–17:   Display instructions.

Line 18:   Wait for user to press a key.

Line 19:   Invoke CHKDSK, which then directs list of files to SORT
               filter, and direct that output to file DIRS.$$$.

Line 20:   Send the directory and subdirectory names to a file,
               SORTED.$$$. The first line in the file shows the name of
               the file used for input, DIRS.$$$.

Line 21:   Change the name of DIRS.$$$ FILE.$$$, so that FIND
               inserts a new name in Line 22.

Line 22:   Put all the lines in FILE.$$$ that contain a backslash (\)
               except those containing the word "Directory" into file
               SORTED.$$$.

Line 23:   Erase the temporary file, FILE.$$$.

Line 24:   Display SORTED.$$$ through MORE filter.

```
1.    ECHO OFF
2.    :    :: DIRS.BAT ::
3.    :    *** List of Files in All Directories ***
4.    CLS
5.    ECHO   DIRS.BAT Provides a sorted list of
6.    ECHO   files in all directories.   List is
7.    ECHO   alphabetical within subdirectories,
8.    ECHO   with root directory entries mixed in.
9.    ECHO   <Alt 255>
10.   ECHO   Syntax is:  DIRS [drive letter]
11.   ECHO   Colon following drive letter not allowed.
12.   ECHO   If no drive specified, default is used.
13.   ECHO   <Alt 255>
14.   ECHO   Insert disk to be checked in Drive %1:
15.   ECHO      (If two colons at end of above line,
```

```
16.    ECHO            press Control-Break and restart)
17.    ECHO     <Alt 255>
18.    PAUSE
19.    CHKDSK %1: /V | SORT > DIRS.$$$
20.    FIND "Directory" DIRS.$$$ > SORTED.$$$
21.    RENAME DIRS.$$$ FILE.$$$
22.    FIND "\" FILE.$$$ | FIND /v "Directory"  >> SORTED.$$$
23.    ERASE FILE.$$$
24.    MORE < SORTED.$$$
```

SUMMARY

In this chapter, we've covered how to redefine keys using ANSI.SYS. Calling other batch files with the COMMAND command was also used in a pair of utilities, REMOVE.BAT and REMOVER.BAT. Some additional uses of the DOS filters, such as FIND, were explained.

In the next chapter, we'll move on to some very creative techniques in learning how to customize the most often-used batch file of all: AUTOEXEC.BAT. A line-by-line dissection of my own AUTOEXEC.BAT file reveals a wealth of new tricks. You won't want to type in this long file yourself, but, you should pick up some techniques you can apply to your own start-up file.

13

Customizing
AUTOEXEX.BAT

INTRODUCTION

This chapter will concentrate on the dozens of ways a customized AUTOEXEC.BAT file can help you by setting up your computer at the start of a session with the parameters and programs you've selected in advance. We'll dissect a typical "power-user's" AUTOEXEC.BAT file to see exactly how it works. The sample shown is extremely long but is not intended for use as-is. I use a similar one daily, although I'll likely have made a few enhancements by the time you read this. It is tailored for my own needs, however. You should be able to extract ideas from it to apply to your own AUTOEXEC.BAT file.

As we've seen, one key advantages of using batch files is that you may replace a long, complex command (or command series) with a short "command" as a batch filename.

For example, the word-processing program I use most often has the following start-up syntax:

```
D:\DW4\DW4PG D:\DW4\PROFILE.PRF,D:\DW4,D:\DW4,C:\DW4,C C:\
```

The group of characters leading off this gibberish is the name of the word-processing start-up command file, including its full pathname. Next, the user must specify the full pathname where the word-processing program can find its user profile (or customization parameter listing), a drive and directory where program files are to be found, where temporary files should be stored, and where program files are to be looked for if they cannot be found in the primary path. This is quite a command to remember to type in. No one in their right mind would be willing or able to type in such a complex command line every time the word processing program is loaded. So, instead, the I have created a batch file called W.BAT. By typing W <ENTER>, I can quickly load my word-processing program with a couple keystrokes.

Actually, W.BAT does more:

```
ECHO OFF
D:
C:\FINDER\WF
CD C:\WP
D:\DW4\DW4PG D:\DW4\PROFILE.PRF,D:\DW4,D:\DW4,C:\DW4,C C:\
C:
CD \
```

The first line of this batch file turns ECHO off so that we don't have to see the following commands. Next, we change the logged drive to D:, my 2-megabyte RAM disk, which has all the word-processing software loaded onto it. The following line loads Wordfinder, a thesaurus program with a 220,000-word synonym list absolutely indispensable for anyone working with words. After that, the batch file changes the directory of C: to WP, or word-processing file directory. The actual word-processing software is not kept there, to avoid cluttering up the working directory. Instead, the program is stored in a subdirectory on the RAM disk, DW4, and accessed from the following line. The last line of the batch file changes the current working directory back to the root directory of C:.

This example was presented as a way to give you ideas for creating your own start-up batch files for programs with complicated procedures. You can use the batch file to change directories, load supporting programs, load the actual software, and then perform another task when you exit the application. That's because DOS keeps batch files active even while you run another program and tries to finish the commands in the file once you exit—as long as the disk with that batch file is still available, and you haven't loaded another command processor using the COMMAND command in the meantime.

If you don't have a hard disk (so the start-up batch files can always be available to DOS) and don't want the inconvenience of having to find and reinsert a certain disk every time you enter or exit a program, you can create a third disk drive in memory, and store all your most-used batch files there. Many multifunction and memory boards come with these RAM disk drivers. DOS 3.0 and above is furnished with VDISK.SYS, which can be used to create a RAM disk of varying sizes.

Your AUTOEXEC.BAT file could then automatically copy all your .BAT files to the RAM disk (which becomes C: if you have two floppy drives in your system; D: if you also have a hard disk).

```
COPY A:\BATCHES\*.BAT C: >NUL
```

This line would copy all the files ending in .BAT contained within subdirectory A:\BATCHES to C:. The ">NUL" appended to the end directs the screen display, as each file is copied, to the NUL device (never-never land), so you don't have to watch the proceedings.

A simple PATH command in your AUTOEXEC.BAT file then tells DOS to first look for system files, including .BAT files, on C:

```
PATH C:\;A:\
```

You may have heard tales of some massive AUTOEXEC.BAT files designed by power users that do everything but clean the floppy-disk drives when the computer is turned on. In truth, most serious users of DOS have found AUTOEXEC.BAT to be an invaluable timesaver.

SAMPLE AUTOEXEC.BAT FILE EXAMINED

Let's examine a "typical" AUTOEXEC.BAT file line by line.

```
1.   ECHO OFF
2.   C:\DOS\ASTCLOCK
3.   PATH D:\BATCHES;C:\BATCHES;C:\DOS;C:\
4.   C:\DOS\NOKEY
5.   CD \DOS
6.   SK
7.   CD \
8.   ECHO ON
9.   PROMPT=$e[0;30;"DIR A:";13p
10.  PROMPT=$e[0;46;"DIR C:";13p
11.  PROMPT=$e[0;25;"C:\BATCHES\COM";13p
12.  PROMPT=$e[0;17;"C:\BATCHES\W";13p
13.  PROMPT=$e[0;50;"C:\BATCHES\MCI";13p
14.  PROMPT=$e[s$e[2;53H$p$e[1;53H$t$h$h$h$h$h$h $d$e[u$n$g
15.  ECHO OFF
16.  NOPARITY
```

```
17.    CLS
18.    ECHO AT S0=0>COM1:
19.    IF EXIST D:\DW4\AF10.KEY GOTO CHOICE
20.    MD D:\DW4
21.    MD D:\BATCHES
22.    COPY C:\BATCHES\W.BAT D:\BATCHES >NUL
23.    COPY C:\BATCHES\X.BAT D:\BATCHES >NUL
24.    COPY C:\BATCHES\COM.BAT D:\BATCHES >NUL
25.    COPY C:\BATCHES\A.BAT D:\BATCHES >NUL
26.    COPY C:\BATCHES\B.BAT D:\BATCHES >NUL
27.    COPY C:\BATCHES\C.BAT D:\BATCHES >NUL
28.    COPY C:\BATCHES\DS.BAT D:\BATCHES >NUL
29.    COPY C:\BATCHES\MOVE.BAT D:\BATCHES >NUL
30.    COPY C:\BATCHES\ED.BAT D:\BATCHES >NUL
31.    COPY C:\BATCHES\KILL.BAT D:\BATCHES >NUL
32.    COPY C:\DW4\*.KEY D:\DW4 >NUL
33.    COPY C:\COMMAND.COM D: >NUL
34.    COPY C:\DW4\*.PG* D:\DW4 >NUL
35.    COPY C:\DW4\PROFILE.PRF D:\DW4 >NUL
36.    COPY C:\DW4\DW4PG.COM D:\DW4 >NUL
37.    COPY C:\DW4\DW4V*.* D:\DW4 >NUL
38.    COPY C:\DW4\DW410.PFT D:\DW4 >NUL
39.    C:\FINDER\WF
40.    SET COMSPEC=D:\COMMAND.COM
41.    :CHOICE
42.    CLS
43.    ECHO
44.    ECHO      ─────────────────────────────────────
45.    ECHO    -         Enter choice:           -
46.    ECHO    -    1.)   Dial MCI Mail           -
47.    ECHO    -    2.)   Load DisplayWrite 4    -
48.    ECHO    -    3.)   Go to DOS               -
49.    ECHO    -                                  -
50.    ECHO      ─────────────────────────────────────
51.    :INPUT
52.    INPUT
53.    IF ERRORLEVEL 49 IF NOT ERRORLEVEL 50 GOTO 1
54.    IF ERRORLEVEL 50 IF NOT ERRORLEVEL 51 GOTO 2
55.    IF ERRORLEVEL 51 IF NOT ERRORLEVEL 52 GOTO 3
56.    GOTO INPUT
57.    :1
58.    CD \BATCHES
59.    ERASE B:MCI.ASC
60.    ERASE C:\WP\MCI.TXT
61.    COMM S2
62.    CD \
```

```
63.   ECHO AT SO=0>COM1:
64.   :2
65.   W
66.   :3
67.   CLS
```

This little monster operates when I first turn on the computer in the morning.

Line 1:   Turns off screen display.

Line 2:   Activates the CLOCK program that sets the system clock to the time stored in the clock on the multifunction board.

Line 3:   Tells DOS where to look for all the batch files and DOS utility programs installed on the hard disk that will be copied to the 2-megabyte RAM disk.

Line 4:   Activates NOKEY, a program that allows running Lotus 1-2-3 and other pesky copy-protected software from a hard disk, without the need to have a key disk in A: This is loaded at start-up, rather than when loading Lotus, because certain other programs like to be loaded in memory last, and this procedure helps avoid potential problems. Note that DOS 3.0 or later versions must be used to call a program directly with the pathname. With DOS 2.x, you must first log onto the directory where the program resides and then activate it.

Lines 5–7:   As an example of the preceding, this is what is done to start up Sidekick.

Line 8:   Turns ECHO on for the PROMPT statements that follow.

Line 9:   Redefines the Alt-A key to call a directory of drive A:

Line 10:   Redefines Alt-C key to call directory of C:

Line 11:   Redefines Alt-P to call a batch file, COM.BAT, which loads a communication program. Note again that DOS 3.0 or later is needed to call a program directly with its pathname.

Line 12:   Redefines Alt-W to call a batch file, W.BAT, which loads the word-processing program.

Line 13:   Redefines Alt-M to call a batch file that loads the telecommunication program and automatically dials up MCI mail, logs on, and downloads awaiting mail.

Line 14:   Changes the system prompt to put the directory time and date in the upper righthand corner of the screen.

Line 15:   Turns ECHO off again.

Line 16:   Activates a program that turns off parity checking by the computer. With parity checking switched on, it is remotely possible that your computer can lock up because of a memory error. If you are running number-intensive programs, like Lotus 1-2-3, you probably want to be alerted should such an error occur. If the corrupted memory were in your spreadsheet in an unknown location, the entire spreadsheet could be inaccurate. A lock-up, while drastic, is better than losing $10,000 somewhere in your spreadsheet because of a memory error that has gone unnoticed.

            Writers, on the other hand, don't care much if a character or two is mislaid. A good spelling checker finds the problem. What we don't want, though, is for the computer to lock up after we've typed for an hour or two and forgotten to SAVE our work. So, I always turn parity checking off with NOPARITY.

Line 17:   Serves a dual purpose. It directs a modem command to a Hayes-compatible modem, telling it to *not* answer the phone. If the modem is switched off, DOS prompts with the "Abort, Retry, Ignore" message telling that the user has forgotten to switch the modem on. After flipping the modem switch, press "R" for Retry.

            If the modem is already on, it is commanded *not* to answer the phone so that the user can receive incoming calls on that line but still can use the active modem to dial out with Sidekick's dialer feature if the user so chooses. A similar Hayes command in a telecommunication software startup batch file can turn autoanswer back on should the user wish to receive a data call. The same batch file turns autoanswer off when exiting telecommunications.

Line 18:   Clears the screen again.

Line 19:   Checks to see if one of the files copied over automatically by the AUTOEXEC.BAT file already resides on the RAM disk. Since the particular RAM disk allows data to remain during a warm boot, it may be unnecessary to copy the files each time AUTOEXEC.BAT is run. If the files exist, this line causes the file to skip the copying and proceed directly to the CHOICE label.

Line 20:   Makes a directory on D: called DW4.

Line 21:   Makes a directory on D: called BATCHES.

Lines 22–38:   Copies the files to the RAM disk.

Line 39:   Activates the thesaurus utility, WORDFINDER.

Line 40:   Sets the COMSPEC to D: so that DOS loads the command processor from the RAM disk.

Line 41:   Start of menu.

Lines 42–50:   Menu that allows user to choose from MCI mail, word processing, and DOS.

Lines 51–52:   Ask for user choice.

Lines 53–55:   Test choice and branch if valid.

Line 56:   Send back for new input if valid choice not entered.

Lines 57–63:   Erase old MCI mail files on disk and call MCI. Since the AUTOEXEC.BAT file is always run when the computer is first turned on, it can perform a regular once-a-day task. Line 58 changes to directory \BATCHES.

Next, Lines 59 and 60 ERASE two files, B:MCI.ASC and C:\WP\MCI.TXT if they exist (otherwise, a FILE NOT FOUND message is displayed harmlessly). Killing these files is necessary because the telecommunication software and word-processing software use macros that won't function as intended if the files are already present when they try to create them.

Line 61 loads the telecommunication software (PC-Talk III) with the "S2" parameter that tells PC-Talk III to immediately begin carrying out the function stored in Shift-F2. That procedure is a function of PC-Talk III, rather than DOS, so that it won't be outlined here. Your own telecommunication software probably has similar function key and "script" capabilities. PC-Talk's "S2" function key as programmed dials up MCI mail, logs on, opens a disk file called MCI.ASC, reads an MCI INBOX, and logs off. At this point, the user has a file on B: called MCI.ASC with the contents of the messages. After manually exiting PC-Talk III, the batch COM.BAT file picks up again and calls W.BAT. My word-processing software is then loaded, and the user is ready to begin the working day. Most often, the next step is to press a macro key within the word processing software, which creates a document called MCI.TXT and loads the ASCII file MCI.ASC into that, paginates it, and presents it for reading.

Lines 64–65:   Call word processing.

Lines 66–67:   Go to DOS and clear screen.

The AUTOEXEC.BAT files for my other DOS computers are all junior versions of this long one. The file for the Tandy 1000 used for telecommunications copies the telecommunication program to the RAM disk and automatically loads PC-Talk.

A computer at home has a larger RAM disk, onto which are loaded many of the word-processing program's overlay files—mainly chiefly macro key definitions used by the WP program to perform certain tasks. It is told through its user-profile program to look on C: for these and A: for all the others. As a result, I can run the program without a lot of disk swapping. As a bonus, because the macros are stored on RAM disk, they operate instantly, without a lot of slow, noisy disk access.

FORCING THE USER TO ENTER A DATE

This next modification for an AUTOEXEC.BAT file is presented separately, since it is of use only to those readers who have computers that do not include a built-in clock that updates the system clock automatically. It *forces* the person booting the computer to enter a date when asked, rather than simply pressing Enter to default to the 1-01-1980 date.

As you know, having date stamping on your files can be invaluable in determining which file was created later than another and is therefore the most recent version. It is also useful to have the correct time entered into the system; however the 00:00:00 default is updated automatically during a given session, stamping your files with consecutive later times. So, if the date is correct, files will be chronologically stamped, at least, even if the exact time is not correct. This assumes that the computer is not turned on and off during the day, of course.

So, our routine requires that the user enter some date other than 1-01-1980. The date doesn't *have* to be the correct one, but as long as the user is forced to enter a valid date, they might as well type in the current date. The routine can be bypassed by exiting the AUTOEXEC.BAT file through Control-C, but doing so also aborts all the other functions of the file.

The routine consists of two parts, one placed within AUTOEXEC.BAT itself, and another stored in your BATCHES subdirectory under the name CURRENT.BAT. The routines look like this:

```
AUTOEXEC.BAT:
 1.  ECHO OFF
 2.  TIME
 3.  :DATE
 4.  DATE
 5.  DATE<C:\BATCHES\CR.ASC >FILE.$$$
 6.  TYPE FILE.$$$ C:\DOS\FIND "Current" >FILE2.BAT
 7.  COMMAND /C FILE2.BAT
 8.  IF NOT EXIST TEMP.$$$ GOTO INSTALL
 9.  CLS
10.  ECHO Enter the current date -- PLEASE -- :
11.  ERASE TEMP.$$$
12.  ERASE FILE2.BAT
13.  ERASE FILE.$$$
14.  GOTO DATE
15.  :INSTALL
16.  CLS
...
```

```
CURRENT.BAT

A. ECHO OFF
B. IF NOT "%4"=="1-01-1980" GOTO END
C. ECHO NO DATE >TEMP.$$$
D. :END
```

To use these, you also need a file called C:\BATCHES\CR.ASC, which can be created using COPY CON:

```
COPY CON:C:\BATCHES\CR.ASC<Enter>
<Enter>
<F6><Enter>
```

Insert the lines labeled AUTOEXEC.BAT in your own AUTOEXEC.BAT file. If you are using DOS 3.0 or later versions, you may place them anywhere, but the beginning is usually the best place. A line-by-line description follows:

Line 1:   Turn off echoing of commands.

Line 2:   Ask user for current time.

Line 3:   DATE routine label.

Line 4:   Ask user for current date.

Line 5:   Access DATE command again, but this time answer it with the contents of CR.ASC (just a carriage return) and redirect its output to FILE.$$$. This has the effect of storing the current system date in the temporary file FILE.$$$.

Line 6:   Type the file using FIND to locate the lines containing the word "Current" (the date line), and redirect the output to a temporary *batch* file, FILE2.BAT. Note that with DOS 3.0 and later versions, you can place these lines anywhere in your AUTOEXEC.BAT file, even before your PATH command, as you can call FIND by typing its pathname. Those with earlier versions of DOS must include this routine *after* their PATH command so that DOS knows how to locate FIND.

Line 7:   Load a second copy of COMMAND.COM, and execute the batch file FILE2.BAT, which will contain a line such as the following:

```
Current date is Tue 1-01-1980
```

Now, while that may appear to be a line listing the current date, when typed as a command (as when it is the only line in the batch file FILE2.BAT), DOS interprets that line as a request to run a batch file called CURRENT.BAT, with four replaceable parameters on the line following: "date" as %1, "is" as %2, "Tue" as %3, and "1980" as %4. We have prepared CURRENT.BAT in advance to check only %4. Our *nested* line-by-line description of CURRENT.BAT is:

Line A: Turn off echoing of commands.

Line B: Check to see if %4 equals 1-01-1980.

Line C: If it does, create the file TEMP.$$$ (contents of TEMP.$$$ do not matter).

Line D: End of the batch file.

We're then automatically returned to the original batch file, to pick up with Line 8:

Line 8:   If the temporary file TEMP.$$$ does not exist (because a date other than 1-01-1980 was entered, go to INSTALL, the label marking the rest of your AUTOEXEC.BAT file.

Line 9:   If TEMP.$$$ does exist, valid date was not entered, so routine loops back to beginning. First, clear the screen.

Line 10:   Echo a request to PLEASE enter date.

Lines 11–13:   Erase the temporary files.

Line 14:   Loop back to DATE label for another try.

Line 15:   INSTALL label; the rest of your file should start here.

Line 16:   Sample next line.

ADDING "ALIASED" DIRECTORIES TO YOUR START-UP FILE

One section of my working AUTOEXEC.BAT file not shown, because not all readers of this book can use it, is a section that sets up "aliased" directories. This is another term for defining a subdirectory with a drive letter name so that you may access that subdirectory simply by using the drive letter name. For users of DOS 3.1 and later versions, this is done with the SUBST command. Its syntax is as follows:

```
SUBST <driveleter> <subdirectory>
```

I define a subdirectory called C:\COMM as drive E:, which is done with a line in my AUTOEXEC.BAT file:

```
SUBST E: C:\COMM
```

My particular application is for receiving and transmitting text files (usually several a day). In effect, I have set up a particular subdirectory, C:\COMM as a separate drive to store files received, those ready for transmitting, and as a holding place while they are "in transit." If I wish to see what files I have on this disk, I just type DIR E: To copy files to that disk, I can just type COPY filename E: My communication program (here, PC-Talk) has been set up so that drive E: is the default for transmitting and receiving files. I don't have to bother to type in C:\COMM, nor even to remember where the files are stored other than the drive specifier E:

You can set up several aliased drives in your AUTOEXEC.BAT file (or define one using EDRIVE.BAT, presented earlier). Keep in mind that DOS allows only drive letters up to drive E: unless you define a higher letter with the LAST-DRIVE= command in your CONFIG.SYS file. I have two floppy drives, one 20-megabyte hard disk, and a 2-megabyte RAM disk created as drive D: on an extended memory card. So E: is the next available drive letter. If you have more than one hard disk, or several RAM disks, you need to allow for drive F: or higher through LASTDRIVE.

SUMMARY

The sample files presented in this chapter should give some ideas for customizing your own AUTOEXEC.BAT file in ways that will help you get started right each time your computer is turned on. You were shown how to set up your hardware the way you want it, define paths and turn your modem's answer feature on or off, load utility programs like Sidekick, and do other once-a-day tasks. Such long batch files may take awhile to run, but you can be opening your mail and doing other "human-initialization" procedures during the minute or so the AUTOEXEC.BAT file runs.

In the next chapter, we'll concentrate on a selection of new DOS commands that help streamline many tasks. Included is an examination of redefining keys, as used in the sample AUTOEXEC.BAT file in this chapter.

14

New DOS Commands

INTRODUCTION

We know almost everything we need to build any DOS commands we want. In this chapter, we'll work more with FOR..IN..DO, which is DOS' provision for looping during batch-file execution. We'll also examine ways of safeguarding your hard disk data with a new FORMAT command, and, for those with DOS 3.2 or later versions, an automated utility that offers a better understanding of how XCOPY works is provided.

All the allowable subcommands in batch files have been covered in some detail, except one. That is FOR..IN..DO. Although we've used this command briefly before, we've waited until this chapter to explain it more completely.

FOR..IN..DO permits a type of looping, related to that of FOR-NEXT or WHILE-WEND loops, so that the batch file can carry out a command repeatedly. The syntax follows this pattern:

```
FOR <%%variable> IN <set> DO <command to carry out>
```

The variable is usually called something like %%a or %%b. Note that a double percent sign marks the variable, which is necessary to keep DOS from confusing the variable with parameters marked with a single percent sign. If ECHO is ON while the command is carried out, you see only a single percent sign displayed when DOS prints each command to the screen.

The members of "set" can be anything that you want, but in practical use are most often a set of filenames that you are having the batch file operate on or using.

Be aware of a subtle difference in this regard between DOS 2.0, 2.1, and 3.x that we have pointed out several times before—only DOS 3.0 and later versions allow using pathnames in all cases where you refer to a file. For example, you cannot call an executable file simply by typing its pathname in versions earlier than 3.0. And, with FOR..IN..DO, you can use pathnames with the filenames only with DOS 3.0 and higher. This might be considered a bug with the earlier DOS that has been corrected.

Each time through the loop, the variable takes on the name of the file being acted on. To give a useless but easy-to-understand example:

```
FOR %%b IN (A:*.*) DO COPY %%b B:
```

this line causes all the files on A: to be copied to B: (just as with COPY A:*.* B:, thus the redundancy). The power of this batch command is that we can be a bit more creative with it—something not always possible with ordinary DOS commands. Examine the following line:

```
FOR %%b IN (A:*.*) IF EXIST B:%%b DO COPY %%b C:
```

Here each file on A: is considered, and if that file also exists on B:, is copied to C:. You end up with a disk containing only the files common to both A: and C:. Or look at this line:

```
FOR %%b IN (A:*.BAS) IF NOT EXIST B:%%b DO COPY %%b C:
```

In this case, any file with the .BAS extension that does *not* exist on the disk in B:, is copied to drive C: The list of filenames can be more complex than that shown:

```
FOR %%b IN (A:*.EXE A:*.COM B:*.EXE B:*.COM) DO COPY %%b C:
```

This line copies all the .COM and .EXE files on the logged directory of both A: and B: to C: The possibilities are limited only by your imagination. Interested in removing duplicate files from your disks? Insert the "main" disk in drive A: and the one that may contain some unwanted duplicate files in B: Make sure that a batch file containing the following line is available, and then execute it:

```
FOR %%b IN (A:*.*) IF EXIST B:%%b DO ERASE B:%%b
```

Of course, you can always substitute a user-supplied parameter for the file list and use the same batch file for different purposes. Suppose you wanted to look at a list of files (or sort a list, or do anything else). The following line would help you.

```
FOR %%b IN (%1 %2 %3) IF EXIST %%b DO MORE<%%b
```

With this line, you could enter up to three file specifications as parameters on your command line. These would be global, such as ''*.TXT'' or ''B:DOCS\LISTS\LIST*.DOC'' or specific, like ''\DOCS\LISTS\LIST4.DOC.'' Remember that paths are only valid with DOS 3.0 and above. When processing this line, the batch file would look on the default drive (or the specified one, if included) for the file, and if it exists, would print it a page at a time through the MORE filter. The IF EXIST syntax keeps the file if the file is not found.

Note that the ''set could also be a set of commands, as in the following example.

```
For %%a in (copy delete) Do %%a B:*.* A:
```

This command would first copy all the files on B: to A:, then delete the files on B:. (You would be asked ''are you sure?'' first.)

The new DOS commands in this chapter make use of several DOS features covered in previous chapters. These include the COMMAND command, using CTTY to redirect output of the standard input and output devices (the keyboard and CRT) to the COM port, CHKDSK, and the use of BASIC to provide expanded interactive functions.

With this information under your belt, we are ready to do some serious DOS command building. Let's get started.

UTILITIES

KEY.BAT

What it does: Turns on (or off) function key definitions that you supply. Two sets may be defined and called interchangeably.

Syntax: KEY   OFF
             KEY   1
             KEY 2

Requirements: DOS 2.0

HOW TO USE IT

DEVICE=ANSI.SYS must be in your CONFIG.SYS file (see Appendix A) and both ANSI.SYS and CONFIG.SYS should be available when DOS boots up.

You may put your own definitions in place of those in lines 21–30 and lines 38–47. Keep in mind that total definitions should be 200 bytes or less. (Count the number of characters in your definitions to determine this.)

Use this command by typing:

```
KEY [off, 1, or 2]
```

When you type KEY OFF, the function keys are restored to their default definitions. KEY 1 or KEY ON changes to definition set 1, and KEY 2 calls up definition set 2. Typing KEY alone with no parameter produces the HELP message.

If you like, you may change the labels to determine which set of function keys are activated to more closely represent the function of that key set. For example, if you need to use the DOS editing keys (such as F3 to redisplay the last command typed in), you might want to call the default or OFF key definition EDIT.

Other times you may want to prevent the user from accessing the DOS editing keys, and replace the definitions with your own, which you might call USER. Still another definition of the function keys might produce the Alt Key sequences described earlier to draw boxes and other figures on the screen. You might call these key definitions DRAW or BOXES. Choose a parameter name that is easy to remember and provide a prompting of the allowable parameters in your HELP screen.

Line-By-Line Description

Line 1:   Turn off screen echoing of commands.

Lines 2–3:   Title remarks.

Line 4:   If parameter %1 is null, display HELP.

Lines 5–10:   Examine parameter %1 and direct file to that label.

Line 11:   If no match, send to HELP.

Lines 12–18: HELP message.

Lines 20–31: Definition set 1.

Lines 32–48: Definition set 2.

Lines 49–61: Restore default definitions.

Lines 62–64: Restore default prompt and exit file.

```
------------------------------------------------------------
1.   ECHO OFF
2.   :     :: KEY.BAT ::
3.   :     *** Defines Keys ***
4.   IF "%1" == "" GOTO HELP
5.   IF %1 == on  GOTO 1
6.   IF %1 == ON  GOTO 1
7.   IF %1 == OFF GOTO OFF
8.   IF %1 == off GOTO OFF
9.   IF %1 == 1  GOTO 1
10.  IF %1 == 2  GOTO 2
11.  GOTO HELP
12.  :HELP
13.  ECHO    You may type KEY followed by:
14.  ECHO         1 (or ON)   Key definitions 1
15.  ECHO         2           Key definitions 2
16.  ECHO         OFF         To restore keys
17.  ECHO    <Alt 255>
18.  GOTO EXIT
19.  :1
20.  ECHO ON
21.  PROMPT $e[0;59;"DIR A:";13p
22.  PROMPT $e[0;60;"DIR B:";13p
23.  PROMPT $e[0;61;"DIR C:";13p
24.  PROMPT $e[0;62;"COPY *.*";p
25.  PROMPT $e[0;63;"BASICA";13p
26.  PROMPT $e[0;64;"FORMAT B:";p
27.  PROMPT $e[0;65;"CHKDSK";p
28.  PROMPT $e[0;66;"CD\";13p
29.  PROMPT $e[0;67;"DIR>FILE";13p
30.  PROMPT $e[0;68;"KEY OFF";13p
31.  GOTO EXIT
32.  :2
```

```
33.   ECHO      This portion disabled until you enter
34.   ECHO       your own definitions.  Then remove
35.   ECHO        these lines and one which follows
36.   GOTO EXIT
37.   ECHO ON
38.   PROMPT $e[0;59;"Your Def 1";p
39.   PROMPT $e[0;60;"Your 2";13p
40.   PROMPT $e[0;61;"Your 3";13p
41.   PROMPT $e[0;62;"Your 4";p
42.   PROMPT $e[0;63;"Your 5";13p
43.   PROMPT $e[0;64;"Your 6";p
44.   PROMPT $e[0;65;"Your 7";p
45.   PROMPT $e[0;66;"Your 8";13p
46.   PROMPT $e[0;67;"Your 9";13p
47.   PROMPT $e[0;68;"Your 10";13p
48.   GOTO EXIT
49.   :OFF
50.     ECHO ON
51.     PROMPT $e[0;59;0;59p
52.     PROMPT $e[0;60;0;60p
53.     PROMPT $e[0;61;0;61p
54.     PROMPT $e[0;62;0;62p
55.     PROMPT $e[0;63;0;63p
56.     PROMPT $e[0;64;0;64p
57.     PROMPT $e[0;65;0;65p
58.     PROMPT $e[0;66;0;66p
59.     PROMPT $e[0;67;0;67p
60.     PROMPT $e[0;68;0;68p
61    GOTO EXIT
62    :EXIT
63.   PROMPT
64.   CLS
```

CONSOLE.BAT

What it does: Changes console device to COM1, COM2, or back to the
                console (CON).

Syntax: CONSOLE *asynchronous port number*

Requirements: DOS 2.0

HOW TO USE IT

If you wish to control your computer from another terminal or device connected through one of the asynchronous ports, this command performs the changeover for you. The syntax for using it is:

```
CONSOLE [1,2, or nothing]
```

Using 1 or 2 as a parameter causes DOS to use the auxiliary console as the standard input and output device instead of the keyboard and screen. Either COM1 or COM2 can be specified, by entering 1 or 2. If you type just CONSOLE with no parameter, DOS switches back to the standard input and output devices. You won't be able to type this command from your keyboard; it must be entered from the new console device.

You can remotely control your computer in this way by hardwiring the two through their COM ports using a null modem device (the null modem is a simple cable or adapter with several of the connections changed, available from many computer stores and Radio Shack outlets). The controlling computer must also have communication software to send the correct commands to the other system.

Line-By-Line Description

Line 1:   Turn off screen echoing of commands.

Lines 2–3:   Title remarks.

Line 4:   If no parameter entered, go to CON and restore standard input and output device.

Lines 5–6:   Send to COM2 or COM1 routines.

Lines 7–11:   If 1 or 2 not entered as %1, display HELP.

Lines 12–19:   Set asynchronous port to 9600 baud, even parity, eight-bit word, and one stop bit, and then change to COM1 or COM2.

Lines 20–21:   Change back to keyboard and video screen.

Lines 22–23:   Exit file.

```
--------------------------------------------------------
1.    ECHO OFF
2.    :: CONSOLE.BAT  ::
3.    :   *** Changes console device to COM1 or COM2 ***
4.    IF "%1"=="" GOTO CON
5.    IF %1 == "2" GOTO COM2
6.    IF %1 == "1" GOTO COM1
7.    :HELP
8.    ECHO   You can enter the command CONSOLE [1 or 2]
9.    ECHO   1 is the default.  Other parameters ignored.
10.   ECHO   <Alt 255>
11.   GOTO EXIT
12.   :COM1
13.   MODE COM1:96,E,8,1
14.   CTTY COM1
15.   GOTO EXIT
16.   :COM2
17.   MODE COM2:96,E,8,1
18.   CTTY COM2
19.   GOTO EXIT
20.   :CON
21.   CTTY CON
22.   :EXIT
23.   CLS
--------------------------------------------------------
```

FORMAT.BAT

What it does: Provides new, safer FORMAT command.

Syntax: FORMAT drive to format

Requirements: DOS 2.0

HOW TO USE IT

Before DOS 3.0, it was possible to accidentally reformat an entire hard disk by mistake, simply by typing FORMAT C: and pressing a key when asked if ready. Many distracted users lost valuable data that way.

DOS 3.0 helped correct this error. If you try to format a fixed disk, DOS gives a stern message:

```
Warning, All Data on Non-Removable
Disk Drive x: Will Be Lost!
Proceed with Format (Y/N)?
```

Later versions of DOS have made it even more difficult to inadvertently format a hard disk, asking you to enter the volume label and so forth to confirm the dastardly deed beforehand.

This batch file makes FORMAT a little safer for all DOS users. You cannot accidentally format the default drive you are logged onto by mistake; the drive you wish to format must be specified explicitly. In addition, you may only format A: or B: even if you specify C: That disk (most commonly used as the hard disk) can be formatted only by typing FORMAT2 C:

So, to format A: or B: type:

```
FORMAT A:
FORMAT B:
FORMAT B
FORMAT A
```

Either upper- or lowercase may be used. FORMAT used alone or FORMAT C: displays only the HELP message. To use this, you must rename your FORMAT.COM file as FORMAT2.COM. This allows you to have a batch file by the same name as an external DOS command. FORMAT2 can still be used exactly like the old FORMAT command if you want to format your hard disk (or other C:).

Rename FORMAT.COM by typing:

```
RENAME FORMAT.COM FORMAT2.COM
```

Include a drive letter in the first filename if FORMAT.COM does not reside on the default drive. The new FORMAT command still allows entering switches, like /1 and /8 (to produce single-sided or 8-sector disks), /V (to prompt DOS to ask for a volume name, /4 (to format double-sided disks for a high-capacity drive), /B to format an 8-sector diskette with space allocated for system modules, and /S to produce a system disk. Note that these switches must be allowable by DOS for the type of drive you are using. All five can be used with conventional disk drive, while only /S and /V are allowed with high-capacity or fixed disks.

Line-By-Line Description

Line 1:   Turn off screen echoing of commands.

Lines 2–3:   Title remarks.

Line 4:   If no parameter entered, display HELP.

Lines 5–12:   Check for legal drive specification.

Lines 13–17:   If not legal drive specification, display HELP.

Lines 18–23:   Format specified drive.

Lines 24–25:   Exit file.

```
------------------------------------------------------
1.    ECHO OFF
2.    :: FORMAT.BAT ::
3.    :        *** Anti-Default Drive Formatter ***
4.    IF "%1"=="" GOTO HELP
5.    IF "%1" == "B:" GOTO B
6.    IF "%1" == "b:" GOTO B
7.    IF "%1" == "A:" GOTO A
8.    IF "%1" == "a:" GOTO A
9.    IF "%1" == "B"  GOTO B
10.   IF "%1" == "b"  GOTO B
11.   IF "%1" == "A"  GOTO A
12.   IF "%1" == "a"  GOTO A
13.   :HELP
14.   ECHO     You cannot FORMAT default drive without
15.   ECHO     Explicitly specifying DRIVE
16.   ECHO     Format C: by typing FORMAT2 C:
17.   GOTO EXIT
18.   :A
19.   FORMAT2 A: %2 %3
20.   GOTO EXIT
21.   :B
22.   FORMAT2 B: %2 %3
23.   GOTO EXIT
24.   :EXIT
25.   CLS
------------------------------------------------------
```

SFORMAT.BAT

What it does: Creates a system disk in B:

Syntax: SFORMAT

Requirements: DOS 2.0. Intended for users of floppy-disk-based systems.

HOW TO USE IT

If you make many system disks for users of floppy-disk-based computers in your organization, this command is a shortcut. Simply type SFORMAT. Command presupposes that you have renamed FORMAT.COM as FORMAT2.COM as described in the previous routine, FORMAT.BAT.

You can modify this command to personalize it for your own needs; include /V to be prompted for a volume name, and so on.

Line-By-Line Description

Line 1:   Turn off screen echoing of commands.

Lines 2–3:   Title remarks.

Line 4:   If no parameter entered, go do it.

Lines 5–10:   If any parameter entered, display HELP message.

Lines 11–12:   Format the disk.

Lines 13–14:   Exit file.

```
-------------------------------------------------------
1.   ECHO OFF
2.   :    ::   SFORMAT.BAT  ::
3.   :        *** Creates System Disk in Drive B: ***
4.   IF "%1" =="" GOTO FORMAT
5.   :HELP
6.   ECHO  This command creates a system disk in Drive B:
7.   ECHO  Insert COMMAND.COM Disk in default drive, then
8.   ECHO  type SFORMAT.  No parameters allowed.
9.   ECHO  <Alt 255>
10.  GOTO EXIT
11.  :FORMAT
12.  FORMAT2 B: /S
13.  :EXIT
14.  CLS
-------------------------------------------------------
```

1FORMAT.BAT

What it does: Creates a single-sided, eight-sector disk in B:

Syntax: 1FORMAT

Requirements: DOS 2.0

HOW TO USE IT

Shows how to create a special command to format the type of disks you use most often (other than the default type) using a new command. In this case, file creates a single-sided, eight-sector disk with no system in B:. You might use this command if you frequently had to make blank disks to distribute to users of IBM or compatible computers and you weren't sure which DOS they use. Since these disks can be read by all versions of PC-DOS and most versions of MS-DOS for compatibles, they would provide a neutral medium of exchange for users with 5 1/4-in. disk drives.

File assumes you have changed the name of FORMAT.COM as outlined earlier and that you always want to format in B:.

Line-By-Line Description

Line 1:   Turn off screen echoing of commands.

Lines 2–3:   Title remarks.

Line 4:   If no parameter specified, go format the disk.

Lines 5–10:   Display help message.

Lines 11–12:   Format the disk.

Lines 13–14:   Exit file.

```
---------------------------------------------------------
1.   ECHO OFF
2.   :       :: 1FORMAT.BAT  ::
3.   : *** Creates 1-sided eight-sector disk in drive B: ***
4.   IF "%1" =="" GOTO FORMAT
5.   :HELP
6.   ECHO  This command creates a single-sided eight-sector disk
7.   ECHO  in drive B:, readable by DOS 1.1  Type 1FORMAT
```

```
 8.   ECHO   No parameters required or allowed.
 9.   ECHO   <Alt 255>
10.   GOTO EXIT
11.   :FORMAT
12.   FORMAT2 B: /1 /8
13.   :EXIT
14.   CLS
------------------------------------------------
```

DUPE.BAT

What it does: Provides prompted file copying

Syntax: DUPE filename

Requirements: DOS 2.0 or later; hard disk (recommended).

HOW TO USE IT

Two files are involved, DUPE.BAT and DUPER.BAT, and both must be available. Type DUPE "filename.ext" to initiate the process. You may use wildcards in the file name, if you wish:

```
DUPE B:*.BAS
```

would initiate copying of BASIC files on B: only. You will be shown each filename and asked to enter "Y", "N", or "Q." If you enter "N" (upper- or lowercase is acceptable) or any other character, the program assumes you do not want to copy the file. Entering "Q" ends the copying process. This is a command similar to XCOPY provided with DOS 3.2 and later versions, with its prompted copying facility. This command, however, may be used with any version of DOS 2.0 or later.

Line-By-Line Description: DUPE.BAT

Line 1:   Turn off echoing of commands.

Lines 2-3:   Title remarks.

Line 4:   If no parameter entered, show help.

Line 5:   If the temporary file C:\TEMP.$$$ exists, erase it.

Line 6:   For each of the file specifications pointed to by %1, repeat these steps: If C:\TEMP.$$$ does not exist, call a second copy of COMMAND.COM and run the batch file DUPER, using %%a as the first parameter on the command line.

Line 7:   Go to the end.

Lines 8–15:   Display help.

Lines 16–17:   End of the routine.

Line-By-Line Description: DUPER.BAT

Line 1:   Turn off echoing of commands.

Lines 2–3:   Title remarks.

Line 4:   ECHO the file being processed to screen.

Lines 5–6:   Ask if it should be copied.

Line 7:   If Y entered, go to COPYIT.

Line 8:   If Q entered, go to QUIT.

Line 9:   If N entered, return without copying.

Line 10:   No match, so go back for another keypress.

Lines 11–14:   Copy the file.

Lines 15–16:   Create TEMP.$$$ as flag to QUIT.

Line 17:   End of file. Control returns to original command processor and DUPE.BAT for next filename.

```
-------------------------------------------------------
1.  ECHO OFF
2.  :    :: DUPE.BAT ::
3.  : *** Prompted file copying ***
4.  IF "%2"=="" GOTO HELP
5.  IF EXIST C:\TEMP.$$$ ERASE C:\TEMP.$$$
```

```
 6.  FOR %%a IN (%1) DO IF NOT EXIST C:\TEMP.$$$ COMMAND /C
     DUPER %%a %2
 7.  GOTO END
 8.  :HELP
 9.  ECHO     Syntax:
10.  ECHO          DUPE [d:][filename.ext] destination
11.  ECHO      You will be asked if you want to copy the
12.  ECHO      file, or individual files that meet the
13.  ECHO      specification.  Wildcards are permitted.
14.  ECHO      Substitute drive specification for [d:]
15.  ECHO <Alt 255>
16.  :END
17.  CLS
---------------------------------------------------------


---------------------------------------------------------
 1.  ECHO OFF
 2.  :       ::: DUPER.BAT :::
 3.  : *** File Copier ***
 4.  ECHO %1
 5.  :INPUT
 6.  INPUT Copy this file to %2 (Y/N/Q)?
 7. IF ERRORLEVEL 89 IF NOT ERRORLEVEL 90 GOTO COPYIT
 8. IF ERRORLEVEL 81 IF NOT ERRORLEVEL 82 GOTO QUIT
 9. IF ERRORLEVEL 78 IF NOT ERRORLEVEL 79 GOTO RETURN
10. GOTO INPUT
11. :COPYIT
12. COPY %1 %2
13. ECHO Copying %1 to %2
14. GOTO RETURN
15. :QUIT
16. ECHO DONE>C:\TEMP.$$$
17. :RETURN
---------------------------------------------------------
```

COPIER.BAT

What it does: Provides prompted XCOPY commands.

Syntax: COPIER source destination

Requirements: DOS 3.2 or later.

HOW TO USE IT

Enter COPIER, followed by the source and destination disk drive/directory/filename specifications you want to use with XCOPY. This routine is good for inexperienced users who are unlikely to learn how to use XCOPY's switches.

Line-By-Line Description

Line 1:   Turn off screen echoing of commands.

Lines 2–3:   Title remarks.

Line 4:   If %2 not blank, start routine.

Lines 5–16:   Display HELP, then END.

Lines 17–26:   Offer choices.

Lines 27–32:   Check for valid input.

Line 33:   If no valid key pressed, loop back.

Lines 34–41:   Invoke XCOPY as requested.

```
------------------------------------------------------
1.   ECHO OFF
2.   :    :: COPIER.BAT ::
3.   : *** Prompted XCOPY Commands ***
4.   IF NOT "%2"=="" GOTO START
5.   ECHO Type:
6.   ECHO COPIER source destination
6.   ECHO where the source is the disk and/or directory
7.   ECHO and/or filename of files you want copied,
8.   ECHO and destination is the disk and/or directory
9.   ECHO and/or filename of the files to be copied to.
10.  ECHO <Alt 255>
11.  ECHO You will be asked whether you want prompted copy
12.  ECHO alone, copy only of files not backed up since
13.  ECHO they were last changed, copy of files in
14.  ECHO  subdirectories below the source directory, or
15.  ECHO both (copy of files changed in subdirectories).
16.  GOTO END
17.  :START
```

```
18. ECHO <Alt 255>
19. ECHO  1. Prompted Copy from %1 to %2
20. ECHO  2. Prompted Copy from %1 to %2
21. ECHO        -- Backup changed files.
22. ECHO  3. Prompted Copy from %1 to %2,
23. ECHO        -- All files in %1's subdirectories
24. ECHO  4. Prompted Copy from %1 to %2
25. ECHO        -- Changed files in %1 subdirectories
26. ECHO <Alt 255>
27. :INPUT
28. INPUT Enter choice:
29. IF ERRORLEVEL 49 IF NOT ERRORLEVEL 50 GOTO 1
30. IF ERRORLEVEL 50 IF NOT ERRORLEVEL 51 GOTO 2
31. IF ERRORLEVEL 51 IF NOT ERRORLEVEL 52 GOTO 3
32. IF ERRORLEVEL 52 IF NOT ERRORLEVEL 53 GOTO 4
33. GOTO INPUT
34. :1
35. XCOPY %1 %2 /P
36.  :2
37. XCOPY %1 %2 /P /M
38. :3
39. XCOPY %1 %2 /P /S
40. :4
41. XCOPY %1 %2 /P /S /M
```

FUNCTION.BAT

What it does: Loads BASIC with new function key definitions.

Syntax: FUNCTION   0
                FUNCTION   1
                FUNCTION 2

Requirements: DOS 2.0

HOW TO USE IT

Although DOS can have its own function key definitions, you may load BASIC automatically with your desired set of BASIC function key definitions, using this command.

First, you must create special function key files, using FUNCTION.BAS. You may create as many as you want. This command draws on two of them. If you have read the rest of the book, you'll be able to modify this file to use three or four or more function key files. Note that FUNCTION.BAS creates a BASIC program that is run by FUNCTION.BAT.

RENAME the files you want to access so that they are named KEYDEFS1.BAS and KEYDEFS2.BAS. Then you may load BASIC with the desired definitions by typing:

FUNCTION [0,1,or 2]

If 0 operates a parameter, the normal function key definitions are used. If 1 or 2 is specified, then your function key definition file 1 or 2 is loaded and the file itself erased from memory. Note that if your computer uses GW-BASIC instead of BASICA, substitute for the BASICA command the command BASIC or whatever summons BASIC with your computer.

Line-By-Line Description

Line 1:	Turn off screen echoing of commands.
Lines 2–3:	Title remarks.
Line 4:	If no parameter used, go to HELP.
Lines 5–7:	If 0 to 2 entered, go to appropriate module.
Lines 8–15:	Display HELP message.
Lines 16–23:	Load BASICA and appropriate function key definition file.
Lines 24–25:	Exit file.

Listing 14-1. ECHO OFF and FUNCTION KEYS Programs.

```
----------------------------------------------------------
1.    ECHO OFF
2.:       :: FUNCTION.BAT ::
3.    : *** Loads Basic With Function Key Definitions ***
4.    IF "%1" =="" GOTO HELP
5.    IF "%1" == "0" GOTO 0
6.    IF "%1" =="1"  GOTO 1
7.    IF "%1" =="2"  GOTO 2
8.    :HELP
9.    ECHO  TYPE FUNCTION [0, 1 or 2] to load BASIC
10.   ECHO  with your choice of function key definitions
11.   ECHO     0 = Normal function keys
```

Listing 14-1. Continued

```
12. ECHO     1 = Definition Set #1
13. ECHO     2 = Definition Set #2
14. ECHO     <Alt 255>
15. GOTO EXIT
16. :0
17. BASICA
18. GOTO EXIT
19. :1
20. BASICA A:KEYDEFS1.BAS
21. GOTO EXIT
22. :2
23. BASICA A:KEYDEFS2.BAS
24. :EXIT
25. CLS
```

```
10 ' ****************
20 ' *              *
30 ' * FUNCTION KEYS *
40 ' *              *
50 ' ****************
60 SCREEN 0,0,0
70 KEY OFF
80 COLOR 7,0
90 DIM DEFINITION$(10)

95 ' *** TURN ON FUNCTION KEYS ***

100 ON KEY(1) GOSUB 770
110 ON KEY(2) GOSUB 780
120 ON KEY(3) GOSUB 790
130 ON KEY(4) GOSUB 800
140 ON KEY(5) GOSUB 810
150 ON KEY(6) GOSUB 820
160 ON KEY(7) GOSUB 830
170 ON KEY(8) GOSUB 840
180 ON KEY(9) GOSUB 850
190 ON KEY(10) GOSUB 860
200 ON KEY(15) GOSUB 870
210 KEY 15,CHR$(0)+CHR$(79)
220 KEY (15) ON

225 ' *** ASK FOR KEY TO DEFINE ***

230 CLS
```

Listing 14-1. Continued

```
240 LOCATE 2,4
250 COLOR 23,0
260 PRINT"Press Function Key to Be Defined : "
270 COLOR 7,0
280 LOCATE 4,4
290 PRINT"Press ";:COLOR 0,7:PRINT" END ";:COLOR 7,0:PRINT"
    key to finish."

295 ' *** SHOW CURRENT DEFS ***

300 PRINT
310 FOR I=1 TO 10
320 PRINT TAB(2)"KEY ";:COLOR 0,7:PRINT
    "F";MID$(STR$(I),2);:COLOR 7,0
330 PRINT TAB(12)"  : Current definition
    :";TAB(40);DEFINITION$(I);
340 IF M$(I)=CHR$(13) THEN PRINT TAB(57)" C/R" ELSE PRINT
350 NEXT I

355 ' *** TURN KEYS ON AND WAIT ***

360 ROW=1:COL=1:WIDE=65:DEEP=15:GOSUB 1000
370 KEY(1) ON:KEY(2) ON:KEY(3) ON:KEY(4) ON:KEY(5) ON
380 KEY(6) ON:KEY(7) ON:KEY(8) ON:KEY(9) ON:KEY(10) ON
390 GOTO 390

395 ' *** TURN KEYS OFF ***

400 KEY(1) OFF:KEY(2) OFF:KEY(3) OFF:KEY(4) OFF:KEY(5) OFF
410 KEY(6) OFF:KEY(7) OFF:KEY(8) OFF:KEY(9) OFF:KEY(10) OFF

415 ' *** GET DEF FOR SPECIFIED KEY ***

420 CLS
430 ROW=1:COL=1:WIDE=70:DEEP=10:GOSUB 1000
440 LOCATE 2,5
450 PRINT "Enter definition for key F";MID$(STR$(K),2);"."
460 LOCATE 3,4
470 IF DEFINITION$(K)<>"" THEN PRINT DEFINITION$(K) ELSE
    PRINT STRING$(15,175)
480 LOCATE 4,4
490 PRINT STRING$(15,254);
500 LOCATE 4,2
510 CU=0
520 B=0
530 TEMP$=STRING$(15,254)
```

Listing 14-1. Continued

```
540 A$=INKEY$:IF A$="" GOTO 540
550 IF A$=CHR$(13) GOTO 660
560 IF A$<>CHR$(8) THEN GOTO 580
570 IF CU=0 THEN GOTO 540 ELSE MID$(TEMP$,CU,1)=CHR$(254)
    :IF CU-1>-1 THEN CU=CU-1:GOTO 600
580 CU=CU+1
590 MID$(TEMP$,CU,1)=A$
600 LOCATE 4,4
610 PRINT STRING$(15,32);
620 LOCATE 4,4
630 PRINT TEMP$;
640 IF INSTR(TEMP$,CHR$(254))=0 GOTO 680
650 GOTO 540
660 B=INSTR(TEMP$,CHR$(254))
670 B=INSTR(TEMP$,CHR$(254))
680 IF B<>0 THEN DEFINITION$=LEFT$(TEMP$,B-1) ELSE
    DEFINITION$=TEMP$
690 IF LEN(DEFINITION$)<1 GOTO 750

695 ' *** ADD CARRIAGE RETURN? ***

700 LOCATE 6,4
710 PRINT"End with a carriage return?  (Y/N)"
720 A$=INKEY$:IF A$="" GOTO 720
730 IF A$="Y" OR A$="y" THEN M$(K)=CHR$(13) ELSE M$(K)=""
740 IF LEN(DEFINITION$)>15 OR LEN(DEFINITION$)>14 AND
    M$(K)=CHR$(13) THEN BEEP:LOCATE 7,4:PRINT"Too long! 15
    characters please!":FOR DELAY=1 TO 2000:NEXT
    DELAY:CLS:GOTO 420
750 DEFINITION$(K)=DEFINITION$
760 GOTO 230

765 ' *** DETERMINE WHICH KEY WAS PRESSED ***

770 K=1:RETURN 400
780 K=2:RETURN 400
790 K=3:RETURN 400
800 K=4:RETURN 400
810 K=5:RETURN 400
820 K=6:RETURN 400
830 K=7:RETURN 400
840 K=8:RETURN 400
850 K=9:RETURN 400
860 K=10:RETURN 400

865 ' *** WRITE DEF FILE TO DISK ***
```

Listing 14-1. Continued

```
870 OPEN "O",1,"KEYDEFS.BAS"
880 FOR N=1 TO 10
890 IF DEFINITION$(N)="" GOTO 930
900 L$=STR$(N)+"  KEY"+STR$(N)+","+CHR$(34)
    +DEFINITION$(N)+CHR$(34)
910 IF M$(N)=CHR$(13) THEN L$=L$+"+CHR$(13)"
920 PRINT #1,L$
930 NEXT N
940 N=N+1
950 PRINT #1,STR$(N)+" NEW"
960 CLOSE 1

965 ' *** RUN THE FILE ***

970 RUN "KEYDEFS.BAS"
980 CLOSE
990 END

995 ' *** DRAW A BOX ***

1000 LOCATE ROW,COL
1010 PRINT CHR$(201);
1020 FOR N=COL+1 TO COL+WIDE-1
1030 PRINT CHR$(205);
1040 NEXT N
1050 PRINT CHR$(187)
1060 FOR N=ROW+1 TO ROW+DEEP-1
1070 LOCATE N,COL
1080 PRINT CHR$(186);
1090 LOCATE N,COL+WIDE
1100 PRINT CHR$(186);
1110 NEXT N
1120 LOCATE ROW+DEEP,COL
1130 PRINT CHR$(200);
1140 FOR N=COL+1 TO COL+WIDE-1
1150 PRINT CHR$(205);
1160 NEXT N
1170 PRINT CHR$(188)
1180 RETURN
```

BASICB.BAT

What it does: Changes default drive and loads BASIC.

Syntax: BASICB

Requirements: DOS 2.0

HOW TO USE IT

Many users like to store BASIC files they are creating on a data disk in drive B: (or in a special subdirectory on C: or another favorite place.) A batch file can change directories for you, log onto the drive you want and then load BASICA so that when you save files, they automatically go on the disk or directory you want. Then, when you leave BASIC, you can be logged back onto the drive you prefer.

This file as written assumes that the desired data drive is B:, and that the drive to be returned to is A:. You may customize it by adding a new drive specification or directory of your choice:

```
B:
CD \FILES
BASICA
CD \
A:
```

This would be an alternative way of doing a more complex change. Invoke this command by typing BASICB. You could also combine this with the previous file to allow going directly to BASIC with the function key definitions you have set up to help speed programming. Again, if your BASIC is called by a command other than BASICA, make the appropriate change in line 5 of the batch file.

Line-By-Line Description

Line 1:   Turn off screen echoing of commands.

Lines 2–3:   Title remarks.

Line 4:   Change default drive to B:

Line 5:   Load BASICA.

Line 6:   Change default drive to A:

```
1.  ECHO OFF
2.  :        :: BASICB.BAT  ::
3.  :        *** Change Default Drive, Go Basic ***
4.  B:
```

```
5.   BASICA
6.   A:
----------------------------------------------------------------
```

CHECK.BAT

What it does: Streamlines CHKDSK command.

Syntax: CHECK drive to check

Requirements: DOS 2.0

HOW TO USE IT

CHKDSK, a useful external DOS command, finds "loose" sectors on your disk, retrieves them, and tells you how much space is used by files on that disk and how much memory you have free and in total. This module is a simpler way of calling the command. You don't have to remember that the spelling is CHKDSK, not CHCKDSK, CKDDSK, or another variation. In addition, it is not necessary to use the pesky colon (:) when entering the drive specification. Just type:

```
CHECK A
CHECK B
CHECK C
CHECK
```

With the last is used, the default drive is checked. The /F switch, which tells the program to fix errors that are found in the directory or file allocation table, is automatically applied. If you do not want to take the chance on having CHKDSK fix something that you would rather work on in a different way (that is, you are an advanced user with access to other utilities), delete the /F from the batch file. CHECK displays error messages if problems are located. A listing of the error messages' meanings can be found in your DOS manual.

Line-By-Line Description

Line 1:   Turn off screen echoing of commands.

Lines 2–3:   Title remarks.

Line 4:   If no parameter entered, go to DEFAULT.

Lines 5–6:   Otherwise, run CHKDSK on specified drive.

Lines 7–8:   Run CHKDSK on default drive.

Line 9:   Exit file.

```
-------------------------------------------------------
1.    ECHO OFF
2.    :         :: CHECK.BAT  ::
3.    :         *** Checks Disk Space and System Memory ***
4.    IF "%1" == "" GOTO DEFAULT
5.    CHKDSK %1: /F
6.    GOTO EXIT
7.    :DEFAULT
8.    CHKDSK /F
9.    :EXIT
-------------------------------------------------------
```

COMPARE.BAT

What it does: Provides a list of files that are found both on the disk in drive A: and the disk in drive B:

Syntax: COMPARE

Requirements: DOS 2.0. Works best with two floppy disks.

HOW TO USE IT

Insert the first disk in drive A:, then insert the second disk in B:. You must have changed to the directories that you wish to compare. A list of the files on both disks is displayed on the screen. For an enhancement, see if you can change this routine so that it compares files on a hard disk and a floppy disk.

Line-By-Line Description

Line 1:   Turn off screen echoing of commands.

Lines 2–3:   Title remarks.

Lines 4–7:   Display instructions and wait.

Line 8:   Clear the screen.

Line 9:   Log onto A:

Line 10:   Repeat for all the files on A:, if they exist on B:; display file-
             name and message on screen.

```
----------------------------------------------------------
1.   ECHO OFF
2.   :          :: COMPARE.BAT  ::
3.   :          *** Lists Common Files ***
4.   CLS
5.   ECHO    Insert first disk in drive A:
6.   ECHO    Insert second disk in drive B:
7.   PAUSE
8.   CLS
9.   A:
10.  FOR %%b IN (*.*) DO IF EXIST B:%%b ECHO %%b is on
     both disks.
----------------------------------------------------------
```

NOPE.BAT

What it does: Provides a list of files that are *not* found both on the disk
                in drive A: and the disk in drive B:.

Syntax: NOPE

Requirements: DOS 2.0. Works best with two floppy disks.

HOW TO USE IT

Insert the first disk in drive A:, then insert the second disk in B:. You must
have changed to the directories that you wish to compare. A list of the files that
are on the disk in drive A: but that are not to be found on drive B: are displayed
to the screen. This batch file could also be changed to compare files on the
floppy disk and the hard disk or that reside in two different directories on a hard
disk. Can you find a way to do it?

Line-By-Line Description

Line 1:   Turn off screen echoing of commands.

Lines 2–3:   Title remarks.

Lines 4–7:   Display instructions and wait.

Line 8:   Clear the screen.

Line 9:   Log onto A:

Line 10:   Repeat for all the files on A:, if they do not exist on B:, display filename and message on screen.

```
----------------------------------------------------------
1.   ECHO OFF
2.   :       :: NOPE.BAT  ::
3.   :       *** Lists Files NOT Common ***
4.   CLS
5.   ECHO    Insert first disk in drive A:
6.   ECHO    Insert second disk in drive B:
7.   PAUSE
8.   CLS
9.   A:
10.  FOR %%b IN (*.*) DO IF NOT EXIST B:%%b ECHO %%b is on
     the disk in drive A: only.
----------------------------------------------------------
```

UPDATE.BAT

What it does: Streamlines updating to a new version of DOS.

Syntax: UPDATE

Requirements: DOS 2.0. Intended for floppy-disk-based systems.

HOW TO USE IT

When you get a new version of DOS, it is a good idea to update all the disks on which you have a system with the new DOS. This is accomplished by using SYS to put the invisible system files on the old disk and by copying the new visible DOS files to the new disk.

This batch file assumes that you want to copy COMMAND.COM, FORMAT.COM, and CHKDSK.COM to the updated system disk but only if those programs are already on that disk. You may add other programs you wish to copy alongside those already listed in line 16. Or you can substitute *.* for the filenames. In that case, the batch file copies *all* the files that are common to both the new DOS disk and the one being updated to the update disk. This method should be used with caution; you may have some different files with the same names on both disks. The old files will be destroyed.

This file assumes that any disk containing COMMAND.COM already is a system disk and that any disk that does not have COMMAND.COM is not. It transfers the new system to disks that have COMMAND.COM and skips updating otherwise. You may update many disks, and halt operation by pressing Control-C.

Line-By-Line Description

Line 1:	Turn off screen echoing of commands.
Lines 2–3:	Title remarks.
Line 4:	If %1 is not null, display HELP message.
Lines 5–12:	Offer opportunity to press key to continue or hit Control-C to stop updating.
Lines 13–14:	Clear screen and Log onto A:
Line 15:	If COMMAND.COM is on the disk in B:, transfer new system files to that disk.
Line 16:	If COMMAND.COM is not on that disk, go to EXIT.
Line 17:	Copy other files to B:, if they exist on A: and B:
Line 18:	Repeat.
Lines 19–22:	Display HELP message.
Line 23:	Exit file.

```
------------------------------------------------------------
1.    ECHO OFF
2.    :         :: UPDATE.BAT  ::
3.    :         *** Updates DOS Disks ***
4.    IF NOT "%1" =="" GOTO HELP
5.    :BEGIN
6.    CLS
7.    ECHO    Insert new DOS disk in drive A:
8.    ECHO    Insert disk to be updated  in drive B:
9.    ECHO    <Alt 255>
10.   ECHO      (Hit Control-C to Cancel)
11.   ECHO    <Alt 255>
12.   PAUSE
13.   CLS
14.   A:
15.   IF EXIST B:COMMAND.COM SYS B:
16.   IF NOT EXIST B:COMMAND.COM GOTO EXIT
17.   FOR %%b IN (COMMAND.COM FORMAT.COM CHKDSK.COM) DO
      IF EXIST COPY %%b B:
18.   GOTO BEGIN
19.   :HELP
20.   ECHO   You may add other filenames to those within
21.   ECHO   parentheses if you want them updated on second
22.   ECHO   disk as well.  Separate with space
23.   :EXIT
------------------------------------------------------------
```

SUMMARY

In this chapter, we learned to redefine function keys, redirect the console device to another computer to remotely control our system and explored various ways to make the FORMAT command safer and easier to use. FIND was put to work in new ways to compare files on a pair of floppy disks and to display a list of files unique to the two disks or that were shared between the two. Another utility was supplied to update DOS disks for floppy-disk systems.

15

Building
Complex Menu
Systems

INTRODUCTION

This chapter will show you how to build menu systems that allow the advanced user and the neophyte to perform complex series of tasks by choosing options from a list. We'll also look at some tricks with the RAM disk device driver, VDISK.SYS, and a way to switch from no RAM disk to one of your choosing—and then back again—by selecting from a menu.

We'll review some of the menu methods discussed previously in this book to allow you to choose from among the various options while introducing a few new tricks.

The first method of making a menu system is the simplest: offering menu choices numbered from 1 to 9 (or from 0 to 9) and then creating batch files with the same root names that carry out those functions.

UTILITY

MENU.BAT

What it does: Allows calling individual programs from a DOS menu.

Syntax: MENU

Requirements: DOS 2.0

HOW TO USE IT

You may substitute your own favorite programs for those included in the menu. Then create batch files that will call up those programs, and name them 1.BAT, 2.BAT, 3.BAT, and so on to correspond with their menu entries. If you are using DOS 3.0 or later versions, your batch files can call programs by using pathnames:

```
ECHO OFF
:      :: 1.BAT ::
C:\PROGS\WP\WS
```

Otherwise, you'll need to log onto the directory where the program resides to call it. These files can also include lines to take care of any other tasks you want to carry out both before and after using the application, such as changing directory and then changing it back again, or copying a data file over to the directory that will be used.

Note that entering a parameter displays a help message, but other than that only one type of error trap is easy to use with this type of batch file. If the user types a number other than the ones shown, a BAD COMMAND OR FILE NAME message is displayed. If you wish, you could create dummy batch files with other numbers, to supply error messages:

```
ECHO OFF
:      :: 6.BAT ::
ECHO  No such menu choice! Try again!
PAUSE
CLS
MENU
```

Line-By-Line Description

Line 1:   Turn off screen echoing of commands.

Lines 2–3:   Title remarks.

Line 4:   If %1 is not null, display help message.

Lines 5–14:   Display the menu choices.

Lines 15–18:   Help message.

Line 19:   Exit file.

```
---------------------------------------------------------
1.   :       :: MENU.BAT ::
2.   :       *** Call programs from DOS menu ***
3.   IF NOT "%1" == "" GOTO HELP
4.   CLS
5.   ECHO     Enter the following to run these programs:
6.   ECHO   <Alt 255>
7.   ECHO           1.) Word Processing
8.   ECHO           2.) Spreadsheet
9.   ECHO           3.) DataBase Program
10.  ECHO           4.) BASIC
11.  ECHO           5.) Communications
12.  ECHO   <Alt 255>
13.  ECHO     -- ENTER CHOICE AND PRESS ENTER --
14.  GOTO EXIT
15.  :HELP
16.  ECHO     You should create batch files that call up
17.  ECHO     your individual menu entries.  These files
18.  ECHO     Should be called  1.BAT, 2.BAT, 3.BAT, etc.
19.  :EXIT
---------------------------------------------------------
```

USING VDISK.SYS

The next type of menu system that we'll look at uses INPUT.COM to allow entering number choices directly and then a series of subroutines within the batch file that carries out each of the numbered selections. For an example, we'll build a menu system that allows choosing your own VDISK.SYS configuration.

As you know, VDISK.SYS is a device driver supplied with DOS 3.0 and later versions that allows setting up one or more RAM disks using available memory. Many memory cards are supplied with drivers that perform a similar function. You may use part of your 640K of system memory not needed for applications or, if you have a PCAT or later model computer with extended memory capabilities, you may allocate part of extended memory for a RAM disk. Third party software, such as those supplied with memory cards conforming to the Lotus-Intel memory specification (also called EMS) or an enhanced version supported by Quadram, AST, and others (called EEMS) may also allow setting up electronic disks in memory outside the 640K recognized by DOS.

RAM disks are typically faster even than hard disks but, because they are volatile (their contents disappear when the computer is turned off or loses power) you must remember to back up any data to a magnetic disk at intervals. Of course, if you use the RAM disk solely for programs and continue to store data on regular disks, this volatility is of less concern.

VDISK and similar device drivers must be set up through a line or lines in your CONFIG.SYS file, conforming to the following syntax:

```
DEVICE=VDISK.SYS <size sector-size directory-entries> /E
```

The first parameter, *size* defines how many thousand bytes you want to set aside for the RAM disk. DOS allows you to allocate more memory than you have to spare after your application programs are loaded—so set the size of your RAM disk with care. RAMDISK.BAT lets you switch back and forth among different size RAM disks if your needs change during a work session.

The sector size may be either 128, 256, or 512 bytes. The largest size, 512 bytes, matches the actual sector size used by DOS, and is efficient from the standpoint that relatively large chunks of data can be read from a disk into memory at one time. Since a file even one byte longer than 512 bytes requires allocation of an entire extra sector, on average 256 bytes are wasted. (Actually, DOS allocates in minimum numbers of clusters—at least *four* with DOS 3.0 or later—so the waste in truth is four times that. For simplicity's sake, just think of the sectors, however.)

Because you may set sector size to 128 or 256 bytes with RAM disks, the average amount of space wasted can be cut in half or even in quarters. DOS at the same time needs to read two or three times as many sectors to obtain the same amount of data, but with speedy RAM disks this is seldom a consideration, whereas the amount of electronic disk space wasted *is* important. Accordingly, DOS sets a default value for sector size at 128 bytes with RAM disks, and we will use this value with RAMDISK.BAT.

The number of directory entries also should be set to realistically allow for the number of files you expect to store in your RAM disk. Each directory entry takes up 32 bytes of the RAM disk so that just setting the entries for 512 or some other large number is an inefficient use of resources. DOS' default value, 64 entries, is used in our utilities.

The optional /E switch may be used only if your computer has extended memory installed. If you try to use the switch anyway, DOS ignores the request to create a RAM disk and displays an error message.

Utility RAMDISK.BAT allows you to choose from among various combinations of RAM disks. It then replaces your current CONFIG.SYS file with one containing a line that instructs DOS to create the properly sized RAM disk. Then, the batch file reboots your computer. To accomplish the reboot, you need a short machine language utility called BOOT.COM, which can be typed in directly with DEBUG (it's only 17 bytes long), as a DEBUG script, or with the BASIC program that follows (the same loader portion used for INPUT.COM and YESNO.COM can be recycled, if you enter the new DATA lines, and substitute line 9 for 7 or 8 with the earlier programs). If you are unsure how to use DEBUG, review Chapter 3. A line-by-line discussion of how RAMDISK.BAT works appears in the section that follows.

BOOT.COM

```
1 ' *****************
2 ' *               *
3 ' *  BASIC LOADER *
4 ' *               *
5 ' *****************

6 ' *** Use ONE of these lines with correct DATA lines ***

9 F$="BOOT.COM":L=19: 'Use this line with BOOT.COM DATA

10 OPEN F$ AS #1 LEN = 1
20 FIELD #1,1 AS A$

25 ' *** Read Bytes From DATA ***

30 WHILE N<L
40 N=N+1
50 C=N MOD 9
60 IF C=0 GOTO 150
70 READ B
80 CU=CU+B
90 LSET A$ = CHR$(B)
100 PUT #1
110 WEND

115 ' *** Test Checksum Last Group ***
```

```
120 READ CHECK
130 N=N+6
140 IF CHECK=CU THEN GOTO 180 ELSE GOTO 170

145 ' *** Test Checksum Individual Groups ***

150 READ CHECK
160 IF CHECK=CU THEN CU=0:GOTO 30

165 ' *** Error Found ***

170 PRINT "Error in line ";INT(N/9)*10+180
180 CLOSE
----------------------------------------------------
185 ' *** Program Data For BOOT.COM ***
190 DATA 186,64,0,142,218,187,114,0,911
200 DATA 199,7,52,18,234,0,0,255,765
210 DATA 255,255
----------------------------------------------------
```

```
BOOT.COM

C>DEBUG
-a 100
xxxx:0100 MOV DX,040
xxxx:0103 MOV DS,DX
xxxx:0105 MOV BX,072
xxxx:0108 MOV WORD PTR BX,1234
xxxx:010C JMP FFFF:0000
xxxx:0110 <Enter>
-r CX
CX 0000
:11
-n BOOT.COM
-w
Writing 0011 Bytes
```

UTILITIES

RAMDISK.BAT

What it does: Allows adding or deleting RAM disks automatically.

Syntax: RAMDISK

Requirements: DOS 2.0

HOW TO USE IT

Type RAMDISK from the DOS prompt. The routine first asks you if you want to delete all RAM disks or whether you wish to add one. If you ask to delete RAM disks, any lines containing VDISK.SYS in your CONFIG.SYS file are stripped off.

When you *add* a RAM disk, the routine asks you to choose from among available sizes, ranging from 64K to 512K. A 360K size is also offered to allow creating a RAM disk the same size as a floppy disk. DOS' default sector size (128 bytes) and directory entry numbers (64) are used.

To keep this routine as short and simple as possible, one idiosyncrasy was left in: Blank lines are inserted into your CONFIG.SYS file. It would have been possible to avoid them by COPYing the old CONFIG.SYS file to a temporary filename and assembling new CONFIG.SYS files from a library of possible lines. The system actually used here, however, works more directly. The blank lines do no harm, since CONFIG.SYS is always be allocated a minimum of 2048 bytes of disk space, the extra lines are unlikely to push the file past that minimum. And on bootup DOS ignores the extra lines. As a famous Vulcan once remarked, "A difference that makes no difference is no difference."

Line-By-Line Description

Line 1:   Turn off screen echoing of commands.

Lines 2–3:   Title remarks.

Lines 4–5:   Log onto C: and change to top directory. Since system will be rebooted after the batch file is over, there is no need to keep track of which subdirectory the batch file was called from.

Line 6:   Clear the screen.

Line 7:   Echo null character (blank line) to screen.

Lines 8–11:   Offer choice of deleting or adding RAM disks.

Lines 12–13:   Ask for choice.

Lines 14–16:   Test for valid choice and loop back if invalid. Otherwise go to DELETE or ADD labels.

Line 17:   Start of DELETE.

Line 18:   Type contents of CONFIG.SYS, filtered through FIND with the /V switch. This tells FIND to locate only lines that do *not* contain the string specified, in this case "VDISK.SYS." The output of FIND is redirected to a temporary file called CONFIG.$$$.

Line 19:   The old version of CONFIG.SYS is erased.

Line 20:   The temporary file is renamed as CONFIG.SYS.

Line 21:   As function is completed, go to END.

Line 22:   Start of ADD routine.

Line 23:   Clear the screen.

Lines 24–31:   Display options for sizes of RAM disk.

Lines 32–33:   Input user's choice.

Lines 33–43:   Check for valid entry, and branch when found.

Line 44:   Loop back to INPUT if no valid key pressed.

Lines 45–69:   Set environment variable SIZE with value equal to RAM disk size selected.

Lines 70–71:   Echo line which sets RAM disk size through the MORE filter to the file CONFIG.SYS. The double greater-than signs cause the text to be appended to the end of the existing CONFIG.SYS file.

Line 72:   END of routine.

Line 73:   Call BOOT.COM, which reboots the system using the new CONFIG.SYS settings.

```
1.  ECHO OFF
2.  :       :: RAMDISK.BAT ::
3.  :       *** Installs/Removes RAM disks ***
```

```
 4.   C:
 5.   CD \
 6.   CLS
 7.   ECHO <Alt 255>
 8.   ECHO  Select mode:
 9.   ECHO  1. Delete all RAM disks
10.   ECHO  2. Add a RAM disk
11.   ECHO <Alt 255>
12.   :INPUT
13.   INPUT Enter choice:
14.   IF ERRORLEVEL 49 IF NOT ERRORLEVEL 50 GOTO DELETE
15.   IF ERRORLEVEL 50 IF NOT ERRORLEVEL 51 GOTO ADD
16.   GOTO INPUT
17.   :DELETE
18.   TYPE C:\CONFIG.SYS | FIND /V "VDISK.SYS" >C:\CONFIG.$$$
19.   ERASE C:\CONFIG.SYS >NUL
20.   RENAME CONFIG.$$$ CONFIG.SYS
21.   GOTO END
22.   :ADD
23.   CLS
24.   ECHO Choose size of RAM disk:
25.   ECHO <Alt 255>
26.   ECHO  1.  64K      5. 320K
27.   ECHO  2. 128K      6. 384K
28.   ECHO  3. 192K      7. 448K
29.   ECHO  4. 256K      8. 512K
30.   ECHO             9. 360K
31.   ECHO  <Alt 255>
32.   :INPUT
33.   INPUT Enter choice:
34.   IF ERRORLEVEL 49 IF NOT ERRORLEVEL 50 GOTO 1
35.   IF ERRORLEVEL 50 IF NOT ERRORLEVEL 51 GOTO 2
36.   IF ERRORLEVEL 51 IF NOT ERRORLEVEL 52 GOTO 3
37.   IF ERRORLEVEL 52 IF NOT ERRORLEVEL 53 GOTO 4
38.   IF ERRORLEVEL 53 IF NOT ERRORLEVEL 54 GOTO 5
39.   IF ERRORLEVEL 54 IF NOT ERRORLEVEL 55 GOTO 6
40.   IF ERRORLEVEL 55 IF NOT ERRORLEVEL 56 GOTO 7
41.   IF ERRORLEVEL 56 IF NOT ERRORLEVEL 57 GOTO 8
42.   IF ERRORLEVEL 57 IF NOT ERRORLEVEL 58 GOTO 9
43.   GOTO INPUT
44.   :1
45.   SET SIZE=64
46.   GOTO NEXT
47.   :2
48.   SET SIZE=128
49.   GOTO NEXT
```

```
50. :3
51. SET SIZE=192
52. GOTO NEXT
53. :4
54. SET SIZE=256
55. GOTO NEXT
56. :5
57. SET SIZE=320
58. GOTO NEXT
59. :6
60. SET SIZE=384
61. GOTO NEXT
62. :7
63. SET SIZE=448
64. GOTO NEXT
65. :8
66. SET SIZE=512
67. GOTO NEXT
68. :9
69. SET SIZE=360
70. :NEXT
71. ECHO DEVICE=C:\DOS\VDISK.SYS %SIZE% | MORE >>CONFIG.SYS
72. :END
73. BOOT
-----------------------------------------------------------
```

CHAR.BAT

What it does: Provides skeleton for custom key input menus.

Syntax: CHAR

Requirements: DOS 2.0

HOW TO USE IT

As printed, this routine merely accepts one keyboard character and then echoes it to the screen. You may type it in, *adding* the lines left out and represented by ellipses for the sake of brevity. That is, instead of printing lines such as:

```
:A
ECHO A
GOTO END
:B
```

```
    ECHO B
    GOTO END
```

it was left to the reader to type these in without being given more than a model. You can type in this routine once, and then recycle it for your own menus or other batch files requiring capturing a keystroke. Simply delete the lines not needed for your particular batch file. The most common keys needed, the uppercase letters from A to Z (INPUT.COM converts to uppercase, remember), the numerals 0 to 9, plus Enter, the hyphen, and period, are all included. You should substitute the result of your choice for the simple echoing of screen characters provided.

Line-By-Line Description

Line 1:   Turn off echoing of screen commands.

Lines 2–3:   Title remarks.

Lines 6–7:   Enter character.

Lines 8–46:   Test for valid character and branch.

Line 47:   Loop back if invalid.

Lines 48–135:   Results desired for each key pressed.

```
--------------------------------------------------------
1.   ECHO OFF
2.   :        :: CHAR.BAT
3.   :        *** Checks for keyboard characters ***
4.   ECHO OFF
5.   ECHO Enter character:
6.   :INPUT
7.   INPUT
8.   IF ERRORLEVEL 65 IF NOT ERRORLEVEL 66 GOTO A
9.   IF ERRORLEVEL 66 IF NOT ERRORLEVEL 67 GOTO B
10.  IF ERRORLEVEL 67 IF NOT ERRORLEVEL 68 GOTO C
11.  IF ERRORLEVEL 68 IF NOT ERRORLEVEL 69 GOTO D
12.  IF ERRORLEVEL 69 IF NOT ERRORLEVEL 70 GOTO E
13.  IF ERRORLEVEL 70 IF NOT ERRORLEVEL 71 GOTO F
14.  IF ERRORLEVEL 71 IF NOT ERRORLEVEL 72 GOTO G
15.  IF ERRORLEVEL 72 IF NOT ERRORLEVEL 73 GOTO H
16.  IF ERRORLEVEL 73 IF NOT ERRORLEVEL 74 GOTO I
17.  IF ERRORLEVEL 74 IF NOT ERRORLEVEL 75 GOTO J
```

```
18.   IF ERRORLEVEL 75 IF NOT ERRORLEVEL 76 GOTO K
19.   IF ERRORLEVEL 76 IF NOT ERRORLEVEL 77 GOTO L
20.   IF ERRORLEVEL 77 IF NOT ERRORLEVEL 78 GOTO M
21.   IF ERRORLEVEL 78 IF NOT ERRORLEVEL 79 GOTO N
22.   IF ERRORLEVEL 79 IF NOT ERRORLEVEL 80 GOTO O
23.   IF ERRORLEVEL 80 IF NOT ERRORLEVEL 81 GOTO P
24.   IF ERRORLEVEL 81 IF NOT ERRORLEVEL 82 GOTO Q
25.   IF ERRORLEVEL 82 IF NOT ERRORLEVEL 83 GOTO R
26.   IF ERRORLEVEL 83 IF NOT ERRORLEVEL 84 GOTO S
27.   IF ERRORLEVEL 84 IF NOT ERRORLEVEL 85 GOTO T
28.   IF ERRORLEVEL 85 IF NOT ERRORLEVEL 86 GOTO U
29.   IF ERRORLEVEL 86 IF NOT ERRORLEVEL 87 GOTO V
30.   IF ERRORLEVEL 87 IF NOT ERRORLEVEL 88 GOTO W
31.   IF ERRORLEVEL 88 IF NOT ERRORLEVEL 89 GOTO X
32.   IF ERRORLEVEL 89 IF NOT ERRORLEVEL 90 GOTO Y
33.   IF ERRORLEVEL 90 IF NOT ERRORLEVEL 91 GOTO Z
34.   IF ERRORLEVEL 49 IF NOT ERRORLEVEL 50 GOTO 1
35.   IF ERRORLEVEL 50 IF NOT ERRORLEVEL 51 GOTO 2
36.   IF ERRORLEVEL 51 IF NOT ERRORLEVEL 52 GOTO 3
37.   IF ERRORLEVEL 52 IF NOT ERRORLEVEL 53 GOTO 4
38.   IF ERRORLEVEL 53 IF NOT ERRORLEVEL 54 GOTO 5
39.   IF ERRORLEVEL 54 IF NOT ERRORLEVEL 55 GOTO 6
40.   IF ERRORLEVEL 55 IF NOT ERRORLEVEL 56 GOTO 7
41.   IF ERRORLEVEL 56 IF NOT ERRORLEVEL 57 GOTO 8
42.   IF ERRORLEVEL 57 IF NOT ERRORLEVEL 58 GOTO 9
43.   IF ERRORLEVEL 48 IF NOT ERRORLEVEL 49 GOTO 0
44.   IF ERRORLEVEL 46 IF NOT ERRORLEVEL 47 GOTO ENTER
45.   IF ERRORLEVEL 45 IF NOT ERRORLEVEL 46 GOTO HYPHEN
46.   IF ERRORLEVEL 62 IF NOT ERRORLEVEL 63 GOTO PERIOD
47.   GOTO INPUT
48.   :ENTER
49.   ECHO ENTER
50.   GOTO END
51.   :HYPHEN
52.   ECHO HYPHEN
53.   GOTO END
54.   :PERIOD
55.   ECHO PERIOD
56.   GOTO END
57.   :A
58.   ECHO A
59.   GOTO END
60.   ...
...   ...
135.  ...
136.  :END
------------------------------------------------------------
```

Menu System

What it does: Provides many menu functions with allowances for user customization.

Syntax: MAINMENU

Requirements: DOS 2.0

HOW TO USE IT

This menu system has room for you to add batch files for your own applications and introduces the concept of batch file subroutines.

A batch file can have a single section that is called by other sections of the file quite simply. Just set an environment variable (here we called it FROM) with the name of the portion of the batch file you want the routine to go to when finished. Then, include a line that reads: GOTO %FROM% at the end of your "subroutine" to direct control to the desired location.

You need to prepare batch files that call your specific application programs and call them LOTUS.BAT, DB.BAT, WP.BAT, and so on. If you elect to name them something else, make appropriate changes in the APPLICAT.BAT file.

This menu system lets you use various DOS commands and utilities like the Norton Utilities. You can also leave bulletins for other users of your computer. In the USERS Menu, you should substitute your users' names. You may also change the routines to provide for different utilities and functions. Add a line in the batch files, which call them to return you to MAINMENU when finished.

For the portions that call BASIC function keys, you should have FUNCT1.BAS and FUNCT2.BAS programs prepared with FUNCTION.BAT in Chapter 14.

Because these menus all operate more or less the same way using principles discussed fully in this book, line-by-line descriptions of each would be repetitive. Only a few new techniques are used.

For example, note the interesting use of INPUT.COM in several of the files as a replacement for PAUSE. Unlike PAUSE, you may substitute any prompt you like, yet the batch file still continues when a key is pressed. In this case, the ERRORLEVEL is simply ignored.

In BULLETIN.BAT, COPY CON works *within* the batch file to allow the user to create bulletins. The user is directed to type F6 and hit Enter when finished typing the bulletin. This returns processing to the batch file, where the routine adds the bulletin just typed to the existing bulletin message base. Also note in this routine how environment variables store the TO and FROM information for each bulletin.

The extensive use of Alt-key combinations in these routines demonstrates quite clearly why I have left such enhancements up to the reader until this point.

Abbreviations had to be used to make the listings even readable: when you see <18 Alt 205>, it means you should type Alt 255 18 times. Better yet, use your word processor to enter these files, and *copy* the characters. Since all the menus use the same layout, design one and copy it for all the other routines.

Listing 15-1. Menus.

```
ECHO OFF
:       :: MAINMENU.BAT
:    *** Main Menu ***
ECHO <Alt 255>
ECHO <Alt 201><18 Alt 205><Alt 187>
ECHO <Alt 186>        Main        <Alt 186>
ECHO <Alt 200><18 Alt 205><Alt 206><18 Alt 205><Alt 187>
ECHO                     <Alt 186>      Menu        <Alt 186>
ECHO                     <Alt 200><18 Alt 205><Alt 188>
ECHO <Alt 201><18 Alt 205><Alt 203><18 Alt 205><Alt 187>
ECHO <Alt 186> 1. Applications  <Alt 186> 4. DOS Commands <Alt
186>
ECHO <Alt 186> 2. Directories   <Alt 186> 5. Bulletins    <Alt
186>
ECHO <Alt 186> 3. Utilities     <Alt 186>                 <Alt
186>
ECHO <Alt 186>                   <Alt 186>                 <Alt
186>
ECHO <Alt 200><18 Alt 205><Alt 202><18 Alt 205><Alt 188>
:INPUT
INPUT Enter your choice (1-5) :
IF ERRORLEVEL 53 IF NOT ERRORLEVEL 54 GOTO BULLETIN
IF ERRORLEVEL 52 GOTO DOS
IF ERRORLEVEL 51 GOTO UTILITY
IF ERRORLEVEL 50 GOTO DIRECTORIES
IF ERRORLEVEL 49 GOTO APPLICATIONS
GOTO INPUT
:APPLICATIONS
APPLICAT
:UTILITY
UTILITY
:DIRECTORIES
DIRECT
:BULLETIN
BULLETIN
:DOS
CLS
ECHO Enter DOS command:
PROMPT=To return to menu type MAINMENU.$_$n$g
```

Listing 15-1. Continued

```
ECHO OFF
:   :: UTILITY.BAT ::
:  *** Utilities routine ***
CLS
:START
ECHO <Alt 255>
ECHO <Alt 201><18 Alt 205><Alt 187>
ECHO <Alt 186>     Utility        <Alt 186>
ECHO <Alt 200><18 Alt 205><Alt 206><18 Alt 205><Alt 187>
ECHO                        <Alt 186>      Menu        <Alt 186>
ECHO                        <Alt 200><18 Alt 205><Alt 188>
ECHO <Alt 201><18 Alt 205><Alt 203><18 Alt 205><Alt 187>
ECHO <Alt 186> 1. Format        <Alt 186> 4. DOS Commands <Alt
186>
ECHO <Alt 186> 2. BASIC         <Alt 186> 5. Norton Util. <Alt
186>
ECHO <Alt 186> 3. Delete Files  <Alt 186> Q  Quit         <Alt
186>
ECHO <Alt 186>                  <Alt 186>                  <Alt
186>
ECHO <Alt 200><18 Alt 205><Alt 202><18 Alt 205><Alt 188>
:INPUT
INPUT Enter your choice (1-5) :
IF ERRORLEVEL 81 IF NOT ERRORLEVEL 82 GOTO RETURN
IF ERRORLEVEL 53 IF NOT ERRORLEVEL 54 GOTO NORTON
IF ERRORLEVEL 52 GOTO DOS
IF ERRORLEVEL 51 GOTO PURGE
IF ERRORLEVEL 50 GOTO BASIC
IF ERRORLEVEL 49 GOTO FORMAT
GOTO INPUT
:RETURN
MAINMEN
:FORMAT
ECHO <Alt 255>
ECHO <Alt 201><18 Alt 205><Alt 187>
ECHO <Alt 186>     Format        <Alt 186>
ECHO <Alt 200><18 Alt 205><Alt 206><18 Alt 205><Alt 187>
ECHO                        <Alt 186>      Menu        <Alt 186>
ECHO                        <Alt 200><18 Alt 205><Alt 188>
ECHO <Alt 201><18 Alt 205><Alt 203><18 Alt 205><Alt 187>
ECHO <Alt 186> 1. Format A:     <Alt 186>                  <Alt
186>
ECHO <Alt 186> 2. Format B:     <Alt 186>                  <Alt
186>
ECHO <Alt 186> 3. Format C:     <Alt 186> Q  Quit          <Alt
186>
```

Listing 15-1. Continued

```
ECHO <Alt 186>                    <Alt 186>                    <Alt
186>
ECHO <Alt 200><18 Alt 205><Alt 202><18 Alt 205><Alt 188>
:INPUT
INPUT Enter your choice (1-3) :
IF ERRORLEVEL 81 IF NOT ERRORLEVEL 82 GOTO START
IF ERRORLEVEL 51 IF NOT ERRORLEVEL 52 GOTO C
IF ERRORLEVEL 50 GOTO B
IF ERRORLEVEL 49 GOTO A
GOTO INPUT
:A
FORMAT A:
UTILITY
:B
FORMAT B:
UTILITY
:C
ECHO <ALT 7>
ECHO ============================
ECHO ARE YOU CERTAIN YOU WANT TO
ECHO FORMAT YOUR HARD DISK?
ECHO ============================
YESNO
IF ERRORLEVEL 78 IF NOT ERRORLEVEL 79 GOTO START
FORMAT C:
:BASIC
ECHO <Alt 255>
ECHO <Alt 201><18 Alt 205><Alt 187>
ECHO <Alt 186>      BASIC       <Alt 186>
ECHO <Alt 200><18 Alt 205><Alt 206><18 Alt 205><Alt 187>
ECHO                     <Alt 186>     Menu       <Alt 186>
ECHO                     <Alt 200><18 Alt 205><Alt 188>
ECHO <Alt 201><18 Alt 205><Alt 203><18 Alt 205><Alt 187>
ECHO <Alt 186> 1. BASIC Logged A <Alt 186> 4.BASIC FUNCT 2 <Alt
186>
ECHO <Alt 186> 2. BASIC Logged B <Alt 186>                <Alt
186>
ECHO <Alt 186> 3. BASIC FUNCT 1  <Alt 186> Q  Quit        <Alt
186>
ECHO <Alt 186>                    <Alt 186>                <Alt
186>
ECHO <Alt 200><18 Alt 205><Alt 202><18 Alt 205><Alt 188>
:INPUT
INPUT Enter your choice (1-4) :
IF ERRORLEVEL 81 IF NOT ERRORLEVEL 82 GOTO START
IF ERRORLEVEL 52 IF NOT ERRORLEVEL 53 GOTO FUNCT2
```

Listing 15-1. Continued

```
IF ERRORLEVEL 51 GOTO FUNCT1
IF ERRORLEVEL 50 GOTO LOGB
IF ERRORLEVEL 49 GOTO LOGA
GOTO INPUT
:FUNCT2
BASICA FUNCT2
MAINMENU
:FUNCT1
BASICA FUNCT2
MAINMENU
:LOGB
B:
BASICA
MAINMENU
:LOGA
A:
BASICA
MAINMENU
:PURGE
ECHO TYPE PURGE filename
GOTO END
:NORTON
C:
CD\NORTON
NU
GOTO START
:DOS
CLS
ECHO Enter DOS command:
:END
PROMPT=To return to menu type MAINMENU.$_$n$g
ECHO OFF
:   :: DIRECT.BAT ::
:   *** Directories routine ***
CLS
:START
ECHO <Alt 255>
ECHO <Alt 201><18 Alt 205><Alt 187>
ECHO <Alt 186>  Directories    <Alt 186>
ECHO <Alt 200><18 Alt 205><Alt 206><18 Alt 205><Alt 187>
ECHO                  <Alt 186>    Menu      <Alt 186>
ECHO                  <Alt 200><18 Alt 205><Alt 188>
ECHO <Alt 201><18 Alt 205><Alt 203><18 Alt 205><Alt 187>
ECHO <Alt 186> 1. Directory A:  <Alt 186>                  <Alt
186>
ECHO <Alt 186> 2. Directory B:  <Alt 186>                  <Alt
```

Listing 15-1. Continued

```
186>
ECHO <Alt 186> 3. Directory C:   <Alt 186> Q  Quit         <Alt
186>
ECHO <Alt 186>                    <Alt 186>                 <Alt
186>
ECHO <Alt 200><18 Alt 205><Alt 202><18 Alt 205><Alt 188>
:INPUT
INPUT Enter your choice (1-3) :
IF ERRORLEVEL 81 IF NOT ERRORLEVEL 82 GOTO RETURN
IF ERRORLEVEL 51 IF NOT ERRORLEVEL 52 GOTO DIRC
IF ERRORLEVEL 50 GOTO DIRB
IF ERRORLEVEL 49 GOTO DIRA
GOTO INPUT
:RETURN
MAINMENU
:DIRA
DIR A: | SORT
INPUT Press a key when ready to return
CLS
MAINMENU
:DIRB
DIR B: | SORT
INPUT Press a key when ready to return
CLS
MAINMENU
:DIRC
DIR C: | SORT
INPUT Press a key when ready to return
CLS
MAINMENU


ECHO OFF
: :: BULLETIN.BAT ::
:  *** Bulletins ***
:START
CLS
ECHO <Alt 255>
ECHO <Alt 201><18 Alt 205><Alt 187>
ECHO <Alt 186>     Bulletins    <Alt 186>
ECHO <Alt 200><18 Alt 205><Alt 206><18 Alt 205><Alt 187>
ECHO                 <Alt 186>     Menu       <Alt 186>
ECHO                 <Alt 200><18 Alt 205><Alt 188>
ECHO <Alt 201><18 Alt 205><Alt 203><18 Alt 205><Alt 187>
ECHO <Alt 186> 1. Post Bulletin  <Alt 186>               <Alt
186>
ECHO <Alt 186> 2. Read Bulletin  <Alt 186>               <Alt
```

Listing 15-1. Continued

```
186>
ECHO <Alt 186> 3. Erase Bulletin <Alt 186> Q  Quit        <Alt
186>
ECHO <Alt 186>                    <Alt 186>                <Alt
186>
ECHO <Alt 200><18 Alt 205><Alt 202><18 Alt 205><Alt 188>
:INPUT
INPUT Enter your choice (1-5) :
IF ERRORLEVEL 81 IF NOT ERRORLEVEL 82 GOTO RETURN
IF ERRORLEVEL 51 IF NOT ERRORLEVEL 52 GOTO ERASE
IF ERRORLEVEL 50 GOTO READ
IF ERRORLEVEL 49 GOTO POST
GOTO INPUT
:RETURN
MAINMENU
:POST
SET FROM=PNEXT
GOTO USERS
:PNEXT
ECHO Enter Bulletin.
ECHO Press F6 and Enter when Finished.
ECHO 0        10        20       30       40       50
ECHO !---+----+----+----+----+----+----+----+----+----!
COPY CON:TEMP.$$$
COPY C:\BATCHES\%BULL%.ASC+TEMP.$$$ TEMP2.$$$
ERASE C:\BATCHES\%BULL%.ASC
COPY TEMP2.$$$ C:\BATCHES\%BULL%.ASC
BULLETIN
:READ
SET FROM=RNEXT
GOTO USERS
:RNEXT
MORE<C:\BATCHES\%BULL%.ASC
INPUT Press a key to continue.
CLS
ECHO Would you like to erase these bulletins?
YESNO
IF ERRORLEVEL 89 IF NOT ERRORLEVEL 90 GOTO KILL
BULLETIN
:KILL
ERASE C:\BATCHES\%BULL%.ASC
BULLETIN
:ERASE
SET FROM=%ENEXT%
GOTO USERS
:ENEXT
```

Listing 15-1. Continued

```
CLS
ECHO Would you like to erase %BULL%'s bulletins?
YESNO
IF ERRORLEVEL 89 IF NOT ERRORLEVEL 90 GOTO KILL
BULLETIN
:USERS
CLS
ECHO <Alt 255>
ECHO <Alt 201><18 Alt 205><Alt 187>
ECHO <Alt 186>      Users       <Alt 186>
ECHO <Alt 200><18 Alt 205><Alt 206><18 Alt 205><Alt 187>
ECHO                    <Alt 186>      Menu         <Alt 186>
ECHO                    <Alt 200><18 Alt 205><Alt 188>
ECHO <Alt 201><18 Alt 205><Alt 203><18 Alt 205><Alt 187>
ECHO <Alt 186> 1.  User #1       <Alt 186> 5.  User #5      <Alt
186>
ECHO <Alt 186> 2.  User #2       <Alt 186> 6.  User #6      <Alt
186>
ECHO <Alt 186> 3.  User #3       <Alt 186>                  <Alt
186>
ECHO <Alt 186> 4.  User #4       <Alt 186> Q Quit           <Alt
186>
ECHO <Alt 200><18 Alt 205><Alt 202><18 Alt 205><Alt 188>
:INPUT
INPUT Enter your choice (1-6) :
IF ERRORLEVEL 81 IF NOT ERRORLEVEL 82 GOTO RETURN
IF ERRORLEVEL 54 IF NOT ERRORLEVEL 55 GOTO 6
IF ERRORLEVEL 53 GOTO 5
IF ERRORLEVEL 52 GOTO 4
IF ERRORLEVEL 51 GOTO 3
IF ERRORLEVEL 50 GOTO 2
IF ERRORLEVEL 49 GOTO 1
GOTO INPUT
:6
SET BULL=6
GOTO %FROM%
:5
SET BULL=5
GOTO %FROM%
:4
SET BULL=4
GOTO %FROM%
:3
SET BULL=3
GOTO %FROM%
:2
```

Listing 15-1. Continued

```
SET BULL=2
GOTO %FROM%
:1
SET BULL=1
GOTO %FROM%
ECHO OFF



: :: APPLICAT.BAT ::
:  *** Applications Menu ***
:START
CLS
ECHO <Alt 255>
ECHO <Alt 201><18 Alt 205><Alt 187>
ECHO <Alt 186>   Applications   <Alt 186>
ECHO <Alt 200><18 Alt 205><Alt 206><18 Alt 205><Alt 187>
ECHO                   <Alt 186>     Menu        <Alt 186>
ECHO                   <Alt 200><18 Alt 205><Alt 188>
ECHO <Alt 201><18 Alt 205><Alt 203><18 Alt 205><Alt 187>
ECHO <Alt 186> 1. LOTUS          <Alt 186> 4. DOS Commands <Alt
186>
ECHO <Alt 186> 2. Word Processng <Alt 186> 5. Telecom       <Alt
186>
ECHO <Alt 186> 3. Data Base      <Alt 186> Q  Quit          <Alt
186>
ECHO <Alt 186>                   <Alt 186>                   <Alt
186>
ECHO <Alt 200><18 Alt 205><Alt 202><18 Alt 205><Alt 188>
:INPUT
INPUT Enter your choice (1-5) :
IF ERRORLEVEL 81 IF NOT ERRORLEVEL 82 GOTO RETURN
IF ERRORLEVEL 53 IF NOT ERRORLEVEL 54 GOTO TELECOM
IF ERRORLEVEL 52 GOTO DOS
IF ERRORLEVEL 51 GOTO DATABASE
IF ERRORLEVEL 50 GOTO WP
IF ERRORLEVEL 49 GOTO LOTUS
GOTO INPUT
:RETURN
MAINMENU
:LOTUS
LOTUS
:WP
WP
:DB
DB
:TELECOM
COM
```

Listing 15-1. Continued

```
:DOS
CLS
ECHO Enter DOS command:
PROMPT=To return to menu type MAINMENU.$_$n$g
```

SUMMARY

In this chapter we presented a complex menu system that called other batch files, used "subroutines" in which environment variables told the batch file where to "return," and applied other sophisticated techniques. A new machine language utility, BOOT.COM, was introduced to allow resetting the computer after you make changes in the CONFIG.SYS file while adding and deleting RAM disks.

In the next chapter, we'll look at some of the ways DOS can make adjustments in your hardware, including setting up a printer, adjusting communication parameters, and turning a modem on and off.

16

Working Your Hardware

INTRODUCTION

In this chapter, we'll customize DOS a bit to take control of the computer's hardware, including the parallel and serial ports, your display adapter, and a Hayes-compatible modem. Routines will be presented that allow setting up a printer, redirecting output of a printer to the COM port, adjusting communication parameters, and centering the screen on boot-up. Also supplied are a menu that allows you to switch from one display adapter to another without learning the syntax of the MODE command, and two small utilities that turn a Hayes modem on and off and disable or enable its speaker.

We'll start with the MODE command, is an external DOS command that allows exerting a bit of control over your IBM or compatible computer's hardware. This complex, multifunction command can control the protocol characteristics of either of two asynchronous communication adapter ports (COM1 or COM2), three parallel printer ports (LPT1, LPT2, or LPT3), as well as your video display.

Because of this flexibility, MODE can be a bit difficult to understand and its syntax impossible to remember. So, we'll set up five new commands of our

237

own, each with an easy-to-remember name and streamlined syntax, to perform all these functions. Where necessary, we can even use BASIC programs for prompting and to allow the operator to choose from several options.

First, you'll need to know MODE's several different uses. To set the characteristics of an IBM printer (or a compatible printer, such as an Epson printer, that accepts the same commands), the syntax is as follows:

```
MODE LPT#: characters per line,lines per inch,P
```

You must replace "#" by the number of the printer to be used, either LPT1, LPT2, or LPT3. The other parameters are optional. If you want to leave that printer characteristic as it is, just use a comma instead of the parameter. Characters per line can be specified as either 80 or 132; line spacing 6 or 8. The "P" parameter, specifies continuous retries on time-out errors. This allows your program to keep trying if the printer is momentarily disconnected.

So, we might enter:

```
MODE LPT1: 80
MODE LPT1: ,132
MODE LPT2: ,,P
```

Each of these sets one parameter and one only. Of course, all may be used on a single line.

In its second "mode," the command can switch back and forth between the monochrome display adapter and color graphics display adapter (if you have both) or set the characteristics of the color graphics adapter. The syntax is:

```
MODE [type of display],shift,[T]
```

Taking the last two parameters first, if you replace shift with either "R" or "L" the display shifts one character to the right or left, to help align the screen. You may repeat the R or L parameter to move more than one character, but the screen can be "moved" only two positions in either direction from its powerup position. By specifying "T," you can request a test pattern to help in this alignment. The monochrome adapter cannot be adjusted in this manner; this portion of the command works only with the color graphics adapter.

The first parameter, type of display, can be one of the following choices:

MONO: Make the monochrome screen the active display.

40:     40-character-wide color/graphics display.

80:     80-character-wide color/graphics display.

BW40: 40-character-wide color/graphics display, but with color image disabled, producing black-and-white only.

BW80: 80-character-wide color/graphics display, but with color image disabled, producing black-and-white only.

CO40: 40-character-wide color display.

CO80: 80-character- wide color display.

Note that only programs that use color display color even if the color/graphics display adapter is set for a color display.

As you may know, both modems and serial printers are devices that can use the asynchronous port of the IBM computer. MODE lets you set this port to handle this type of communication, using the following syntax:

MODE COM#: baud,parity,databits,stopbits,P

The "#" should be replaced by either 1 or 2, depending on whether you want to send the command to COM1 or COM2. Many users have two asynchronous ports, and use one for their modem, and the other for a serial printer. Baud rate, parity, data bits, and stop bits are the communication settings that must match those of the device receiving the information. As with using MODE to set the LPT device, the P parameter commands continuous retries on time-out errors. Also as with the previous LPT command, you may omit a parameter by using a comma instead. The first two digits of the baud rate can be used instead of the full value, for example, 96 instead of 9600.

You can force DOS to direct output destined for your parallel printer to a serial printer instead, by using MODE in the following manner:

MODE LPT#:=COM#:

Various values can be used to replace both # in the above, so that LPT2 can be directed to COM2 or another configuration.

The batch files in this chapter break down each of these commands into more easily handled chunks. PRINTER.BAT calls a BASIC program, PRINTER.BAS, that prompts for each of the printer parameters, and writes a setup file that you can call (with a batch file, if you wish) any time you want that particular setup.

PAR.BAT redirects parallel output to the serial printer, while COMM.BAT either uses the default settings built into the program (or those you supply as a replacement) or an alternaive set of parameters. CENTER.BAT centers your screen, while ADAPTER.BAT and ADAPTER.BAS supplies a menu useful for setting the monochrome or color graphics adapter to your choice of configuration.

UTILITIES

PRINTER.BAT

What it does: Calls BASIC program, which allows writing printer setup batch files.

Syntax: PRINTER

Requirements: DOS 2.0 or later.

HOW TO USE IT

Type PRINTER. The BASIC program loadeds automatically and asks you about all the parameters can be set. You can supply the name of a setup file and this will be stored on your disk. If you give this file a name ending in .BAT, you may invoke those settings by typing the file's root name at any time from DOS. Or, you can install the files name or the file itself in a batch file of your own (such as AUTOEXEC.BAT).

Line-By-Line Description (PRINTER.BAT)

Line 1:   Turn off screen echoing of commands.

Lines 2–3: Title remarks.

Line 4:   Call up PRINTER.BAS.

PRINTER.BAS, like all BASIC programs in this book, is set off with remarks that show each portion's function.

```
-----------------------------------------------------------
1.   ECHO OFF
2.   :        :: PRINTER.BAT ::
3.   :        *** Calls PRINTER.BAS ***
4.   BASICA PRINTER.BAS
-----------------------------------------------------------
```

Listing 16-1. PRINTER.BAS Program

```
------------------------------------------------------
10 ' ****************
20 ' *              *
30 ' * PRINTER SETUP *
40 ' *              *
50 ' ****************
60 CLS
70 ROW=1:COL=10:WIDE=26:DEEP=5
80 GOSUB 420
90 LOCATE 3,12
100 COLOR 0,7

105 ' *** Choose Name of Setup ***

110 PRINT"Parallel Printer Setup"
120 COLOR 7,0
130 LOCATE 10,2
140 PRINT"Name of printer setup: ";TAB(47);
150 LINE INPUT PRINTER$

155 ' *** Enter printer number ***

160 LOCATE 11,2
170 PRINT"Enter printer number (1,2, or 3) :";
180 PN$=INKEY$:IF PN$='' GOTO 180
190 PN=VAL(PN$):IF PN<1 OR PN>3 THEN BEEP:GOTO 180
200 PRINT TAB(47)PN$

205 ' *** Set characters per line ***

210 LOCATE 12,2
220 PRINT SPACE$(40);
230 LOCATE 12,2
240 PRINT"Enter 80 or 132 characters per line:";TAB(45);
250 INPUT COLUMN$
260 IF COLUMN$="80" OR COLUMN$="132" GOTO 270 ELSE GOTO 210

265 ' *** Set lines per inch ***

270 LOCATE 13,2
280 PRINT"Enter 6 or 8 lines per inch :";TAB(45);
290 INPUT LINES.PER.INCH$
300 IF LINES.PER.INCH$="6" OR LINES.PER.INCH$="8" GOTO 310 ELSE GOTO 270

305 ' *** Specify timeout action ***

310 LOCATE 14,2
320 PRINT "Continuous retries on timeout? (Y/N) :";TAB(47);
330 TIMEOUT$=INKEY$:IF TIMEOUT$="" GOTO 330
```

Listing 16-1. Continued

```
340 PRINT TIMEOUT$
350 IF TIMEOUT$="Y" OR TIMEOUT$="y" THEN TIMEOUT$="P" ELSE TIMEOUT$=""

355 ' *** Write file to disk ***

360 OPEN "O",1,PRINTER$
370 PRINT #1," .
    ECHO OFF"
380 PRINT #1,"MODE LPT";PN$;":
    ";COLUMN$;",";LINES.PER.INCH$;
390 IF TIMEOUT$="P" THEN PRINT#1,",P" ELSE PRINT #1,""
400 CLOSE 1

405 ' *** Return to DOS ***

410 SYSTEM

415 ' *** Draw A Box ***

420 LOCATE ROW,COL
430 PRINT CHR$(201);
440 FOR N=COL+1 TO COL+WIDE-1
450 PRINT CHR$(205);
460 NEXT N
470 PRINT CHR$(187)
480 FOR N=ROW+1 TO ROW+DEEP-1
490 LOCATE N,COL
500 PRINT CHR$(186);
510 LOCATE N,COL+WIDE
520 PRINT CHR$(186);
530 NEXT N
540 LOCATE ROW+DEEP,COL
550 PRINT CHR$(200);
560 FOR N=COL+1 TO COL+WIDE-1
570 PRINT CHR$(205);
580 NEXT N
590 PRINT CHR$(188)
600 RETURN
```

PAR.BAT

What it does: Redirects Parallel printer output to a serial printer.

Syntax: PAR

Requirements: DOS 2.0 or later.

HOW TO USE IT

Examine line 4, and change "LPT1" or "COM2" to suit your own configuration. That is, if you want to send the output from LPT2 to COM1, substitute the proper values in that line of the batch file. Type PAR to summon batch file.

Line-By-Line Description

Line 1:   Turn off screen echoing of commands.

Lines 2–3: Title remarks.

Line 4:   Redirect printer output to asynchronous port.

```
----------------------------------------------------------
1.    ECHO OFF
2.    :       :: PAR.BAT ::
3.    :       *** Redirects Parallel Output to Serial
                  Printer ***
4.    MODE LPT1:=COM2
----------------------------------------------------------
```

COMM.BAT

What it does: Sets asynchronous port to either your most-used settings or an alternate set you have specified.

Syntax: Comm

                Comm Alt

Requirements: DOS 2.0 or later.

HOW TO USE IT

Substitute settings you prefer for those listed in lines 17 and 20. Then, type either COMM or COMM ALT to set the asynchronous port to the first or second set of parameters. Or, you could have line 17 set COM1, and line 20 set COM2 by changing line 20 to specify COM2 instead of COM1. Then, ALT would configure the alternate port, instead of using an alternate configuration.

Line-By-Line Description

Line 1:   Turn off screen echoing of commands.

Lines 2–3:   Title remarks.

Lines 4–5:   If %1 parameter is HELP, goto HELP message.

Line 6:   If no parameter entered, goto default settings.

Lines 7–8:   If ALT entered, goto alternate settings.

Line 9:   If no match, goto default anyway.

Lines 10–15:   Display HELP message.

Lines 16–18:   Configure for default settings.

Lines 19–20:   Configure for alternate settings.

Lines 21–22:   Exit file.

```
--------------------------------------------------------------
1.    ECHO OFF
2.    :       :: COMM.BAT ::
3.    :          *** Sets Communications Parameters ***
4.    IF "%1"=="help" GOTO HELP
5.    IF "%1" == "HELP" GOTO HELP
6.    IF "%1" == "" GOTO DEFAULT
7.    IF "%1" == "ALT" GOTO ALT
8.    IF "%1" == "alt" GOTO ALT
9.    GOTO DEFAULT
10.   :HELP
11.   ECHO      Type COMM
12.   ECHO      If you add "ALT", alternate settings
13.   ECHO      will be used.
14.   ECHO      <Alt 255>
15.   GOTO EXIT
16.   :DEFAULT
17.   MODE COM1:1200,8,1
18.   GOTO EXIT
19.   :ALT
20.   MODE COM1:300,7,1
21.   :EXIT
22.   CLS
--------------------------------------------------------------
```

CENTER.BAT

What it does: Centers screen automatically.

Syntax: CENTER

Requirements: DOS 2.0 or later.

HOW TO USE IT

If you use a non-IBM display, you may find that it is consistently centered improperly. Call this CENTER command or include line 4 in your AUTOEXEC.BAT file to produce a properlycentered screen automatically.

As written, file assumes that screen must be moved two characters to the right. You can cut this to one character by removing one of the Rs or by directing the centering in the other direction, by substituting Ls. Once the proper amount of correction has been determined, you'll not have to make this adjustment in the batch file again.

Call the command by typing CENTER from DOS.

Line-By-Line Description

Line 1:   Turn off screen echoing of commands.

Lines 2–3: Title remarks.

Line 4:   Center the screen.

```
-------------------------------------------------------
1.    ECHO OFF
2.    :       :: CENTER.BAT ::
3.    :       *** Centers Screen Automatically ***
4.    MODE CO80,R,R
-------------------------------------------------------
```

ADAPTER.BAT

What it does: Calls ADAPTER.BAS, which allows choosing display adapter from a menu.

Syntax: ADAPTER

Requirements: DOS 2.0 or later.

HOW TO USE IT

Type ADAPTER, and follow the prompts from the BASIC program. You should not try to set a display adapter that you do not have installed in your computer. ADAPTER.BAS writes a batch file, "DISP.BAT" that you can call at any time (Type DISP) to reproduce the settings you enter. When the program ends, control returns to the batch file, which calls DISP.BAT before exiting to DOS.

Line-by-Line Description (DISPLAY.BAT)

Line 1:   Turn off screen echoing of commands.

Lines 2–3:   Title remarks.

Line 4:   Load DISPLAY.BAS.

Line 5:   Call DISP.BAT.

```
---------------------------------------------------------
1.   ECHO OFF
2.   :      :: ADAPTER.BAT ::
3.   :      *** Choose Display From Menu ***
4.   BASIC ADAPTER.BAS
5.   DISP.BAT
---------------------------------------------------------


---------------------------------------------------------
10 ' **************
20 ' *            *
30 ' * ADAPTER.BAS *
40 ' *            *
50 ' **************
60 KEY OFF
70 SCREEN 0,0,0
80 DATA BW40,BW80,CO40,CO80,MONO

85 ' *** Read Display Choices to array ***

90 FOR N=1 TO 5
100 READ PARAM$(N)
110 NEXT N
```

```
115 ' *** Check to see which adapter in use for BASIC ***

120 CLS
130 DEF SEG=0
140 IF (PEEK(1040) AND 48)=48 THEN ADAPTER=1 ELSE ADAPTER=0
150 PRINT"Currently activated adapter is ";
160 IF ADAPTER=1 THEN PRINT "monochrome"; ELSE PRINT
    "color";
170 PRINT"."

175 ' *** Switch? (BASIC only) ***

180 PRINT"Do you wish to switch to the other?"
190 A$=INKEY$:IF A$="" GOTO 190
200 IF A$="Y" OR A$="y" GOTO 210 ELSE GOTO 240
210 IF ADAPTER=0 THEN POKE 1040,(PEEK(1040) OR
    48):ADAPTER=1:GOTO 240
220 POKE 1040,(PEEK(1040) AND 207) OR 16
230 ADAPTER=0

235 ' *** Choose display type ***

240 CLS
250 LOCATE 4,2
260 PRINT "Choose display characteristics:
270 LOCATE 6,2
280 PRINT"1.) Black-and-white, 40 columns."
290 PRINT TAB(2)"2.) Black-and-white, 80 columns."
300 PRINT TAB(2)"3.) Color, 40 columns."
310 PRINT TAB(2)"4.) Color, 80 columns."
320 PRINT TAB(2)"5.) Monochrome'
330 PRINT
340 PRINT TAB(8)"Enter choice ==>";
350 A$=INKEY$:IF A$="" GOTO 350
360 A=VAL(A$)
370 IF A<1 OR A>5 GOTO 350
380 PRINT A$

385 ' *** Print batch file to disk ***

390 OPEN "O",1,"DISP.BAT"
400 PRINT #1," .
    ECHO OFF"
410 PRINT #1,"MODE "+PARAM$(A)
420 CLOSE 1
430 SYSTEM
-------------------------------------------------------
```

ANSWER.BAT

What it does: Turns on or off autoanswer feature of Hayes-compatible modem.

Syntax: ANSWER ON or ANSWER OFF

Requirements: DOS 2.0 or later.

HOW TO USE IT

You may wish to use a Hayes-compatible modem with Sidekick or another program as an autodialer, in which case the modem should be left on at all times. To avoid having the modem answer that line while you are using another application program, this batch file can be invoked at any time from DOS command mode, or the relevant lines can be inserted in your own batch files to turn the modem autoanswer feature on and off as you enter and exit applications. To use it, type ANSWER ON or ANSWER OFF. Uppercase or lowercase letters can be used, and if you forget a parameter, the routine prompts you.

Line-By-Line Description

Line 1:   Turn screen echoing of commands off.

Lines 2-3:   Title remarks.

Line 4:   Check if parameter entered, if not, branch to ASK.

Line 5:   Go to label specified by %1. If ON or OFF not entered, error will result.

Line 6:   Start ASK routine.

Line 7:   Clear the screen.

Lines 8–11:   Present choices.

Lines 12–13:   Ask for INPUT.

Lines 14–15:   Test for valid key.

Line 16:   If no valid key pressed, loop back for another key.

Lines 17–19: Turn modem autoanswer on, for two rings. User may change this value.

Lines 20–21: Turn off autoanswer feature.

Line 22:   End of routine.

```
------------------------------------------------------
1.  ECHO OFF
2.  :       :: ANSWER.BAT ::
3.  :    *** Turns modem answer on and off ***
4.  IF "%1"=="" GOTO ASK
5.  GOTO %1
6.  :ASK
7.  CLS
8.  ECHO  Would you like to turn autoanswer
9.  ECHO      1.  ON
10. ECHO      2.  OFF
11. ECHO <Alt 255>
12. :INPUT
13. INPUT Enter choice:
14. IF ERRORLEVEL==49 IF NOT ERRORLEVEL 50 GOTO ON
15. IF ERRORLEVEL==50 IF NOT ERRORLEVEL 51 GOTO OFF
16. GOTO INPUT
17. :ON
18. ECHO COM1: >AT S0=2
19. GOTO END
20. :OFF
21. ECHO COM1: >AT S0=0
22. :END
------------------------------------------------------
```

SPEAKER.BAT

What it does: Turns on or off internal speaker of Hayes-compatible modem.

Syntax: SPEAKER ON or SPEAKER OFF

Requirements: DOS 2.0 or later.

HOW TO USE IT

To avoid bothering others, you may wish to turn off the internal speaker of your Hayes-compatible modem. This batch file can be invoked at any time from

DOS command mode, or the relevant lines can be inserted in your own batch files to turn the modem speaker on and off as you wish. For example, you may want the speaker on while calling online networks and performing other telecommunication task (so you can listen for a carrier tone) while you may want the speaker off when using the modem for ordinary autodialing through Sidekick.

To use the routine, type SPEAKER ON or SPEAKER OFF. Uppercase or lowercase letters can be used, and if you forget a parameter, the routine prompts you.

Line-By-Line Description

Line 1:   Turn off screen echoing of commands.

Lines 2–3:   Title remarks.

Line 4:   Check if parameter entered, if not, branch to ASK.

Line 5:   Go to label specified by %1. If ON or OFF not entered, error will result.

Line 6:   Start ASK routine.

Line 7:   Clear the screen.

Lines 8–11: Present choices.

Lines 12–13: Ask for INPUT.

Lines 14–15: Test for valid key.

Line 16:   If no valid key pressed, loop back for another key.

Lines 17–19: Turn speaker on.

Lines 20–21: Turn speaker off.

Line 22:   End of routine.

```
--------------------------------------------------------------
1.   ECHO OFF
2.   :       :: SPEAKER.BAT ::
3.   :    *** Turns modem speaker on and off ***
```

```
 4.  IF "%1"=="" GOTO ASK
 5.  GOTO %1
 6.  :ASK
 7.  CLS
 8.  ECHO  Would you like to turn speaker
 9.  ECHO      1.  ON
10.  ECHO      2.  OFF
11.  ECHO <Alt 255>
12.  :INPUT
13.  INPUT Enter choice:
14.  IF ERRORLEVEL==49 IF NOT ERRORLEVEL 50 GOTO ON
15.  IF ERRORLEVEL==50 IF NOT ERRORLEVEL 51 GOTO OFF
16.  GOTO INPUT
17.  :ON
18.  ECHO AT M1 >COM1:
19.  GOTO END
20.  :OFF
21.  ECHO AT M0 > COM1:
22.  :END
```

SUMMARY

Working your computer's hardware is one of the most useful capabilities of batch file programming. This chapter introduced some of the ways you can control the printer, CRT screen, modem, and other peripherals through batch file utilities.

In the next chapter, we'll look at some ways of working with data from DOS.

17

Manipulating
Data From DOS

INTRODUCTION

Most of your application programs produce files of some sort, whether word-processing text files, spreadsheet data files, or computerized databases. Organizing, manipulating, viewing, and otherwise handling these files is an important part of your DOS housekeeping chores.

We've had a few file-handling batch files (such as COMPARE.BAT, in Chapter 13), which were included to whet your interest or to introduce certain DOS and batch file commands and subcommands. Now we introduce a selection of more new DOS commands that let you streamline many complex file-handling tasks. These include routines that help you find text within ASCII files, use DOS' commands to build a phone directory and disk cataloger, as well as create and erase entire directory paths. Other utilities in this chapter let you transmit a group of files to another computer *without* a telecommunication program and sort your Sidekick directory automatically.

A VARIED GROUP OF UTILITIES

FINDER.BAT locates a given string in one file to many files. Unlike the FIND filter, you may use wildcards in your file specification with FINDER.BAT. HELP.BAT may be customized by you to include help messages on any of your application programs so that a new user can type the HELP filename, and receive some brief instructions on how to use that program.

PHONES.BAT is a simple DOS telephone directory, using only batch file commands. You may add entries from DOS, and search for all entries with a given area code, last name, or first name. Entries can be deleted using PHONEDEL.BAT.

DISKS.BAT supplies an accessible catalog of all the files on your hard disk. Database maintenance has been kept to a minimum. If you've added significant files, simply start the file over from scratch—the cataloging function takes a few minutes but is automatic and can be done while you have lunch.

SCRAP.BAT erases all the files in a directory and removes the directory.

UNDUPE.BAT checks two disks, and if a file is found to exist on both, removes the duplicate on Drive B: This will be useful for cleaning up duplicate files on two working disks.

CANCEL.BAT deletes all files from all subdirectories in the path you specify but does not disturb the subdirectories themselves. Use this command when you want to alter the path of subdirectories, or selectively remove a subdirectory or two. When you remove one subdirectory, all the files and subdirectories in it (and their files as well) must be erased first.

DIRDEL.BAT removes a chain of empty directories. This command can be used in conjunction with CANCEL.BAT. Or, you can use SCRAP.BAT, which removes both files and directories from a path you specify.

ZAP.BAT erases all the files in the current directory—without prompting you "Are You Sure?" and, as a result, should be used with caution.

FONESORT.BAT sorts a Sidekick telephone directory, for those who can never remember Sidekick's syntax or who don't want the bother of loading the phone directory into the notepad and sorting from there.

This chapter brings together everything we have learned previously in this book. There are only a few new techniques here, though familiar methods are combined in new and interesting ways.

FINDER.BAT

What it does: Locates a string in one or more files.

Syntax: FINDER *string to find file specification*

Requirements: DOS 2.0 or later.

HOW TO USE IT

You may type FINDER [string to search for] [file specification]. Unlike the FIND filter, you may use wildcards in the file specification. FINDER looks through the file you name (or several files if a global filename is used) and display the lines containing the string. If NO file specification is used, FINDER searches through all the files on the logged directory.

Note: this file *adds* the strings found to a file, FOUND.$$$. You can use the command to add the output of FINDER to this file, without destroying the information from the previous use of FINDER. If you want FOUND.$$$ to contain only the information from the current use of FINDER.BAT, erase the old version of FOUND.$$$ first, or rename it so that it can be retained:

Example:

```
RENAME FOUND.$$$ newname.$$$
```

Line-By-Line Description

Line 1:   Turn off screen echoing of commands.

Lines 2–3:   Title remarks.

Line 4:   If %1 is null, display HELP message.

Line 5:   Otherwise, go to FIND.

Lines 6–12:   HELP message.

Lines 13–15:   Check to see if ALL or one file is to be checked.

Lines 16–18:   Check all files on logged drive.

Lines 19–20:   Check file specified.

Lines 21–22:   Display the file, FOUND.$$$

Line 23:   Erase temporary file, FOUND.$$$

Line 24:   End of batch file.

```
----------------------------------------------------------
 1.    ECHO OFF
 2.    :        :: FINDER.BAT ::
 3.    :        *** Locates strings in files ***
 4.    IF "%1" == "" GOTO HELP
 5.    GOTO FIND
 6.    :HELP
 7.    ECHO     Type FINDER [string] [file specification]
 8.    ECHO     If no file specification used, all files
 9.    ECHO     will be searched.  Unlike FIND filter,
10.    ECHO     you may use wildcards in file spec.
11.    ECHO   <Alt 255>
12.    GOTO END
13.    :FIND
14.    IF "%2" == "" GOTO ALL
15.    GOTO SOME
16.    :ALL
17.    FOR %%a IN (*.*) DO FIND "%1" %%a >>FOUND.$$$
18.    GOTO EXIT
19.    :SOME
20.    FOR %%a IN (%2) DO FIND "%1" %%a >>FOUND.$$$
21.    :EXIT
22.    MORE<FOUND.$$$
23.    ERASE FOUND.$$$
24.    :END
----------------------------------------------------------
```

SUPERFND.BAT

What it does: FIND with wildcards, and switches.

Syntax: SUPERFND searchstring filespec [/V] [/C] [/N]

Requirements: DOS 2.0 or later versions, hard disk.

HOW TO USE IT

This version of the FIND command also allows use of wildcards but adds the ability to append FIND's filters. With this version, if you do not add a file specification, it doesn't automatically search through all files on the current directory.

Line-By-Line Description

Line 1:   Turn off echoing of commands.

Lines 2–3:   Title remarks.

Line 4:   If second parameter not blank, go to START.

Line 6–18:   HELP.

Lines 19–20:   FIND string.

Line 21:   End of routine.

```
------------------------------------------------------------
1.  ECHO OFF
2.  :    :: SUPERFND ::
3.  :   *** FIND with wildcards, and switches ***
4.  IF NOT "%2"=="" GOTO START
5.  :HELP
6.  ECHO Type:
7.  ECHO    SUPERFND searchstring filename [/C][/V][/N]
8.  ECHO    <Alt 255>
9.  ECHO * The search string should be the string you want.
10. ECHO    to locate in your text files.
11. ECHO * The filename should be the filenames, including
12. ECHO    wildcards that you want searched.
13. ECHO * The switches can be any of the FIND switches:
14. ECHO       /C -- Count lines
15. ECHO       /N -- Number the lines
16. ECHO       /V -- Find only lines without the string.
17. ECHO    <Alt 255>
18. GOTO END
19. :START
20. FOR %%a IN (%2) DO FIND %3 "%1" %%a
21. :END
------------------------------------------------------------
```

HELP.BAT

What it does: Displays help messages you create.

Syntax: HELP filename

Requirements: DOS 2.0 or later.

HOW TO USE IT

You should add labels to the batch file that are the same as the root filename of any application you wish to provide a help message for. Then follow the label with a short help message that tells the user how to load, use, or gain further information about the program.

Once installed, the user can gain help on the covered applications by typing HELP filename.
Example:

HELP HELP
or
HELP

Provides explanation of HELP.BAT.

Line-By-Line Description

Line 1:   Turn screen echoing of commands off.

Lines 2–3:   Title remarks.

Line 4:   If %1 is null, go to HELP.

Lines 5–7:   Explanation of file.

Line 8:   Go to label marked by %1.

Lines 9–18:   HELP message.

Line 19:   Exit file.

```
-----------------------------------------------------------
1.   ECHO OFF
2.   :       :: HELP.BAT ::
3.   :       *** Displays HELP on Your Programs ***
4.   IF "%1" == "" GOTO HELP
5.   ECHO      If 'Label Not Found' Message is displayed
6.   ECHO      No HELP available for that program
7.   ECHO   <Alt 255>
8.   GOTO %1
```

```
 9.   :HELP
10.   ECHO       This is a single file containing HELP
11.   ECHO       Messages for a number of programs or
12.   ECHO       files.  You need to write HELP lines
13.   ECHO       like this one for each program you
14.   ECHO       want to provide HELP for.  Then label
15.   ECHO       those lines with the filename of the
16.   ECHO       program.  End with GOTO EXIT line.
17.   ECHO    <Alt 255>
18.   GOTO EXIT
19.   :EXIT
------------------------------------------------------------
```

PHONES.BAT

What it does: Allows building a list of phone numbers and names you
                can check from DOS.

Syntax: PHONES   ADD
                PHONES FIND field to search search string

Requirements: DOS 2.0 or later.

HOW TO USE IT

To add new entries, type PHONES ADD. You can then type as many lines of
entries as you wish. Each phone number and name should be on a different line.
You must type last name first, followed by first name. Names must be enclosed
in brackets. You may separate them with a space or comma, but you should be
consistent for the best appearance. Phone number should include area code in
parentheses. You can enter name or phone number first or last if you wish, but
for the best appearance during retrieval, you should be consistent.

When done making entries, hit ENTER, followed by F6 and another ENTER.

To access your phone directory, type PHONES FIND [AC, LAST, or FIRST]
[string to find]

FIND can be entered in all upper- or lowercase but not a mixture. The second
parameter, which can be AC, LAST, or FIRST can also be in upper- or lowercase. You would enter AC to search for an area code, LAST to look for a last
name, and FIRST to look for a first name. The "string to find" should be the area
code or name you are looking for. Case DOES count here so that you must use
the same format as when you entered the information in your file. It is recommended that you use all uppercase for entries in the file and to retrieve names.

The display shows all matches. Some unwanted entries may also match:

PHONES FIND LAST JOHNSON

This will locate Bill Johnson, as well as Tommy Johns in your file.
Example:

PHONES FIND AC 216
PHONES FIND FIRST CATHY

To delete names from your file, use PHONEDEL.BAT, which follows this one.

Line-By-Line Description

Line 1:	Turn off screen echoing of commands.
Lines 2–3:	Title remarks.
Line 4:	If %1 is null, go to HELP.
Lines 5–8:	Check for ADD or FIND and send to those modules if found.
Lines 9–15:	Display HELP message.
Lines 16–24:	Show ADD module instructions.
Line 25:	Copy from CONSOLE to temporary file TEMP.$$$.
	User terminates this step with F6 and ENTER.
Line 26:	Add temporary file TEMP.$$$ to PHONES.LST file.
Line 27:	Erase TEMP.$$$
Line 28:	Go to exit.
Lines 29–30:	Send to AC, LAST or FIRST. If some other label entered by user by mistake, file will crash here.
Lines 31–39:	Search PHONES.LST for string %3.
Line 40:	Exit file.

```
----------------------------------------------------------
1.    ECHO OFF
2.    :       :: PHONES.BAT ::
3.    :         *** Maintains Phone Directory ***
4.    IF "%1"=="" GOTO HELP
5.    IF "%1"=="ADD" GOTO ADD
6.    IF "%1"=="add" GOTO ADD
7.    IF "%1"=="FIND" GOTO FIND
8.    IF "%1"=="find" GOTO FIND
9.    :HELP
10.   ECHO    TYPE PHONES [FIND or ADD] [AC or LAST or FIRST]
               [string to find]
11.   ECHO    Second and third parameters valid only if first
               is FIND
12.   ECHO    Enter AC, LAST or FIRST to search for area code,
               last name
13.   ECHO    or first name, plus the string to look for.
14.   ECHO    <Alt 255>
15.   GOTO EXIT
16.   :ADD
17.   ECHO    Enter [lastname,firstname](area code)phone number
18.   ECHO    <Alt-255>
19.   ECHO    Be sure to include "[" and "]" around name,
20.   ECHO    and put parentheses around area code.  Separate
21.   ECHO    area code from phone number with NOTHING ELSE.
22.   ECHO    <Alt 255>
23.   ECHO    End each entry with [ENTER]
24.   ECHO    End session with [ENTER]+F6+[ENTER]
25.   COPY CON:TEMP.$$$
26.   COPY C:\BATCHES\PHONES.LST /A +TEMP.$$$ /A
27.   ERASE TEMP.$$$
28.   GOTO EXIT
29.   :FIND
30.   GOTO %2
31.   :AC
32.   FIND "(%3" C:\BATCHES\PHONES.LST
33.   GOTO EXIT
34.   :LAST
35.   FIND "[%3" C:\BATCHES\PHONES.LST
36.   GOTO EXIT
37.   :FIRST
38.   FIND "%3]" C:\BATCHES\PHONES.LST
39.   GOTO EXIT
40.   :EXIT
----------------------------------------------------------
```

PHONEDEL.BAT

What it does: Removes files from PHONE directory.

Syntax: PHONEDEL *name to delete*

Requirements: DOS 2.0 or later.

HOW TO USE IT

Type PHONEDEL followed by the name to delete. You must use the same case as the entry in your phone directory. It is recommended that you use all uppercase for entries in the file and use uppercase to retrieve or delete names.

Line-By-Line Description

Line 1:   Turn off echoing of screen commands.

Lines 2–3:   Title remarks.

Line 4:   If parameter entered go to START.

Lines 5–9:   Otherwise, display HELP.

Line 10:   Start deletion.

Line 11:   Log onto C:

Line 12:   Log onto Batches subdirectory.

Line 13:   Type Phone data and filter through FIND, looking for all lines that do *not* include %1. Redirect to temporary file PHONE.$$$.

Line 14.   Erase old phone list.

Line 15.   Rename temporary file as new list.

Line 16.   End.

```
------------------------------------------------------
 1. ECHO OFF
 2. :       :: PHONEDEL.BAT ::
 3. :   *** Deletes Entries from phone directory ***
 4. IF NOT "%1"=="" GOTO START
 5. :HELP
 6. CLS
 7. ECHO  Type PHONEDEL name-to-delete
 8. ECHO  You must use all uppercase.
 9. GOTO END
10. :START
11. C:
12. CD BATCHES
13. TYPE PHONE.LST - FIND /V "%1" >PHONE.$$$
14. ERASE PHONE.LST
15. RENAME PHONE.$$$ PHONE.LST
16. :END
------------------------------------------------------
```

DISKS.BAT

What it does: Catalogs a fixed disk and finds files within the catalog.

Syntax: DISKS   ADD
          DISKS FIND file to find

Requirements: DOS 2.0 or later.

HOW TO USE IT

You may construct a new or updated catalog of your hard disk by typing DISKS ADD. To locate a file, type DISKS FIND [file to find]. Global filenames are not allowed; but you can specify part of the file name. You cannot search for CHAP10.*, but you may find CHAP10.TXT by searching for just CHAP10. Search will be for all files in all subdirectories of a given partition. If you know part of a pathname, you may include it, but only from the file's actual subdirectory upward. This would be useful if several files have the same name but are found in different subdirectories. The pathname will be displayed, except for files in the root directory.
Examples:

```
DISKS FIND CHAP10
DISKS FIND CHAP10.TXT
DISKS FIND \WS\CHAP10.TXT
```

Line-By-Line Description

Line 1:   Turn off screen echoing of commands.

Lines 2–3:   Title remarks.

Line 4:   If %1 is null, go to HELP module.

Lines 5–8:   If ADD or FIND entered, send to that label.

Lines 9–11:   Display HELP message.

Lines 12–16:   Display warning about ADD step.

Line 17:   Find all file names in all directories and send to temporary file TEMP.

Line 18:   Send only those lines in TEMP with a backslash (that is, the filenames, to file DISKS.LST.

Line 19:   Erase the temporary file.

Line 20:   Go to exit.

Lines 21–22:   Start FIND.

Line 23:   Find %2 in DISKS.LST.

Line 24:   Exit.

```
------------------------------------------------------
1.   ECHO OFF
2.   :      :: DISKS.BAT ::
3.   :      *** Catalogs a Hard Disk ***
4.   IF "%1"=="" GOTO HELP
5.   IF "%1"=="ADD" GOTO ADD
6.   IF "%1"=="add" GOTO ADD
7.   IF "%1"=="FIND" GOTO FIND
8.   IF "%1"=="find" GOTO FIND
9.   :HELP
10.  ECHO    To find file type: DISKS FIND [file to find]
11.  GOTO EXIT
12.  :ADD
13.  CLS
```

```
14.  ECHO     Process will take a few minutes.  Please wait.
15.  ECHO     <Alt 255>
16.  PAUSE
17.  CHKDSK C: /V > TEMP
18.  FIND "\" TEMP > C:\BATCHESDISKS.LST
19.  ERASE TEMP
20.  GOTO EXIT
21.  :FIND
22.  CLS
23.  FIND "%2" C:\BATCHES\DISKS.LST
24.  :EXIT
     -------------------------------------------------------
```

SCRAP.BAT

What it does: Removes files and directories in one step.

Syntax: SCRAP directory-list

Requirements: DOS 2.0 or later.

HOW TO USE IT

You may remove all the files and directories from a given path in one step with this command. Type SCRAP, followed by the directories, in their reverse order. You'll be shown the files in each subdirectory and asked to okay purging. You may stop at any time by pressing Control-BREAK. Replying "N" to any ARE YOU SURE prompt also stops the file, since a directory that contains files cannot be removed.
Example:

```
SCRAP PITT PA EAST MARKETS
```

Line-By-Line Description

Line 1:   Turn off screen echoing of commands.

Lines 2–3:   Title remarks.

Lines 4–12:   Clear screen, display instructions.

Line 13:   Log onto each directory to arrive at lowest directory to be removed.

Line 14:   Display files on current directory.

Lines 15–18:   Show warning.

Line 19:   Erase all files on current directory, except those beginning
                 with $ (a quirk of DOS).

Line 20:   Erase files beginning with $.

Line 21:   Change to next highest directory.

Line 22:   Display warning message.

Line 23:   Pause to allow user to hit Control-Break.

Line 24:   Remove the previous directory.

Line 25:   Shift to next parameter.

Line 26:   If it is not null, repeat.

Line 27:   Exit file.

```
1.  ECHO OFF
2.  :  :: SCRAP.BAT ::
3.  :      *** Removes Directories and Files ***
4.  CLS
5.  ECHO   Remove directories and their files in one step.
6.  ECHO   Type SCRAP, then list directories in reverse
7.  ECHO   order.  You'll be shown directories of each
8.  ECHO   subdirectory and asked to okay purging.
9.  ECHO   You may stop at any time by pressing Control-Break
10. ECHO   <Alt 255>
11. ECHO   Disk to be processed must be in default drive.
12. PAUSE
13. FOR %%b IN (%9 %8 %7 %6 %5 %4 %3 %2 %1) DO IF NOT
    "%%b"=="" CD %%b
14. :ERASE
15. DIR
16. ECHO   <Alt 255>
17. ECHO      Will erase this directory.
18. ECHO   <Alt 255>
19. ECHO Y | ERASE *.*
```

```
20. ERASE $*.*
21. CD ..
22. ECHO   REMOVING DIRECTORY %1
23. PAUSE
24. RD %1
25. SHIFT
26. IF NOT "%1"=="" GOTO ERASE
27. :EXIT
```

UNDUPE.BAT

What it does: Checks disks for duplicate files and erases files found on both disks from disk in B:

Syntax: UNDUPE

Requirements: DOS 2.0 or later.

HOW TO USE IT

There are no parameters to enter, simply type UNDUPE. You should have first disk in A: and the second disk in B: Files found in both A: and B: will be erased from B: If you use subdirectories, log onto the two directories you wish to use for this step.

You may alter the file for slightly different operation. Change lines 12 and 13 to the following:

```
12.   C:
13.   FOR %%b IN (*.*) DO IF EXIST A:%%b ERASE A:%%b
```

This change, useful for those with fixed disks, checks the files on Drive A: against those on the fixed disk, and erase those files on A: that are duplicated on the fixed disk directory. This would be helpful if you were transferring files manually (and hadn't used HCOPY.BAT) and wanted to delete files from the floppy disk that had already been copied to the fixed disk.

Line-By-Line Description

Line 1:   Turn off screen echoing of commands.

Lines 2–3:   Title remarks.

Line 4:   Clear the screen.

Lines 5–11:   Display instructions and wait while user mounts disks.

Line 12:   Log onto A:

Line 13:   Check each file on A:, and if it exists also on B: erase it
                    from B:

```
1.     ECHO OFF
2.     :      :: UNDUPE.BAT ::
3.     :      *** Removes duplicate files ***
4.     CLS
5.     ECHO    Place first disk in A:
6.     ECHO    Place second disk in B:
7.     ECHO    <Alt 255>
8.     ECHO    Files found in both A: and B:
9.     ECHO    will be erased from B:
10.    ECHO    <Alt 255>
11.    PAUSE
12.    A:
13.    FOR %%b IN (*.*) DO IF EXIST B:%%b ERASE B:%%b
```

CREATE.BAT

What it does: Creates a new path.

Syntax: CREATE subdirectory list

Requirements: DOS 2.0 or later.

HOW TO USE IT

Type CREATE, followed by a list of the subdirectories you want created, in the order that you want them. Start this command from the directory that you want to be the parent of all the new subdirectories. The directory names you enter should be legal filenames. You may enter as many as you wish on the command line. There should be enough space on your disk to allow the extra space taken up by the directory entries themselves (about 1000 bytes each).

Once a primary path has been created, you may log onto each directory and create more directories and paths, using this same command. You might first create the following path:

MARKETS EAST PENN PITT

Then, logging onto the MARKETS subdirectory (which contains EAST), you could create SOUTH GA ATLANTA in one more step, and WEST CA SANFRAN in another. Repeat for each subdirectory you wish to create. It would be helpful to have a chart of your proposed tree structure to see the most efficient way of creating a given path with CREATE.
Example:

CREATE BOOKS FICTION US PRE1900

Line-By-Line Description

Line 1:   Turn off screen echoing of commands.

Lines 2–3:   Title remarks.

Line 4:   If %1 is not null, go to CREATE.

Lines 5–11:   Display HELP message.

Lines 12–14:   Create new directory named %1, then log onto that directory.

Line 15:   Shift to next parameter.

Line 16:   If it is not null, go back and repeat.

Line 17:   Begin Exit from file.

Line 18:   Change back to root directory.

Line 19:   Clear screen.

```
1.  ECHO OFF
2.  :    :: CREATE.BAT ::
3.  :    *** Creates new Paths ***
```

```
 4.    IF NOT "%1"=="" GOTO CREATE
 5.    :HELP
 6.    ECHO      List subdirectories you want created
 7.    ECHO      in the order you want them.  Call this
 8.    ECHO      command from the directory you want to
 9.    ECHO      start the new subdirectories in.
10.    ECHO <Alt 255>
11.    GOTO EXIT
12.    :CREATE
13.    MD %1
14.    CD %1
15.    SHIFT
16.    IF NOT "%1"=="" GOTO CREATE
17.    :EXIT
18.    CD
19.    CLS
```

CANCEL.BAT

What it does: Removes all files from the list of subdirectories you supply.

Syntax: CANCEL subdirectory list

Requirements: DOS 2.0 or later.

HOW TO USE IT

Type CANCEL, and then list the subdirectories to purge, in their REVERSE
order. That is, start with the subdirectory farthest down the path and list all those
that are the parent and grandparent of the starting directory. You must specify a
complete path from the first directory back to the root or the directory onto
which you are logged when you start this command. You are shown each
directory that will be purged and are given two chances to preserve it. Hit
Control-C or Control-Break when asked to stop the entire batch file, or answer
"N" to the "Are You Sure?" prompt. You may specify only nine directories deep
for this command.
Example:

CANCEL PITT PA EAST MARKETS

Line-By-Line Description

Line 1:   Turn off screen echoing of commands.

Lines 2–3:   Title remarks.

Line 4:   If %1 is not null, go to DELETE module.

Lines 5–10:   Display HELP message.

Lines 11–12:   For each of the parameters %9 to %1, change to that direc-
                tory, if it exists. Since you have entered the directory
                names in reverse order, the first parameter encountered by
                this line (%9, %8, %7, or some smaller number) contains
                the name of the FIRST (highest) subdirectory to use. %1
                contains the name of the last subdirectory. So, line 12
                eventually logs onto the deepest subdirectory to be purged.

Line 13:   Display files in the directory.

Lines 14–16:   Offer chance to abort batch file.

Lines 17–19:   Explain that erasing all files underway.

Line 20:   If any files are in this directory, erase them.

Line 21:   Shift to the next parameter.

Line 22:   Return to the root directory (this method isn't the most effi-
                cient way to proceed from subdirectory to subdirectory; a
                more efficient method will be demonstrated in
                SCRAP.BAT).

Line 23:   If %1 is not null, go back and repeat the previous steps but
                with one fewer directory.

Line 24:   Exit the file.

```
1.   ECHO OFF
2.   :       :: CANCEL.BAT ::
3.   :       *** Removes Files from  Subdirectories ***
4.   IF NOT "%1"=="" GOTO DELETE
```

```
 5.    :HELP
 6.    ECHO     List subdirectories to purge
 7.    ECHO     in their reverse order on the disk, with
 8.    ECHO     a space between each.
 9.    ECHO   <Alt 255>
10.    GOTO EXIT
11.    :DELETE
12.    FOR %%b IN (%9 %8 %7 %6 %5 %4 %3 %2 %1) DO CD %%b
13.    DIR
14.    ECHO      HIT CONTROL C TO ABORT
15.    ECHO   <Alt 255>
16.    PAUSE
17.    ECHO   <Alt 255>
18.    ECHO      Erasing all files above except directories
19.    ECHO   <Alt 255>
20.    IF EXIST *.* ERASE *.*
21.    SHIFT
22.    CD \
23.    IF NOT "%1"=="" GOTO DELETE
24.    :EXIT
------------------------------------------------------
```

DELDIR.BAT

What it does: Deletes empty subdirectories.

Syntax: DELDIR subdirectory list

Requirements: DOS 2.0 or later.

HOW TO USE IT

This command can be used to delete directories that have been purged with the CANCEL.BAT file. You may only delete directories that have no files or other subdirectories in them. To do this in one stop, you should either remove files manually before running this module, use CANCEL.BAT, or use SCRAP.BAT, which follows. Using two batch files like CANCEL.BAT and DELDIR.BAT is less dangerous.

Type DELDIR followed by a list of the directories to be removed, in reverse order.

Example:

```
DELDIR PITT PA EAST MARKETS
```

Line-By-Line Description

Line 1:   Turn off screen echoing of commands.

Lines 2–3:   Title remarks.

Line 4:   If %9 is null, go to 8. There are a number of lines in this file. Each in turn tests to see if the parameter is null, and if it is, sends control to the next test. This method was used for clarity. However, a more efficient way to do it would be to use the following line in place of line 4:

```
FOR %%b IN (%9 %8 %7 %6 %5 %4 %3 %2 %1) DO IF NOT %%b=="" GOTO %%b
```

You would then remove the line following each label (IF %..) The batch file would also operate faster, since DOS would not have to test each IF statement. Once a parameter has been arrived at that is NOT null, then all the other parameters that follow are also not null.

Line 5:   If parameter is not null, remove the directory at the bottom.

Lines 6–29: These lines are the same as 4 and 5.

Line 30:   Go to exit routine.

Lines 31–35: Display HELP message.

Line 36:   Exit the file.

```
----------------------------------------------------------
1.   ECHO OFF
2.   :        :: DELDIR.BAT ::
3.   :        *** Deletes Subdirectories ***
4.   IF "%9"=="" GOTO 8
5.   RD \%1\%2\%3\%4\%5\%6\%7\%8\%9
6.   :8
7.   IF "%8"=="" GOTO 7
8.   RD \%1\%2\%3\%4\%5\%6\%7\%8
9.   :7
10.  IF "%7"=="" GOTO 6
11.  RD \%1\%2\%3\%4\%5\%6\%7
12.  :6
13.  IF "%6"=="" GOTO 5
```

```
14.    RD \%1\%2\%3\%4\%5\%6
15.    :5
16.    IF "%5"=="" GOTO 4
17.    RD\%1\%2\%3\%4\%5
18.    :4
19.    IF "%4"=="" GOTO 3
20.    RD \%1\%2\%3\%4
21.    :3
22.    IF "%3"=="" GOTO 2
23.    RD \%1\%2\%3
24.    :2
25.    IF "%2"=="" GOTO 1
26.    RD \%1\%2
27.    :1
28.    IF "%1"=="" GOTO HELP
29.    RD \%1
30.    GOTO EXIT
31.    :HELP
32.    ECHO    Type names of EMPTY directories
33.    ECHO    to be deleted, in the same order
34.    ECHO    as they appear on your disk.
35.    ECHO    <Alt 255>
36.    :EXIT
```

ZAP.BAT

What it does: Deletes all files in current directory.

Syntax: ZAP

Requirements: DOS 2.0 or later.

HOW TO USE IT

This command can delete all files from the current directory without bothering with the ARE YOU SURE? prompt. Use it with extreme caution.

Line-By-Line Description

Line 1:   Turn off echoing of screen commands.

Lines 2–3:   Title remarks.

Line 4:   Erase all files except those beginning with $.

Line 5:   Erase all files beginning with $.

```
--------------------------------------------------------
1.   ECHO OFF
2.   :      :: ZAP.BAT ::
3.   :  *** Deletes all files in current directory ***
4.   ECHO Y - ERASE *.*
5.   ERASE $*.*
--------------------------------------------------------
```

FONESORT.BAT

What it does: Sorts a Sidekick phone directory.

Syntax: FONESORT

Requirements: DOS 2.0 or later.

HOW TO USE IT

When you simply type FONESORT from the DOS prompt, this routine sorts your Sidekick phone directory without the need to load it into the notepad and save it again.

Line-By-Line Description

Line 1:   Turn off echoing of screen commands.

Lines 2–3:   Title remarks.

Line 4:   Display message at start of function.

Line 5:   Type existing phone directory through SORT filter. Sorts on fourth character in the phone directory listing, which should be last name if you use the most common arrangement:

                 DB Busch, David 1-216-555-1111

Line 6:   Erase old phone directory.

Line 7:   Copy temporary file as new phone directory. Note that RENAME doesn't allow using pathnames (to prevent you from renaming across paths and thus moving a file). So, this method is used—copying the file, then erasing the old version. You could also log onto the subdirectory where the files reside and rename them there.

Line 8:   Erase temporary file.

```
-------------------------------------------------------
1.  ECHO OFF
2.  :      :: FONESORT.BAT ::
3.  :  *** Sorts Sidekick Phone Directory ***
4.  ECHO Sorting....
5.  TYPE C:DOSPHONE | SORT /+4>C:TEMP.$$$
6.  ERASE C:DOSPHONE
7.  COPY C:TEMP.$$$ C:DOSPHONE
8.  ERASE C:TEMP.$$$
9.  ECHO Finished.
-------------------------------------------------------
```

SUMMARY

The utilities in this chapter have supplied a broad range of new capabilities, including new ways of using FIND to locate text within an ASCII file, a system for installing HELP files on your hard disk, a utility to remove duplicate files, and a dangerous new capability—deleting all the files in a directory *without* seeing DOS' Are You Sure (Y/N)? prompt.

Some of these routines handled files. In the final batch files presented in this book in the next chapter, we'll discover some new ways of manipulating files.

18

Handling Files

INTRODUCTION

This chapter includes some utilities that you can use for handling and manipulating files in creative ways. For example, TRANS.BAT came in very handy during the writing of this book. For some applications, it can replace an entire communication program, with a single short batch file. By typing TRANS filename and substituting several filenames, the routine automatically directs each file to the asynchronous port. The files should be ASCII text or a BASIC program stored in ASCII form. With this file, I transfered all the batch files in this book from one computer to another with incompatible disk formats.

In some of these later routines, we'll offer suggestions for you to make changes to customize them further for your own needs. For example, FSORT is a limited file-sorting utility (it isn't set up to sort by a column other than 1) that automatically replaces a given file with a file of the same name that has been sorted. With what you have learned so far, you should be able to easily modify it to allow entering a replaceable parameter to sort on a different column or, better yet, prompt the user (with INPUT.COM) to enter the column to sort on interactively.

HCOPY, a handy new version of COPY that you can use to transfer programs or data to your hard disk, copies a file to drive C: and then erases it from the old disk. LOOK.BAT and LIST.BAT display ASCII files in handy paged format.

LOOK.BAT shows a single file, while LIST.BAT can show as many files as you can type on the command line.

A selection of other routines, described more fully as they are presented, allow you to perform other useful tasks.

UTILITIES

TRANS.BAT

What it does: Sends a list of files to the serial port.

Syntax: TRANS filenames...

Requirements: DOS 2.0 or later.

HOW TO USE IT

If you use other than COM1 for this application, change line 12 to COM2. You may also alter the baud rate, parity, word length, and stop bits if you use other settings.

Then type TRANS and a list of the files you want to send. Wildcards or multiple names can be used.
Example:

```
TRANS  FILE1.DAT  FILE2.DAT  CHAP10.TXT
```

Line-By-Line Description

Line 1:   Turn off screen echoing of commands.

Lines 2–3:   Title remarks.

Line 4:   If %1 is not null, go to INIT.

Lines 5–9:   Display HELP message.

Lines 10–11:   Set serial port configuration.

Lines 12–13:   Send files to serial port.

Line 14:   SHIFT to next parameter.

Line 15:   If it is not null, repeat operation.

Lines 16–17:   Exit file.

```
-----------------------------------------------------
1.    ECHO OFF
2.    :       :: TRANS.BAT ::
3.    :       *** Uploads a list of files ***
4.    IF NOT "%1"=="" GOTO INIT
5.    :HELP
6.    ECHO   Type filenames to be uploaded.
7.    ECHO   You may use wildcards, or multiple names.
8.    ECHO   <Alt 255>
9.    GOTO EXIT
10.   :INIT
11.   MODE COM1:1200,E,7,1
12.   :TRANS
13.   FOR %%b IN (%1) DO TYPE %%b>COM1
14.   SHIFT
15.   IF NOT "%1"=="" GOTO TRANS
16.   :EXIT
17.   CLS
-----------------------------------------------------
```

FSORT.BAT

What it does: Replaces a file with a sorted version of that file. Sorts by first column only.

Syntax: FSORT filenames...

Requirements: DOS 2.0 or later.

HOW TO USE IT

Type FSORT and as many filenames as you wish on the command line. This module sorts them each in turn. Files should be ASCII files, and sort begins with the first character on each line.
Example:

```
FSORT  INFO.DAT  LIST.LST
```

Line-By-Line Description

Line 1:   Turn off screen echoing of commands.

Lines 2–3:   Title remarks.

Line 4:   If %1 is not null, go to SORT.

Lines 5–10:   Display HELP message.

Lines 11–12:   Sort the file and store in TEMPFILE.

Line 13:   Erase original file.

Line 14:   Rename TEMPFILE with original filename.

Line 15:   SHIFT to next parameter.

Line 16:   If it is not null, repeat.

Lines 17–18:   Exit the file.

```
---------------------------------------------------------
1.    ECHO OFF
2.    :       :: FSORT.BAT :::
3.    :       *** Sorts Files ***
4.    IF NOT "%1"=="" GOTO SORT
5.    :HELP
6.    ECHO    Enter the files to sort on the command
7.    ECHO    line.  Enter as many as you wish.  Global
8.    ECHO    filenames are not allowed.
9.    ECHO    <Alt 255>
10.   GOTO EXIT
11.   :SORT
12.   SORT < %1 > TEMPFILE
13.   ERASE %1
14.   RENAME TEMPFILE %1
15.   SHIFT
16.   IF NOT "%1"=="" GOTO SORT
17.   :EXIT
18.   CLS
---------------------------------------------------------
```

HCOPY.BAT

What it does: Copies a file to the fixed disk from Drive A:, and then deletes it from the old disk.

Syntax: HCOPY file to transfer new name

Requirements: DOS 2.0 or later.

HOW TO USE IT

Place the disk containing the file you wish to move and type:

```
HCOPY [file to transfer] [new name]
```

If you are moving one file, a new name may be specified. If a new name is not entered, the old name will be used. If no new name is specified, then a global filename can be used for the file to transfer.
Example:

```
HCOPY  INFO.DAT  NEWINFO.DAT
HCOPY  *.*
```

Drive A: is always used for the source diskette, and the fixed disk is always the destination. The old files are erased from the A: diskette. The drive letters A: and C: are not needed or allowed. See if you can modify this utility to allow moving from one disk directory to another.

Line-By-Line Description

Line 1:   Turn off screen echoing of commands.

Lines 2–3:   Title remarks.

Line 4:   If %1 is null, go to HELP.

Line 5:   Otherwise go to COPY.

Lines 6–12:   Display HELP message.

Lines 13–14: COPY file(s).

Line 15:   ERASE old file(s).

Line 16:   Exit file.

```
-------------------------------------------------
1.    ECHO OFF
2.    :     :: HCOPY.BAT ::
3.    :      *** UPDATE DISK ***
4.    IF "%1" =="" GOTO HELP
5.    GOTO COPY
6.    :HELP
7.    ECHO       Type HCOPY [file to transfer][new name]
8.    ECHO       File will be copied from floppy
9.    ECHO       disk in A: to hard disk C: and
10.   ECHO       then erased from A:  New name optional.
11.   ECHO    <Alt 255>
12.   GOTO EXIT
13.   :COPY
14.   COPY A:%1 C:%2
15.   ERASE A:%1
16.   :EXIT
-------------------------------------------------
```

LOOK.BAT

What it does: Displays a single file in pages.

Syntax: LOOK file to display drive

Requirements: DOS 2.0 or later.

HOW TO USE IT

Type LOOK [file to display] [drive letter]
File to display should be an ASCII file. Drive letter should not include the colon. If drive letter is omitted, the logged directory is used. This is a fast command to use when the proper directory levels are already in use or if you generally do not use subdirectories. Paths cannot be used with this command; use LIST.BAT, which follows.
Example:

```
LOOK CHAP10.TXT B
```

Line-By-Line Description

Line 1:   Turn off screen echoing of commands.

Lines 2–3:   Title remarks.

Line 4:   If %1 is null, go to HELP message.

Line 5:   If %2 is null (no drive letter specified), go to LOOK1.

Line 6:   Otherwise, go to LOOK2.

Lines 7–13:   Display HELP message.

Lines 14–16:   Display file in pages.

Lines 17–18:   Display file in pages.

Line 19:   Exit the file.

```
1.   ECHO OFF
2.   :      :: LOOK.BAT ::
3.   :       *** Displays File in Pages ***
4.   IF "%1" == "" GOTO HELP
5.   IF "%2" =="" GOTO LOOK1
6.   GOTO LOOK2
7.   :HELP
8.   ECHO      Type LOOK [filename] [drive]
9.   ECHO      Colon not needed after drive name.
10.  ECHO      If no drive specified, logged drive
11.  ECHO      will be used.
12.  ECHO   <Alt 255>
13.  GOTO EXIT
14.  :LOOK1
15.  MORE<%1
16.  GOTO EXIT
17.  :LOOK2
18.  MORE<%2:%1
19.  :EXIT
```

COMBINE.BAT

What it does: Combines a list of ASCII files

Syntax: COMBINE filenames....

Requirements: DOS 2.0 or later.

HOW TO USE IT

You may type as many filenames as you want on the command line. This batch file adds them together into a new file, MERGED.ASC, which you may rename to anything you like. See if you can modify this file so that it *erases* the old files after they have been copied to the new, combined file. Or use IN-PUT.COM to offer the user this option.

Line-By-Line Description

Line 1:   Turn off echoing of screen commands.

Lines 2–3:   Title remarks.

Line 4:   If second parameter not blank, go to START.

Lines 5–11: Display HELP.

Line 12:   Start merging.

Line 13:   Copy first and second files to MERGED.ASC.

Line 14:   Shift parameters one place to the left.

Line 15:   Start the NEXT portion of the routine.

Line 16:   Shift the parameters one place to the left again, moving the original %3 into the %1 position.

Line 17:   Test to see if new %1 is blank. If so, branch to END.

Line 18:   Copy %1 to MERGED.ASC in a new temporary file.

Line 19:   Erase the old MERGED.ASC file.

Line 20:   Rename the temporary file as MERGED.ASC.

Line 21:   Go back to see if more parameters remain to be copied.

Line 22:   END.

Line 23:   Display new filename of combined files.

```
-----------------------------------------------------------
1.  ECHO OFF
2.  :   :: COMBINE.BAT ::
3.  :  *** Combines ASCII files ***
4.  IF NOT "%2"=="" GOTO START
5.  :HELP
6.  ECHO Type
7.  ECHO  COMBINE filenamelist
8.  ECHO   The ASCII files will be combined in a
9.  ECHO   new file called MERGED.ASC
10. ECHO  <Alt 255>
11. GOTO END
12. :START
13. COPY %1+%2 MERGED.ASC
14. SHIFT
15. :NEXT
16. SHIFT
17. IF "%1"=="" GOTO END
18. COPY MERGED.ASC+%1 TEMP.$$$
19. ERASE MERGED.ASC
20. RENAME TEMP.$$$ MERGED.ASC
21. GOTO NEXT
22. :END
23. ECHO  New file is MERGED.ASC
-----------------------------------------------------------
```

LIST.BAT

What it does: Shows a list of files you specify.

Syntax: LIST filenames....

Requirements: DOS 2.0 or later.

HOW TO USE IT

You may type as many filenames as you want on the command line. This batch file displays each, conveniently paged for easy viewing. Global filenames are not allowed.
Example:

```
LIST FILE1.DAT  FILE2.DAT  CHAP10.TXT CHAP11.TXT
```

Line-By-Line Description

Line 1:	Turn off screen echoing of commands.
Lines 2–3:	Title remarks.
Line 4:	If %1 is not null, go to SHOW.
Lines 5–10:	Display HELP message.
Lines 11–12:	Display a file.
Line 13:	SHIFT to next parameter on command line.
Line 14:	If new parameter is not null, go to SHOW.
Line 15:	Exit file.

```
-----------------------------------------------------
1.   ECHO OFF
2.   :      :: LIST.BAT ::
3.   :      *** Shows list of files ***
4.   IF NOT "%1"=="" GOTO SHOW
5.   :HELP
6.   ECHO    Type list of file names you
7.   ECHO    want to look at.  Global names
8.   ECHO    are not allowed.
9.   ECHO    <ALT 255>
10.  GOTO EXIT
11.  :SHOW
12.  MORE<%1
13.  SHIFT
14.  IF NOT "%1"=="" GOTO SHOW
15.  :EXIT
-----------------------------------------------------
```

SHOW.BAT

What it does: Shows a list of files you specify, with wildcards allowed.

Syntax: SHOW filename

Requirements: DOS 2.0 or later.

HOW TO USE IT

You may type one or more filenames, using wildcards on the command line. This batch file displays each, conveniently paged for easy viewing. Example:

```
SHOW *.TXT  *.DAT  CHAP??.DOC
```

Line-By-Line Description

Line 1:   Turn off screen echoing of commands.

Lines 2–3:   Title remarks.

Line 4:   If %1 is not null, go to SHOW.

Lines 5–10: Display HELP message.

```
------------------------------------------------------------
1.    ECHO OFF
2.    :      :: SHOW.BAT ::
3.    :      *** Shows list of files ***
4.    IF NOT "%1"=="" GOTO SHOW
5.    :HELP
6.    ECHO    Type list of filenames you
7.    ECHO    want to look at.
9.    ECHO    <ALT 255>
10.   GOTO EXIT
11.   :SHOW
12.   FOR %%a IN (%1) DO COMMAND /C DISPLAY %%a
13.   SHIFT
14.   IF NOT "%1"=="" GOTO SHOW
15.   :EXIT
------------------------------------------------------------
```

```
--------------------------------------------------------
1.    ECHO OFF
2.    :      :: DISPLAY.BAT ::
3.    :      *** Displays files ***
4.    ECHO ----------------------
5.    ECHO Displaying %1
6.    ECHO ----------------------
7.    MORE<%1
--------------------------------------------------------
```

SUMMARY

This chapter has presented the final batch file utilities in this book, a selection of eight short routines that offer a number of functions for handling files. Included was a file that lets you transmit a series of files to another computer, a file- sorting utility, a file that displays ASCII text files in pages, and a file to help you back up your hard disk. Since addititional ideas for batch file utilities have been presented throughout this book, you should have no shortage of ideas on customization. If you want to *really* stretch out, see what can be done with batch files with one of the enhancement products discussed in the following chapter.

19

Batch-File Language Extensions and Utilities

INTRODUCTION

In this book we've presented a few small extensions to batch-file language, such as INPUT.COM, which surmount some of the shortcomings built into DOS. You should know that there are many alternatives that you can use to extend the utility of DOS and provide even more extensive customizing capabilities. This chapter will explore some of them and show you how you can obtain many utilities at low cost or for free.

It's dangerous enough to talk about any sort of hardware or software in a book that will be revised annaully, at best. We've already seen that DOS has under gone eight or more major revisions since 1981 and is likely to see several more before (or even if) OS/2 and its successors take over as the chief operating system for IBM and compatible PCs. IBM and Microsoft are major vendors; when talking about software available in public domain form from individuals, as shareware from small companies, or as offerings from would-be software empires, the odds are even better that today's favorite utility will become tomorrow's discontinued product. Some company names and addresses are given in this chapter for the reader's convenience. Keep in mind that while 90 percent of the information in this book should remain current for a year or two after publication, there are no guarantees that the suppliers listed here will remain at these addresses during that span: You're on your own.

Moreover, the author discovered in researching this book that there are literally thousands of different batch-file utility programs and batch-file extensions available. Programs that perform functions like INPUT.COM and YESNO.COM abound, under names like GETKEY.COM, ANSWER.COM, and so on. It would be impossible to discuss all of them and fruitless given the short life of some products. Use this chapter as a guideline for obtaining and using your own batch-file extensions from the rich resources that surround you.

OBTAINING UTILITIES FROM BULLETIN BOARDS

One often-untapped resource is the on-line bulletin board system (BBS). These are computer systems with dialup access through modems, often set up on a PC with a hard disk, operated by individuals or organizations for the exchange of information and public domain software among their users. Such BBSs may be free of charge or require a modest membership fee. A metropolitan area of any size should have a half dozen or more BBSs available.

Your SYSOP (system operator) may be an individual who enjoys tinkering with computers, someone who enjoys being the focus of attention, an idealist seeking to provide a service for computer-using humanity, a budding entrepreneur seeking to subsidize their computer usage—or a combination of any or all these. BBSs are also operated by software and hardware vendors to support their products, by computer stores as a service to their customers and to generate more business, and by clubs and organizations to benefit their members.

To access a BBS system, you'll need a modem connected to your PC's serial port and telephone lines, proper telecommunication software, and a list of phone numbers. The best way to find your local BBS numbers is to ask other computer users or the sales staff of your computer store. Many boards specialize in certain brands of hardware, so you'll want to find some that deal chiefly with the IBM PC and compatibles.

Each BBS has its own log-on procedure. You probably need to set your communication software for 1200 or 300 baud, 7 bit words, even parity, and one stop bit. Many systems also use 1200/300, 8 bits, no parity, and one stop bit. When you call, press carriage return several times if you don't get a prompt right away. If you see strange characters on the screen, change to the other settings and try again or hang up, change, and dial back. Most BBSs are set up to make it as easy as possible for new users to log on for the first time.

Most likely you'll be asked for your real name, and possibly an address and phone number. BBSs have many problems with prank callers and potential system crashers, so that the trend is for an informal "sign-up" that may involve a voice phone call from the SYSOP to confirm your identity or at least the exchange of on-line messages before you'll be authorized full access to the board. You may be asked to choose a password or have one assigned to you. This is another security measure for the BBS' protection.

A BBS system consists of various sections, including a message section for posting your own bulletins, and, usually an upload and download section where the public domain and shareware software is located. You may upload programs you have written for others to use and download software for your own system. There will often be a listing of other BBSs in the area (or nationwide) for you to expand your bulletin board horizons even further.

Public domain software is not copyrighted and may be used and given to others without restriction. You may change the utility as you wish. "Shareware" may be given to others for evaluation; however, if you decide to keep and use the program, you are supposed to send a modest registration fee ($25 to $75 or a bit more) to an address supplied with the program. You generally must keep the copyright notice and other accompanying information together with the shareware, and shouldn't give modified copies to others. Shareware resembles regular commercial software, except that the method of distribution is more informal. Both public domain and shareware can be as sophisticated and useful as the most costly commercial offerings. For example ProComm and PC-Talk III each rank at the very top among telecommunication programs for the IBM PC.

To download software, you need only to examine the listings provided by your BBS and follow the instructions. If a board is a local call for you, and your phone system doesn't work on a distance or time (message unit) basis, you can download software almost for free. Best of all, bulletin boards try to keep the latest software available, with frequent uploads from SYSOPs and users who frequent other boards around the country. So, you'll often find the very latest software available within weeks of introduction.

The Capital PC User's Group, one of the best-known user groups dedicated to the IBM PC, provides a comprehensive list of utilities and other public domain software that can be downloaded from its board or obtained on disk by mail. At this writing the address is:

Capital PC User's Group
Box 6128
Silver Spring, Md 20906.

We won't give any phone numbers for BBS systems, since the numbers change so often.

ONLINE INFORMATION SYSTEMS

While most BBS' can handle only a single caller (or a few with more sophisticated software and hardware) at one time, the big online information systems are set up to handle hundreds of users at once. The leaders in this field include People/Link, The Source, and CompuServe. Each system has its own personality and resources.

While you might think of on-line information systems as mammoth bulletin boards, they also offer a great deal more, such as on-line "chatting" in CB-like real-time environments, electronic mail facilities, and features like on-line games, IQ tests, airline schedules, and full text databases.

Each has a user section dedicated to IBM computer hardware, software, and other interests, with huge data libraries of public domain programs. None of the information services are free; charges range from $4.95 to $12.50 an hour, and up, depending on the time of day when you log on (it can be more expensive during "prime" time—before 6 p.m.), the speed of your modem (some have a surcharge for 1200 baud or higher), and other factors.

However, when you consider that a valuable utility can be downloaded in fifteen minutes or less, for a dollar or two, the net cost to you can be very little. Each of the major on-line services has its own signup fees and procedures for accessing and using the data libraries. The addresses are shown below:

American People/Link
350 N. Clark St.
Suite 650
Chicago, IL

CompuServe Information Services Inc.
Columbus, OH 43260

The Source
1616 Anderson Rd.
McLean, VA 22102

SOME UTILITY SOFTWARE

Because public domain and shareware can be distributed through so many sources, you'll find that the utilities available through local bulletin boards, user groups may contain many of the same software. It is often worth sorting through what is available on each to locate the gems. What you'll find varies greatly in quality and sophistication. These can include:

- Machine language utilities that can be called from a batch program to carry out a specific function. For example, one program called CP.COM toggles on and off the PC's "print screen" feature. This allows your batch files to control your printer. Other utilities allow inputting characters to batch files as ERRORLEVELS (like INPUT.COM), parsing strings, for example, to extract dates from the output of DATE, or other chores.

- Sample batch files. Many users have developed batch files that perform tasks similar to those in this book. You may find one you like better or with ideas that can be adapted to those in *DOS Customized*.

- Entire systems of extended batch-file capabilities, with names like BAT.COM that can be called from your batch files and provide even more sophisticated input features, more powerful branching and looping capabilities, and use of variables (including string variables) in place of or along with replaceable parameters.

COMMERCIAL BATCH-FILE ENHANCERS OR REPLACEMENTS

A number of products supply extensions or replacements for batch-file language. Some, like Extended Batch Language (EBL) are available as shareware but are so sophisticated you should strongly consider registering for them and obtaining them directly from the vendor. Others, like Personal REXX, are full interpreters that carry out many of the functions of batch files but are more like a true programming language. Command Plus, and Pro Command are two more examples of software you might be interested in. Here is a brief review of each.

Extended Batch Language (EBL)

Adapted from the EXEC2 language of the IBM VM/CMS mainframe system, EBL is available as shareware on many systems or from the vendor.

This utility will be easy for most readers of this book to learn, as you run your batch files normally, invoking EBL's BAT.COM and its features from within the file. BAT.COM takes over processing from COMMAND.COM, and however, then returns control after the commands you've specified have been carried out.

With current versions, you start a section that you want carried out under BAT.COM control with a BAT/P command and then exit with LEAVE. A SHELL command allows carrying out DOS commands from BAT.COM.

EBL allows the use of variables, which can be input by the user while the batch file is running. EBL's strings can be up to 128 characters, with variables given names %0 to %9, or %a to %o. An extension to the extension, BATXV, allows defining even more variables. String commands similar to the MID$, LEFT$, and RIGHT$ statements in BASIC are allowed. Strings can be filtered to change it to uppercase.

Access to other programs' ERRORLEVEL is provided in a variable called %r. Since EBL allows simple arithmetic comparisons with variables, you can write FOR-NEXT loops by incrementing a counter variable and testing it at the end of the loop to see if control should drop down to the next line, branch, or increment and loop back. EBL also allows additional IF comparisons beyond those provided with DOS' batch file language, and more flexible GOTO structures.

EBL offers error trapping that can, through the %r variable, provide an appropriate response by the batch file. Particularly useful is the "GOTO -%1" structure, which sends control to that label if no matching label can be found.

Single key entries, as well as entire strings or disk files, can be entered into EBL variables.

Other features include access to the current date, disk drive, and directory from within a file, and a built-in four-function decimal calculator.

Extended Batch Language is available from:
Seaware Corp.
P.O. Box 1656
Delray Beach, FL 33444

Personal REXX

This is another version of the IBM VM/CMS language, but, unlike EBL, it serves as a replacement for your conventional batch files. REXX offers precision arithmetic functions, direct execution of DOS commands, built-in functions for DOS file I/O, directory access, and screen/keyboard communication.

As such, it is considerably more sophisticated in many ways than the other three programs being reviewed—even though it is modest in cost ($125 at this writing). More like an interpreter than anything else, REXX operates on source files that you prepare.

Personal REXX runs as an interpreter much like BASIC. Using the rules of the REXX language, you prepare a REXX source file in advance. REXX allows variable manipulation and filtering much as EBL does but with many enhancements. It allows permits access to the ERRORLEVEL through variable "rc."

REXX allows more flexible control structures, such as DO..WHILE for the FOR-NEXT-like structure DO N=1 TO 10. A DO FOREVER command can be exited only by an appropriate IF..THEN LEAVE command.

REXX allows specifying different routines to be accessed on errors, much like BASIC's ON ERROR structure. REXX also allows single key entries as well as entry of entire strings or entering data into variables from disk files.

In addition, REXX provides date access and the current disk drive and directory as well as a wealth of other information. Its calculator can also do extended calculations, such as powers.

Personal REXX is available from:

Mansfield Software Group
P.O. Box 532
Storrs, CT 06268

Pro Command

Pro Command, also shares some characteristics with BASIC, except that its language is an expansion of batch-file language, so that batch files can be run by Pro Command as-is or enhanced with extensions provided by the utility.

Pro Command allows great flexibility in choosing and using variable names. Any string of eight characters or less can be preceded by % to mark it as a variable. Parsing and filtering operations are similar to that of the other utilities. Pro Command does not allow global variables, which however, can be defined in one batch file and accessed in another. Its ERRORLEVEL variable is called %errorlvl.

Pro Command has similar control structures to EBL, with self-programmed loops based on incrementing variables and has an extended FOR...IN..DO feature that allows calling a subroutine within the batch file instead of requiring that the entire command fit on the line (or be called by COMMAND /C)

Pro Command allows entering single key or entire strings of characters into a batch file variable as well as taking input from a disk file. Pro Command also includes date access, availability of the current drive and directory to the files as well as number of bytes free on the disk. The Pro Command calculator is a four-function integer feature.

Pro Command is available from:

Innovative Technology
2710 Lancaster Rd.
Unit 101
Ottawa, Ontario
CANADA K1B 4W8

Command Plus

Command Plus is unlike the previous products in that it actually serves as a replacement for the DOS command processor COMMAND.COM. It may be invoked as a secondary command processor (just as COMMAND /C loads a second copy of COMMAND.COM) or you may specify the primary file COM-PLUS.EXE as the main command processor for DOS on bootup.

As you'll recall, this is done with the SHELL command in the CONFIG.SYS file (with DOS 3.0 or later versions). As a replacement for COMMAND.COM, COMPLUS handles all of DOS' internal commands just like COMMAND.COM, with similar—or enhanced—features.

Command Plus' equivalent of batch files are given an extension of .S instead of .BAT. You can still execute regular batch files with COMPLUS by loading COMMAND.COM. The .S files can include up to 15 different variables. Powerful branching and looping features are provided, with comparison, expression evaluation, arithmetic, and Boolean operations undreamed of in simple batch-file programming. There are built-in capabilities for string manipulation, redirection of output to the standard input device, and access to environment variables.

Users writing batch files with Command Plus will also appreciate enhancements to COPY and DELETE, DIR, and other commands. For example you can list multiple filenames on the command line during copy or delete operations, and copy files matching a *range* of characters (say, files from an alphabetized list beginning with the letters A to C).

Command Plus is available from:

ESP Software Systems, Inc.
11965 Venice Blvd.
Suite 309
Los Angeles, California 90066

SUMMARY

In customizing DOS, you needn't be limited to the features provided in the operating system by Microsoft or IBM. Serious PC users have established a long tradition of DOS-add-ons, from the "path extenders" that preceded APPEND to the batch file language enhancements discussed in this chapter. As you've learned from this book, you don't have to do things DOS' way—DOS can be taught to do things your way.

APPENDIX A

Getting Started

THIS APPENDIX WILL GET YOU STARTED USING SOME OF the commands in this book even if you haven't read the book or are a new IBM computer user who needs extra help. We'll go through some simple steps that will allow you to type in and use the commands. It's likely that you won't understand what all the steps do or how they work. For all the background information, you should read the explanations from start to finish, skimming only the material that you fully understand.

WHAT COMMANDS CAN I USE?

The table of contents lists each command and briefly describes what it does. For the most part, if you want to use a given command, you'll probably know enough to be able to use it. Conversely, if you don't know what a command is for, you are better off not using it until you've gained a little more experience with DOS or have read the book more thoroughly.

For example, you might like to send a sorted disk directory to your printer, as supplied by DSORT.BAT, in Chapter 6. That command uses a special DOS feature, SORT, to do this for you. But it's not necessary to learn about SORT to access this new command. All you really need to know is the information in this Appendix, plus the how-to-use-it information included with DSORT.BAT. The various commands were segregated at the end of each chapter for easy access by the reader and a consistent presentation.

On the other hand, you may also notice other commands, like PATHS.BAT or SCRAP.BAT. For these, you really need to understand about paths and how DOS handles subdirectories. Many new users, unless they are learning with a fixed disk-drive system, don't need or use paths until they are more advanced. For that reason, the how-to-use-it explanations with those modules are less basic and more specific. It's more efficient to explain paths once in the book than to repeat this information for each how-to-use-it section. If a command explanation seems confusing to you, you're probably not ready to use it.

Given these guidelines, you should be able to find several dozen new DOS commands to take advantage of right away. There are many that will streamline operations for even the newest user of the IBM computer—but which will remain valuable no matter how experienced you are.

WHICH COMMANDS SHOULD I USE?

Even if you understand a command, you still have to decide whether or not to take the time to type it in and install it on your computer. Obviously, if you rarely use a command, it is not worth the trouble. Also, even though most of the commands in this book make performing a task simpler, many of them require learning an easy syntax nonetheless. For example, using LOOK.BAT, you can view a file in drive B: in easy-to-read pages 23 lines long by typing:

```
LOOK FILENAME.EXT B
```

This is a bit easier than remembering DOS' syntax:

```
MORE < B:FILENAME.EXT
```

It's also a little faster and easier to type because we don't have to hit shift to use the colon. This example was chosen because both the DOS command and the new one are about equally easy to use. You may prefer one or the other. Whichever one you use, however, you must learn the correct syntax.

If you choose many of the commands in this book without regard for your need for them, you'll end up with just as much to learn as if you'd tackled DOS itself. That's not the point of this book. The object is to make new commands that can perform new, most-needed functions as simply as possible.

So, when choosing a command from this book, keep three things in mind:

1. How much will I use this new command?

2. Is it sufficiently easier to use or more powerful that it is worth my while to learn to use this command instead of using DOS to do the same thing?

3. Am I loading up with too many new commands to learn and use comfortably? If so, should I wait and add this command later?

SETTING UP FOR NEW COMMANDS

To get the most use from your new commands, they should be available to you at any time, no matter what disk or directory you happen to be using. To achieve this freedom, there are several things you can do.

First, the command files themselves must be on a disk in an available drive. Users with an IBM PCjr or other IBM computer equipped with only one drive have one easy solution: Keep all the files you want to use available on all your disks. They don't take up much space, and this is the simplest way to keep them always online. You'll need to remember to copy the files over to any new disk you make.

A second solution, if you use a so-called "memory" disk, RAM disk, virtual disk, or other "electronic" disk drive (a disk drive simulated by setting aside a portion of memory) you can copy all the files to that disk, and keep them available. In effect, you have a second disk drive available and are using that.

Those with two disk drives available have a simpler solution. It's common to have a "start-up" disk that contains DOS, as well as many utility programs available in drive A: most of the time. Then drive B: can be used with systemless "data" disks to store programs and files as needed. The "system" disk might contain, besides DOS, a simple text editor, telecommunication program, BASICA, some utilities, and other frequently accessed files. It could also contain all the command files for this book. This solution is recommended. You can always take out your system disk to make two drive copies of nonsystem disks. It is also convenient to take the startup disk out to run application programs, like DisplayWrite 4, that are too large to fit on a system disk. While you are running such a program, you won't need the new commands anyway; when you return to DOS, reinsert your system disk.

Those with the IBM PC-AT and high-capacity disks can easily find room for these files on each of their 1.2-megabyte disks. It might be a good idea to make a special disk with the files already on it, and copy that, using DISKCOPY each time a new "data" disk is needed. For all intents and purposes, most of the 1.2 megabytes will still be available for data, and the disk is not much different from one that would be simply formatted and left devoid of all files.

Users of fixed disk drives have an even easier choice. Just place all the files on your fixed disk. They'll always be available. We show you how to "hide" them away, even if you haven't gotten fully into "paths" yet; there is a way to tell DOS where the files are located.

FIRST STEPS

You need to have on your startup disk a special file, called AUTOEXEC.BAT. When the computer is started up or rebooted, DOS looks for this file. If it is found, DOS carries out the commands in the file, one at a time.

If you already have an AUTOEXEC.BAT file on your disk and have been using it, we'll ask you to make some changes. Just follow these instructions but also be sure to include any lines that already exist in your AUTOEXEC.BAT file, to ensure that they are carried out. Unless you have lines that duplicate the functions of the lines we need, there should be no conflict. Some utility programs say that they should be called as the last step in an AUTOEXEC.BAT file. If that is true, be sure to include that line last, after those presented here.

At your keyboard type:

```
COPY CON:AUTOEXEC.BAT<ENTER>
```

Then type the following lines (but not the comments)

```
DATE REM    If you have a clock card, leave out
TIME REM    these lines and substitute one that will
REM         call the clock-setting utility, such as
REM         PWRUPCLK supplied with the Quadboard.
PATH A:\;A:\BATCHES;B:\;B:\BATCHES
```

End by hitting the F6 function key and pressing ENTER one last time. DOS responds (1) Files Copied, and your new AUTOEXEC.BAT file will be available. The PATH command in the preceding line tells DOS where to look for certain types of files if it cannot find them on the current directory.

It is important that if you are using a fixed disk, you should change "A" to "C", and "B" to "A" in the preceding line. You'll probably want DOS to look on the fixed disk for the files first and not A:.

There is one other thing to do. Log onto the disk drive specified first in the preceding PATH command (either A: or C:). You should be in the top or "root" directory. If you never use subdirectories, you are probably in the root directory already. If you are unsure, you can get there for certain by typing:

```
CD \
```

Next, type in the following line:

```
MD BATCHES
```

This creates a special subdirectory for you to store your commands. Each time you type in one of the new commands, copy it over to the BATCHES directory. The most foolproof way to do this is to type:

```
COPY filename.ext  A:\BATCHES
```

Again, if you are using the hard disk, type:

```
COPY filename.ext  C:\BATCHES
```

The filename should include the drive letter if it is different from the one you are currently using. That is, if you see the A> prompt and want to copy LOOK.BAT on B: to A:\BATCHES, you would enter:

```
COPY  B:LOOK.BAT C:\BATCHES
```

By following these instructions, you can copy all the files in this book into the subdirectory BATCHES. The PATH command in your AUTOEXEC.BAT file has told DOS where to look for them. If you want to know more about subdirectories, look through Chapter 4 in this book.

Certain commands in this book need to have a special program run while DOS is booting up. It's a good idea to do this now so that you'll be ready for those commands when you want them. Follow these steps:

1. Make sure that a file called ANSI.SYS is on the main or root directory of the disk you boot up from, either A: or C:. If it is not, find ANSI.SYS on your DOS disk and copy it over.

2. Check to see if you already have a file called CONFIG.SYS. If so, enter TYPE CONFIG.SYS to see what it says. If may include lines about VDISKs and BUFFERs and so forth. If you set up CONFIG.SYS yourself, you'll know the purpose of these. If someone else has set up DOS for you, you'll probably want to keep the current CONFIG.SYS file. When you follow step 3, merely add the lines that you saw in your existing CONFIG.SYS file to the one you'll type.

3. When you are ready to create a new CONFIG.SYS file, type:

```
COPY CON:CONFIG.SYS<ENTER>
DEVICE=ANSI.SYS<F6><ENTER>
```

As noted, add any other lines you wish to have in your CONFIG.SYS file, before pressing F6. CONFIG.SYS should also be on the main directory of the disk you boot up with.

More advanced users can edit or create both AUTOEXEC.BAT and CONFIG.SYS with EDLIN, or some word-processing programs. But, we've told you enough to get started. COPY CON works fine for as short as these AUTOEXEC.BAT and CONFIG.SYS programs are. Even though it's not possible to edit them, they are easy enough to type in from scratch each time we want to correct an error or make a modification.

That's all the configuring information you need. Now it's time to tackle the commands themselves.

HOW TO TYPE IN THE COMMANDS

At this point you need to make a decision on how you are going to physically type in the lines. You may use COPY CON as above, especially for the shorter commands. Just type:

```
COPY CON:filename of command
```

For example:

```
COPY CON:LOOK.BAT
```

Then type in the lines as they appear in the listing, *leaving out the line numbers*. Type only the lines themselves. The line numbers are for reference only. When you type in the last line, press F6 and hit ENTER to store the new file on disk.

This method is fast, but there is no way to correct a mistake on one line after you have hit ENTER, other than to retype the whole file. With longer commands, this could be frustrating.

EDLIN, if you have learned its commands, allows both entry and editing of ASCII text lines. If you know how to use EDLIN, you may use this. Instructions on using EDLIN are given in Chapter 3.

Many word processors can also produce simple ASCII text (that is, without complex control codes or print formatting characters). The author used PC-Write to produce some of the modules in this book. Because word-processing programs allow flexible screen-oriented editing (as opposed to EDLIN's line-at-a-time editing), they are preferable. Test your word processor to see if it has an ASCII (sometimes called nondocument) mode. Some WP programs, like Word-Star 2000, allow "printing" a document to disk, which places an ASCII image of the file on the disk. When using such a program, however, make sure you'll be able to reload this ASCII file back into the WP for later editing.

PC-Write can be purchased for as little as $10 or obtained free from another user, because it is "shareware." If you find the program useful, you're supposed to send a registration fee to the author.

If you don't have any compatible WP program, however, and don't care to learn EDLIN, a simple BASIC text-file line-editing given is given in Chapter 3. It allows you to enter and view text files a page at a time, select a line to delete, add, or update, and perform other tasks.

HOW TO USE THE NEW COMMANDS

Each command has instructions on how to use it. In most cases you use the command by typing the command's root name (without the extension) and perhaps some parameters. This is similar to how many DOS commands are used:

```
DISKCOPY A: B:
```

DISKCOPY is the name of the command, and "A:" and "B:" are parameters telling the program to copy from A: to B: The instructions for each module explain what parameters, if any, are required, and how to type them in. Some commands use no parameters, and that is noted too.

Many commands that require parameters help you a bit by displaying some instructions when you enter them without any parameters at all or with the incorrect parameters. Some commands simply abort if the parameters are wrong. Again, the key is to read the instructions. If you still don't understand, the command is probably still too advanced for you. It has to wait until you've read the book.

We think, though, that most readers will be able to get something from the commands without reading the book. The ease of using DOS 2.x and 3.x with these new capabilities will lead them to want to read every word.

APPENDIX B

Scan Codes

THE FOLLOWING IS A TABLE OF SCAN CODES FOR THE IBM PC family and many compatibles. Note that some compatible computers, like the Tandy line, may have different scan codes for some keys, because of a nonstandard layout.

When using INPUT.COM, only the second code of an extended scan code is returned, so that Alt-N indicates the same 49 value as the number 1. Possible conflicts in your own batch-file programming should be rare, however.

Table B-1. Scan Codes for the IBM PC

Key	Code	Shift	Control	Alt
A	97	65	1	0;30
B	98	66	2	0;48
C	99	67	3	0;46
D	100	68	4	0;32
E	101	69	5	0;18
F	102	70	6	0;33
G	103	71	7	0;34
H	104	72	8	0;35
I	105	73	9	0;23
J	106	74	10	0;36
K	107	75	11	0;37
L	108	76	12	0;38
M	109	77	13	0;50
N	110	78	14	0;49
O	111	79	15	0;24
P	112	80	16	0;25
Q	113	81	17	0;16
R	114	82	18	0;19
S	115	83	19	0;31
T	116	84	20	0;20

Key			
U	117	85	21	0;22
V	118	86	22	0;47
W	119	87	23	0;17
X	120	88	24	0;45
Y	121	89	25	0;21
Z	122	90	26	0;44
1	49	63		0;120
2	50	64		0;121
3	51	35		0;122
4	52	36		0;123
5	53	37		0;124
6	54	94		0;125
7	55	38		0;126
8	56	42		0;127
9	57	40		0;128
0	48	41		0;129
-	45	95		0;130
=	61	43		0;131
TAB	9	0;15		
SPACE	57			

Table B-2. Extended Scan Codes for Numeric Keypad and Function Keys

Key	Code	Shift	Control	Alt
F1	0;59	0;84	0;94	0;104
F2	0;60	0;85	0;95	0;105
F3	0;61	0;86	0;96	0;106
F4	0;62	0;87	0;97	0;107
F5	0;63	0;88	0;98	0;108
F6	0;64	0;89	0;99	0;109
F7	0;65	0;90	0;100	0;110
F8	0;66	0;91	0;101	0;111
F9	0;67	0;92	0;102	0;112
F10	0;68	0;93	0;103	0;113
F11	0;133			
F12	0;134			
Home	0;71	55	0;119	
Crs-Up	0;72	56		
Pg Up	0;73	57	0;132	
Crs-Lf	0;75	52	0;115	
Crs-Rt	0;77	54	0;116	
End	0;79	49	0;117	
Crs-Dn	0;80	50		
Pg Dn	0;81	51	0;118	
Ins	0;82	48		
Del	0;83	46		
PrtSc			0;114	

APPENDIX C

ANSI.SYS
Commands

To COMMUNICATE WITH ANSI.SYS, YOU NEED TO BE able to send the ESCape character, with an editing program that allows entering the ESC character or by using PROMPT as described in Chapter 4.

CURSOR MOVEMENT COMMANDS

Move Cursor to Specified Location

`ESC[<row;col>H`—Substitute the row (1–25) and column (1-80) you want the cursor to move to for row and col. you do not specify row, cursor is moved to row 1; if you do not indicate column, it is moved to column 1. Omit both, and the cursor is moved to the home position.

`ESC[<row;col>f`—Same as the preceding ESC[<row,col>H.

Move Cursor Down

`ESC[<lines>A`—Moves cursor up lines rows. If you omit the number of lines, DOS moves up one row.

`ESC[<lines>B`—Move cursor down lines rows. Default is again one row. In both these cases, the column in which the cursor appears remains unchanged.

Move Cursor Right

`ESC[<columns>C`—Moves cursor 1–79 columns positions forward. Default is one, and this sequence is ignored if the cursor is already at the far right of the screen; in other words, there is no wraparound to the next line.

Move Cursor Left

`ESC[<columns>D`—Move the cursor 1–79 columns positions backward. The default and lack of wraparound is identical to the sequence preceding.

Save Cursor Position

`ESC[`—Saves current cursor position

Return Cursor to Position Stored by ESC[s

`ESC[u`—Restores cursor to the value it had when the above sequence was delivered.

ERASE SCREEN COMMANDS:

`ESC[2J`—Erases entire CRT screen.

`ESC[K`—Erase from current cursor position to the end of the current line.

CHANGE DISPLAY ATTRIBUTES

Set Foreground Color, Background Color, other

Attibutes

`ESC[<attributem>`—For attribute substitute one or more of the values in Table D-1. If more than one is entered, separate them with semicolons:

Table D-1. Display Attributes

Foreground	Background	
30	40	Black
31	41	Red
32	42	Green
33	43	Yellow
34	44	Blue
35	45	Magenta
36	46	Cyan
37	47	White

Other Attributes	
0	None
1	High intensity
4	Underline
5	Blinking
7	Reverse video
8	Invisible

SET DISPLAY MODE

ESC[<modeh>—For setting the screen width and graphics modes of the display. Also can turn on or off line-wrap capability; that is, carrying over of screen lines past the 80th character to the next line (Table D-2). Substitute for *mode* one of the numerical values.

Table D-2. Display Modes

Display Modes	
0	40 columns wide, 25 rows; black and white
1	40 columns wide, 25 rows; color
2	80 columns wide, 25 rows; black and white
3	80 columns wide, 25 rows; color
4	320 pixels wide, 200 deep color graphics
5	320 pixels wide, 200 deep black & white graphics
6	640 pixels wide, 200 deep black & white graphics

Line Wrap On/Off	
ESC[=7h	Activate line wrap
ESC[=7l	Deactivate line wrap

REDEFINE KEYS

Define a key

`ESC[<oldkey;newkey>p`

`ESC[<oldkey;newkey>13p`—Redefines keys to deliver a different character or string of characters than that provided by DOS as a default. Substitute for *oldkey* the keycode (from Appendix B) of the key to be redefined. Substitute for *newkey* either the key code of the new definition for the old key or else the string of characters to be supplied. Put the string inside quotation marks. *Newkey* can also consist of a combination of a string and a key code.

Keys such as function keys, keypad keys, or keys to be pressed in combination with the Control, Alt, or Shift key require *two* numbers to define them. The first is a zero, followed by the key's code, with a semicolon separating them.

When the key redefinition ends with *13p* instead of simply *p*, the new definition is terminated with a carriage return.

Restore Original Definition

`ESC[<oldkey;oldkey>`—Restores old definition by supplying the original key code as the new definition for that key.

APPENDIX D

Suppliers' Addresses

Online Information Services

American People/Link
350 N. Clark St.
Suite 650
Chicago, IL 60610

CompuServe Information Services Inc.
5000 Arlington Centre Blvd.
Columbus, OH 43260

The Source
1616 Anderson Rd.
McLean, VA 22102

MCI Mail
Box 1001
1900 M St. NW
Washington, D.C. 20036

Hardware Manufacturers

Personal Computers, PC-DOS, TopView

IBM
Entry Systems Division
P.O. Box 1328-C
Boca Raton, FL 33432

Hayes modems
Hayes Microcomputer Products
P.O. Box 105203
Atlanta, GA 30348

Software Vendors

Lotus 1-2-3
Lotus Development Corp.
55 Cambridge Pkwy.
Cambridge, MA 02142

Extended Batch Language
Seaware Corp.
P.O. Box 1656
Delray Beach, FL 33444

Personal REXX
Mansfield Software Group
P.O. Box 532
Storrs, CT 06268

Pro Command
Innovative Technology
2710 Lancaster Rd.
Unit 101
Ottawa, Ontario
CANADA K1B 4W8

Command Plus
ESP Software Systems Inc.
11965 Venice Blvd.
Suite 309
Los Angeles, CA 90066

MS-DOS, Windows
Microsoft Corp.

116011 N.E. 36th Way
P.O. Box 97017
Redmond, WA 98073-9717

CP/M, Concurrent DOS
Digital Research Inc.
P.O. Box DRI
Monterey, CA 93942

dBase products
Ashton-Tate
10150 W. Jefferson Blvd.
Culver City, CA 90230

Glossary

ANSI.SYS   a file supplied with DOS that allows sending special codes which control the keyboard and screen in ways specified by the user.

ASCII   acronym for American Standard Code for Information Interchange—a common numeric code that expresses the alphabet, numbers, punctuation, and special symbols used by computers.

Assembler   a tool that allows more efficient writing of machine language programs through mnemonic abbreviations that are later translated or assembled into code the computer can execute directly.

AUTOEXEC.BAT   ASCII file placed in the root directory of the disk that contains a list of commands which are carried out by DOS automatically during the bootup operation. This file allows the user to load memory-resident programs, specify a PATH to be used by DOS to search for system files, and perform other tasks that configure the system.

BIOS   a computer's Basic Input/Output System or BIOS, is a set of computer code, provided on read-only memory (ROM) chips, that governs basic system-level functions.

Bootstrap   a very short set of computer instructions, that usually do nothing but load into the computer a longer program that carries out the actual loading of the operating system. On hard disks, the boot sector is found on the first sector of the first track of the first surface to be read by the system.

Cluster   the smallest unit of disk space that can be allocated by DOS. For hard disks, a cluster may be 4 sectors (512 bytes each), 2048 bytes, or 16 sectors for a total of 8,192 bytes. Cluster size has a bearing on how efficiently DOS operates. Smaller clusters waste less space on the disk, but larger clusters allow DOS to collect more information at one time.

Command line   the line typed at the prompt (supplied by DOS or another program) including the command to be carried out and the parameters to be used with that command.

Command processor   a program that accepts command lines, interprets them, and oversees their execution. With DOS, COMMAND.COM is almost always the command processor used.

Compatibility box   a capability of IBM's OS/2 to allow running of existing MS-DOS or PC-DOS programs on 80286 and 80386 machines within certain strict limits.

CONFIG.SYS   An ASCII file, interpreted by DOS on booting, if present in the root directory of the boot disk. CONFIG.SYS is acted on *before* AUTOEXEC.BAT but may not contain anything other than specific commands, which specify device drivers to be used, or which set other system configuration factors such as the number of buffers to be allocated, size of the environment, and so on.

Console device   the standard input and output device—the keyboard and CRT screen.

Contiguous   for hard disks or floppy disks, contiguous sectors are arranged consecutively on the disk. DOS tries to allocate sectors to a file contiguously so that the disk drive can read as many sectors of a file as it can with mimimal read/write head movement. As a hard disk fills, though, the unallocated sectors gradually become spread out and fragmented, forcing DOS to choose more and more noncontiguous sectors. Fragmented files can be much slower to access.

Coprocessor   an additional microprocessor that works in tandem with the main processor. IBM PCs and compatibles typically have sockets for an 8087, 80287, or 80387 math coprocessor that offloads number-crunching tasks from the main microprocessor, speeding operation for applications involving much computation, such as spread sheet recalculation.

DEBUG   a tool supplied on the DOS Supplemental disk that allows reading and editing bytes from a disk or memory, simply assembly and dissassembly of machine-language programs, and other functions.

Device driver   a software module that tells DOS how to control a given piece of hardware, such as a printer, monitor, disk drive, or keyboard. ANSI.SYS and VDISK.SYS are device drivers supplied with DOS. Others are supplied by manufacturers of peripherals.

DOS   (Disk Operating System) the control program of the computer, which oversees how the system interfaces with the user and peripherals, including disks.

Dynamic RAM   type of memory that must be electrically refreshed many times each second or else the contents will be lost. PCs and compatibles use dynamic RAM to store programs, data, and the operating system.

EDLIN   DOS's line-oriented text editor.

Environment   an area of memory set aside to keep track of information, such as the system prompt. The user can also define variables to be placed in this environment through the SET command.

FAT (file allocation table)—a special area on the disk that tracks how each cluster is assigned to various files.

File a collection of information, usually data or a program, that has been given a name and allocated sectors by the FAT.

File-oriented backup any backup system that stores information in files, just as they are stored on the disk. Such systems allow easier access or restoration of a particular file.

Filter a DOS program that accepts ASCII data and performs a function on it before passing it through to a file. FIND locates strings within the file or file specification; MORE displays the file or list of files paged for easy reading; SORT sorts the list or file according to the user's specifications.

Hierarchical in disk terminology, the structuring of directories such that each subdirectory has one parent but may have several child directories, branching out in a treelike structure.

High-level format the formatting performed by FORMAT.COM, in which information needed by DOS to use the disk is written.

Image-oriented backup any backup system that creates a mirror image of the disk, without regard to the files themselves. With such systems, the entire disk has to be restored from the backup medium to allow access to the files.

Instructions the basic set of capabilities of a microprocessor, allowing the chip to load information in registers, move it to other registers, increment the data, add or subtract data from registers, and so forth.

Intelligent having sufficient programming built-in to carry out certain tasks independently. An intelligent disk drive can accept requests from DOS, locate the data, and deliver it without detailed instructions on how to do the physical I/O functions.

Interactive allowing user input during run-time.

Label in batch-file language, a marker that DOS uses to determine where to jump following a GOTO command. In batch files, a label is a line prefixed with a colon. On a hard disk, the volume name applied immediately after high-level formatting, if the /V switch was specified or by use of the LABEL command.

Logical a feature that exists only by definition, rather than as a physical entity. For example, your hard disk C: is a physical disk. Using DOS' SUBST command, you may redefine a directory on that disk as a logical disk drive, such as drive E: No physical drive E: exists, but DOS treats the logical drive as if it were real for most functions. See also *physical*.

Low-level formatting the most basic formatting done on the hard disk to prepare it for partitioning and high-level formatting. This is often done by the manufacturer, which locks out bad sectors at this time.

Macro a series of commands that can be triggered at the press of a key or two. Many application programs as well as utilities like SuperKey and ProKey allow users to develop their own macros for frequently used command sequences.

Noncontiguous   not arranged according to consecutive physical sectors on a disk.

Overlays   portions of a program called into memory as needed, overlaying the previous redundant section of the program. Using overlays allows programs that are much bigger than those that would fit into memory all at once.

Parameter   a qualifier that defines more precisely what a program such as DOS is to do.

Partition   a part of a disk drive set aside for use by a particular operating system. One partition on a hard disk is bootable. The others, if any, may become the active partition with the FDISK program.

Path   a listing of directory names in order that defines the location of a particular file.

Peripheral   a device separate from the main computer to which information can be directed, such as a printer, modem, or mass storage device.

Physical   a feature that exists in reality, as opposed to one that exists only because we choose to logically think of it as an entity. Sectors written on a disk are physically consecutive; however, a file may consist of sectors that are physically scattered all over the disk. We can think of the file's sectors as being logically consecutive, even though they are physically not laid out in this manner.

Pixel   a picture element of a screen image—one "dot" of the collection that makes up an image.

Redirection   rerouting input or output to or from the device for which it was originally headed. For example, you may send screen output to the printer using a command like DIR>PRN or send it to a file: DIR>MYFILE.ASC.

Registers   the basic special-purpose memory locations of a microprocessor, used to carry out its instructions during the computing process.

ROM-BIOS   see BIOS.

Serial   passing information one bit at a time in sequential order.

Standard input device   the keyboard.

Standard output device   the CRT screen.

Static RAM   memory that does not need to be refreshed and therefore does not lose its contents when power to the computer is turned off.

Subdirectory   a directory created within another directory, which stores its own separate files.

Switch   an entry on a command line, usually marked with a special character such as a slash, that allows specifying options available with that command. Example:

```
DIR /W
```

Tree-structured directories   the hierarchical structure of a DOS directory using parent and child directories.

Unfragmented   a hard disk that has most of its files stored in consecutive sectors and not spread out over the disk. Such an arrangement allows more efficient reading of data with less time required to move the read/write head to gather the information.

VDISK.SYS   the device driver supplied with DOS 3.0 and later versions that allows creation of virtual disks or "RAM" disks through a line placed in the CONFIG.SYS file.

Virtual disk   an electronic, or "RAM" disk created in memory that mimics a real disk drive—but is much faster. Such disks are also volatile, meaning that they lose their data when power is interrupted to the computer.

Volume   the largest disk entity that DOS can deal with. For example, a single physical disk can be divided into two or more logical disks created as separate volumes. DOS may see one volume as drive C: and the other as drive D: even though both exist on the same physical drive.

Index

About The Author

David D. Busch is a full-time book and magazine writer who has written 20 computer-related books since 1983, including *Sorry About the Explosion*, winner of the Computer Press Association's 1985 Book of the Year Award. He has been a contributing editor and monthly columnist for six computer magazines. David lives in Ohio with his wife and three children.